Self-Care
Isn't Selfish

Chicken Soup for the Soul: Self-Care Isn't Selfish
101 Stories about Looking Out for Yourself
Amy Newmark

Published by Chicken Soup for the Soul, LLC www.chickensoup.com
Copyright ©2025 by Chicken Soup for the Soul, LLC. All Rights Reserved.

No part of this publication may be reproduced, stored in a retrieval system or transmitted in any form or by any means, electronic, mechanical, photocopying, recording or otherwise, without the written permission of the publisher.

CSS, Chicken Soup for the Soul, and its Logo and Marks are trademarks of Chicken Soup for the Soul, LLC.

The publisher gratefully acknowledges the many individuals who granted Chicken Soup for the Soul permission to reprint the cited material.

Front cover image of dog courtesy of iStockphoto.com (©damedeeso), pink wall paper background courtesy of iStockphoto.com (©damedeeso)
Back cover and interior photo courtesy of iStockphoto.com (©bgblue)

Photo of Amy Newmark courtesy of Susan Morrow at SwickPix

Cover and Interior by Daniel Zaccari

Publisher's Cataloging-in-Publication Data

Names: Newmark, Amy, editor.
Title: Chicken soup for the soul : self-care isn't selfish : 101 stories about looking out for yourself / Amy Newmark.
Description: Cos Cob, CT: Chicken Soup for the Soul, LLC, 2025.
Identifiers: LCCN: 2025935328 | ISBN: 978-1-61159-122-4 (paperback) | 978-1-61159-356-3 (ebook)
Subjects: LCSH Self-actualization (Psychology). | Conduct of life. | Happiness. | Health--Literary collections. | Health behavior--Literary collections. | Well-being--Literary collections. | Health--Anecdotes. | Health behavior--Anecdotes. | Well-being--Anecdotes.| Self-help. | BISAC SELF-HELP / Motivational & Inspirational | SELF-HELP / Personal Growth / Happiness | SELF-HELP / Personal Growth / Self-Esteem
Classification: LCC RA776 .C54398 2025 | DDC 613--dc23

Library of Congress Control Number: 2025935328

PRINTED IN THE UNITED STATES OF AMERICA
on acid∞free paper

Self-Care Isn't Selfish

101 Stories about Looking Out for Yourself

Amy Newmark

Chicken Soup for the Soul, LLC
Cos Cob, CT

Changing your life one story at a time®
www.chickensoup.com

Table of Contents

❶
~Make Me-Time~

1. Guilt-Free Mom, *Molly England*...1
2. Finding Time for Me, *Wendy Portfors*..3
3. Recharge Rental, *Bonnie L. Beuth*...7
4. Taking Time, *Teresa Hoy*...9
5. Farmer's Hours, *Kristiana Pastir*..12
6. Put On Your Oxygen Mask First,
    Deborah Henderson Roberts..14
7. Already Possessing the Answers, *Claire McGarry*..................16
8. Ode to a Quiet Bathroom, *Mimi Greenwood Knight*.............20
9. The Young and the Rested, *Aja Moore-Ramos*......................22

❷
~Take Back Your Power~

10. Choosing People Who Choose You, *Elizabeth Yeter*.............26
11. The White Couch, *Dr. Tricia Wolanin*....................................29
12. The Ring of Hope, *Diane Lowe MacLachlan*.........................32
13. A Little Housekeeping, *Connie K. Pombo*.............................36
14. Buying a Ticket to Life, *Tena Beth Thompson*......................39
15. The Power of a Word, *Sandy Newman*..................................42
16. There's a Limit, *Monica A. Andermann*.................................44
17. Your Marriage Is Killing You, *Tina O'Reilly*..........................47

❸
~Get Outside in Nature~

18. A Motorcycle and the Open Road, *Timothy Martin* 51
19. Cabin Life, *Tamra Anne Bolles* 54
20. Forever Changed, *Jonney Scoggin* 57
21. The Best View, *Anna Jensen* 60
22. Three O'Clock on Phantom Lake, *Ilana Long* 63
23. Kleenex Capers, *Connie Kaseweter Pullen* 65
24. The Solitary Cottage, *Dennis McCloskey* 68
25. Tiny Sanctuary, *Tanya Estes* 71
26. Gone Too Soon, *Rachel Chustz* 74

❹
~"No" Is a Complete Sentence~

27. The Strength of No, *Loren Slocum Lahav* 79
28. Silencing the "Should" Monster, *Sydney Logan* 82
29. Finding Me, *Betsy S. Franz* 85
30. The Power of "No" *Margaret Johnson-Hodge* 88
31. Time to Say Goodbye, *Noelle Sterne* 91
32. Recharging Batteries, *Jonet Neethling* 94
33. The Day I Banished Busy-ness, *Kim Forrester* 97
34. No, *Gail Small* 101
35. Saying "Yes" to Myself, *Holly English* 104
36. Just Say No — and Sometimes Yes, *Ann Vitale* 107

❺
~Love Who You Are~

37. Goals for Growing Older, *Kristin Goff* 111
38. You Are More than the Way You Look, *Tina Muir* 115
39. The No-Share Zone, *Deborah Shouse* 119
40. Defending Our Children, *Ceil Ryan D'Acquisto* 122
41. Like Daughter, Like Mother, *Courtney Conover* 126

Table of Contents

42. My Picture-Perfect New Year's Resolution, *Britteny Elrick* ... 130
43. Un-Resolved, *Michele Ivy Davis* 133
44. Running for My Life, *Jenna Schifferle* 136
45. Lord, Make Me a Babe, *Linda Hoff Irvin* 139

❻
~Treat Yourself~

46. Just Socks, *Marilyn Helmer* 143
47. In This Moment, *Shannon Kaiser* 146
48. One Day, *Wendy Hairfield* 149
49. Permission to Joyride, *Rebecca Radicchi* 153
50. Hearts and Hurricanes, *Priscilla Dann-Courtney* 156
51. Every Day a Friday, *Elaine L. Bridge* 159
52. Guest Treatment, *Paula Klendworth Skory* 161
53. The Life You Save May Be Your Own, *Rebecca Josefa* 164
54. Big Red Divorce Boots, *Diane Morrow-Kondos* 168

❼
~Find Your Fitness~

55. Cleansing the Soul, *Machille Legoullon* 172
56. Strength to Be Strong, *Nicole Christine Caratas* 174
57. Finish the Race, *Temeka S. Bailey* 177
58. Time for Health, *Billy Cuchens* 181
59. Cereal for Dinner, *Shannon McCarty* 184
60. Off the Ropes, *Rachel R. Thompson* 188
61. The Joy of a Mortal Body, *Mitali Banerjee Ruths* 191
62. Running for My Life, *Sue LeBreton* 195

❽
~Channel Your Inner Warrior~

63. My Cape's Under My Cardigan, *Ashley Dailey* 200
64. Remember to Breathe, *Marilyn Haigh* 201

65.	Bad Mama Jama, *Regina Sunshine Robinson*	203
66.	Never Underestimate Yourself, *Carole Harris Barton*	206
67.	Riding High Side, *Robin Martin*	210
68.	He Wouldn't Do a Thing Like That! *Michelle Jones*	212
69.	Moment of Truth, *Susan Traugh*	217
70.	The Chief of the Clan, *Elizabeth Rose*	220
71.	Independence Day, *Ellarry Prentice*	222

❾
~You Come First~

72.	Rebuilding a Life, *R'becca Groff*	227
73.	What Breaks You, *Aleksandra Slijepcevic*	230
74.	Getting My Bling Back, *Linda C. Defew*	233
75.	Here to Shine, *Diana Lynn*	237
76.	Being Intentional about Self-Care, *LaQuita Jean Starr*	240
77.	Finding My Footing, *Joan Bailey*	243
78.	Giving Thanks by Letting Go, *Maggie John*	246
79.	Surviving and Thriving, *Terry Hans*	250
80.	Softness in the Vast Blue Sky, *Galen Pearl*	253
81.	What I Deserve, *Diana Lynn*	256

❿
~Reclaim Your Calendar~

82.	Speed Bump, *Veronica Bowman*	260
83.	A Working Man's Chuck-It List, *Timothy Martin*	263
84.	Remember to Remember You, *Joshua J. Mark*	266
85.	Stop Juggling and Put Something Down, *Ann Morrow*	269
86.	The Cleanup, *Judee Stapp*	273
87.	Determined, Distraught, and Demented, *Amy Newmark*	276
88.	The Pie Chart of Me, *Aileen Liang*	281
89.	Itching for a Change, *Priscilla Dann-Courtney*	285
90.	Making Time for Possibilities, *Annmarie B. Tait*	287
91.	No More Overtime, *Anita Love*	290

⓫
~Do What You Love~

92. Lisa Things, *Lisa A. Malkiewicz* 294
93. Following My Heart, *Randi Nelson* 297
94. Escaping Insomnia, *Debby Johnson* 300
95. My Own Beat, *Stephanie Doerr* 302
96. Self-Care Found in a Library Basement, *Jill Keller* 305
97. The Six Months Test, *Pauline Youd* 309
98. Awakened by the Creator Within, *Christine Burke* 312
99. From Plumbing to Prose, *Gary Sprague* 315
100. Warm and Familiar, *Erin Hazlehurst* 317
101. Loving My Inner Child, *L.A. Strucke* 320

Meet Our Contributors 323
Meet Amy Newmark 337
About Chicken Soup for the Soul 339

Chapter 1

Make Me-Time

Guilt-Free Mom

If you want to have enough to give to others, you will need to take care of yourself first. A tree that refuses water and sunlight for itself can't bear fruit for others.
~Emily Maroutian

It was a momentous day — but not like a birthday, anniversary, or when a baby starts walking. It was bigger than that. Today, I did something for myself as a mom, and I felt no guilt. That's right. None.

Sure, in my nine years of motherhood, I've done nice things for myself. I've gotten my nails painted a bold beige (so the almost-instant chips didn't show up as much). I've embarked on the occasional girls' night out to dance and ultimately felt tired by 9 p.m., longing for a cup of tea and my cozy bed. I've gotten a massage and panicked all forty-five epic minutes thinking that I was missing an urgent call from the school about some heinous illness one of my kids had abruptly come down with.

Point being, whenever I do nice things for myself, they always include an element of my kids. Even when I feel "weightless" because I'm out on a date with my husband, dressed up and gripping just a black leather clutch, with the diaper bag nowhere in sight, that "weightlessness" comes with its own baggage. It's indelibly tied with rejoicing in the fact that I'm not carrying changes of clothes, baby wipes, or random trash, aka my kids' treasures.

So, I still think about the kids. I wonder if they're going too long without a diaper change. I fixate on whether whoever's in charge is feeding them the "right" food. Are they napping, behaving, playing, and screaming, all to my exact specifications even though I'm not there? I create them in my thoughts. Their absence is present.

But today. Oh, today. Today, I went to New York City on my own. Steve, my husband, their dad, was in charge. He's competent, capable, and half of the reason that they exist. So, I let go of my duties and spread my sometimes-clipped-feeling wings.

I soared.

I didn't do anything particularly special. I just walked around the city, but that's something I love to do.

And what I love even more is that after nine years of parenting three little kids, I've finally learned how to enjoy my "me time." I didn't really think about my kids or my husband. I just did *me*.

I sat at a juice café, drank a green concoction, and observed every character who walked by on Perry and Hudson Streets. I weaved in and out of the masses of people as they clamored for organic vegetables and artisan jams at the Union Square Greenmarket. I got lost in Tribeca and then found Laughing Man Coffee Company, where I grabbed a coffee that apparently also helps better the world. I peeked into an intimidating pop-up shop in SoHo.

At every turn, I found more of me.

The farther along I travel in this motherhood journey, the more I learn how to redefine myself. I learned today that sometimes I can allow myself to exist without my kids and, more importantly, without guilt. What freedom.

— Molly England —

Finding Time for Me

*If you feel "burnout" setting in, if you feel demoralized
and exhausted, it is best, for the sake of everyone,
to withdraw and restore yourself.*
~Dalai Lama

To pass time, I stared absently out the hospital window until my thoughts were interrupted. "When are we going home?" my husband Brian asked.

"I think you will be able to go home today."

"Good. I don't like it here."

Every night, when visiting hours ended, I dreaded having to leave him and most nights ended in tears — his and mine.

Today, after two weeks, I was determined to take Brian home. The doctor had signed the release document, but I needed to meet with the Palliative Coordinator before we left. She arrived and suggested we go sit in the outdoor garden and talk. She crossed her arms over an envelope nestled in her lap. Her friendly smile and demeanor were comforting. She started our conversation by asking about Brian. I explained about his diagnosis with terminal brain cancer seven months earlier, our life before and after the diagnosis, and my fears. I told her why I wanted to take Brian home and care for him. Before I finished, my tears welled up.

"It won't be easy," she said.

"I know," I said.

As she spoke, I listened with as much attention as I could muster. She described what being a caregiver would entail in the upcoming months. She reached out and placed her hand on my shoulder, and I cried. We sat in silence until I gained control. Then she stood, handed me the envelope, and said, "Good luck." I clutched the envelope to my chest and watched her walk back through the sliding glass doors. I took a deep breath, opened the envelope, and removed a book. Tears streamed down my cheeks as I stared at the title: *A Caregiver's Guide to End-of-Life Care*

I can honestly say that I did not fully understand what being a caregiver for a palliative person would entail. All I knew was that having Brian at home would allow visitors to spend precious time with him without the confines of visiting in a care facility. And my own time with him wouldn't be limited at all.

I waited until my emotions were in check and then went back to Brian's room. Within two hours, we were home.

Before going into the hospital, Brian was able to get into a wheelchair, but now he would remain bedridden for the remainder of his life. I was able to position his hospital bed between the kitchen and living room, near a large window so he could look out.

Now that he was home, I wondered what daily life was going to be like.

The palliative doctor visited weekly, and more than once he said to me, "Remember to take care of yourself. Sometimes, the caregiver dies before the person they are caring for because of the stress and strain."

Time ticked by ever so slowly. Days grew into weeks, and I realized how true his words were with each visit. We had no family close by to help, so I wondered how I would make time for myself. I knew I was under strain, and both my body and mind were fatigued. I tried to put on a brave face when the doctor was at the house, but in truth I was struggling.

One day, I stood at the window as Brian slept, watching as the doctor drove away. I leaned against the kitchen counter, holding myself up by my elbows. I was weary, and the weight of it was crushing me. A good night's sleep was difficult as I kept one eye open, and my ears perked for any noise from Brian. It was catching up with me.

I was startled by the feeling of a cold, wet nose on my leg as Danny nudged me. I looked down into the gentle black eyes of our Border Collie — eyes that melted my soul. I knew she felt my sadness. Those kind eyes yearned to be the centre of my attention.

How do you find time for yourself when you have a twenty-four-hours-a-day, seven-days-a-week commitment to care for a loved one? How do you put yourself first? I was scared to leave Brian's side in case something material in his medical condition changed. Most days, I was overwhelmed with decisions and the weight of the situation. I wanted my husband and my life back. I tried not to think of what the future held.

I lay awake at night with the doctor's warning to care for myself swirling in my mind. I knew it was important, but I couldn't envision how I could change my current situation. Miraculously, a solution came to me one night while I slept. In the morning, I searched several private healthcare agencies and was successful in hiring a university student to be a visitor for Brian. She was contracted to come to our home for four hours weekly, which became my salvation.

I had found a way to have free time, but what would I do? Looking at our golf clubs, I realized that golfing would allow me to be outdoors, get exercise, and let my mind relax. I knew that I had found a way to recharge my batteries!

I chose the golf course in a national park just fifteen minutes from our home. I experienced a sense of freedom every time I walked from the parking lot to the first tee box. I savoured the fresh air as I walked the fairways and enjoyed seeing the deer and rabbits that called the course home. Ducks wandered from the ponds when I approached and squawked to tell me I had broken their solitude. On lucky days, I saw herds of bison that roamed in the park. I lived in the moment and relished my surroundings. I had been given a true gift of time. I was finding strength, both physically and mentally. Each week when I returned home, I felt rejuvenated and ready to face what lay ahead. The timeout was beneficial for both my wellbeing and Brian's.

No one knows what it is like to be a caregiver until they are faced with the situation. It is difficult when we're immersed in the situation. Many days, I felt hopeless and alone. I felt guilty about asking for help. I was fortunate to find a solution that allowed me to give back to myself. I know not all caregivers are so lucky.

When I reflect on my months caring for Brian, many things come to mind that could have made that journey easier for me. If you know someone who is a caregiver, I encourage you to reach out to them. Give them the gift of time for themselves. Offer to come and clean the house, cook a meal, do the laundry, get groceries, or offer to sit with their loved one so the caregiver can take some time out. If the caregiver has children, offer to take the children for a sleepover, out to a movie, or to the park. Young people need time away just as much as the caregiver. Be there as a shoulder to cry on or just to listen when they need to share. Be the most supportive friend you can be. I guarantee that you will feel better for it.

— Wendy Portfors —

Recharge Rental

*The sea, once it casts its spell, holds one
in its net of wonder forever.*
~Jacques Cousteau

I hit a wall. I am the girl who rarely says "no," the one my friends say is the busiest person they know. A sometimes demanding career, chairing a local professional group, helping to found an international professional group, becoming a condominium association board member, participating in writing and Bible classes, caring for a parent's affairs, providing stateside assistance to a deployed Army brother, and caring for two dogs had burned me out. I needed a vacation.

I scheduled a week off from work and searched for beach rentals. At first, the search was futile. Most properties were too expensive, some would not allow dogs, and some were too far away from the beach. At the last minute, I found a property for the right price, with a dog-friendly fenced yard, across the street from the beach. Was this property too good to be true?

I took off for the rental with my dogs in tow. Finding the condo was easy. Inspecting the premises, the first thing I noticed was the same throw rug in their kitchen as in my own. It felt like a good sign. I let the dogs loose to run and roll in the yard and continued my inspection. The condo was very clean, the bed and sofas were all comfortable, and there were plenty of pots, pans and dishes for a week of meals. Settling into this strange place felt like taking a deep breath.

We went on unleashed walks and runs on the beach. Schools of playful dolphins offshore kept pace with my walks. Sitting under the pier in the shade, I traded technical manuals for fiction for the first time in years. Fresh air and sunshine, surfers, cooperative birds and interesting flowers growing in the sand inspired creativity with my digital camera.

I now refer to this place as my recharge rental, and it has become the one calendar entry each year written in stone. Each trip yields a new adventure. One year, I took a boat tour around Cumberland Island, where John F. Kennedy, Jr. was married, and saw wild horses. That trip was especially eventful because such a bad storm hit us on the way back that you could see nothing but torrential rain and wind from the boat windows. Comforting the terrified woman sitting next to me, I learned she too was visiting from Atlanta. When the storm finally subsided, we saw the actual lifeboat from which Navy SEALs rescued Captain Phillips, bullet holes and all.

Every visit, I meet nice people. A man on the beach told me how to recognize shark teeth in the sand. I never found any teeth, but I collected lots of beach glass and unusual shells. Another year, during a beach walk, a woman stopped me because she thought she knew me. It turned out we have a friend in common in Atlanta. One year, I met a local author. Last year, I met the owners of the condo upstairs, joining them for wine and pizza. That's how I found out about and witnessed a turtle hatching where they count the hatched eggs of endangered sea turtles.

Enjoying an annual visit to the beach has allowed me to step out of life's hamster wheel and replenish my energy. An added benefit is that it is the perfect halfway point for my mother's trip home. When my mom visits Atlanta from South Florida, I meet her halfway and drive her in, or travel with her halfway back. This year was the first time she joined me at the condo on her way home. The night before she left, we ate dinner at a wonderful beachside restaurant with live music. The evening was one of the best that either of us could remember. It was the perfect end for her visit to Atlanta, and the perfect beginning of my annual retreat.

— Bonnie L. Beuth —

Taking Time

*A daughter is a mother's gender partner, her closest
ally in the family confederacy, an extension of her self.*
~Author Unknown

Mom stood in the small farmhouse kitchen, staring at the clean dust rag in one hand and the can of furniture polish in the other.

I sat at the dining room table folding laundry. I finished a towel and reached into the basket for another, never taking my eyes off her across the open bar that separated the kitchen from the dining room.

"Mama, do you want me to dust?" I asked.

"Hmm?" she murmured.

It was summer and the middle of the week, so I wasn't in school and Dad was working. My ten-year-old heart picked up its pace as I saw her gaze linger on the clock. I suddenly knew what was preoccupying her — Dad wouldn't be home for two or three hours.

She turned and looked at me.

"Let's read," she blurted, hazel eyes flashing with anticipation. "The dusting can wait."

"Can I bring in Ebony?" I asked, as usual. Ebony was the black cat I'd raised from a kitten. She had to stay outside because Dad didn't want animals in the house.

"Sure. You get Ebony and I'll make us some hot tea."

It didn't matter, summer or winter, Mom loved to drink hot tea.

She also read a lot of romance novels set in England, where they were always drinking afternoon tea. Maybe that's what whetted her appetite for it every time we read.

I quickly set the folded laundry in the basket and rushed outside, careful not to slam the screened door.

Ebony lay stretched out on the cistern, basking in the sun. I scooped her up and hurried inside. I was barely back in the dining room before she was struggling to get down and explore. I let her go and rested my elbows on the open counter to watch Mom in the kitchen.

She had set out her fancy teacups, the pretty white ones with pink flowers. Delicate, painted saucers rested beneath their rounded bottoms. A Lipton tea bag nestled in each cup, the white string and tag dangling over the side.

"Afternoon tea is good for the spirit. It's four o'clock somewhere, right?" she said, her eyes twinkling.

"Too bad we don't have scones," I said. I had no clue what a scone was, only that Mom said everybody in England ate scones with their tea. "What is a scone?"

"Some kind of biscuit, I think," she said.

The teakettle whistled, and Mom poured the hot water into the cups. Steam curled into the air.

I leaned over a cup and drew in a deep breath. The pungent scent of black tea filled my nostrils.

When the liquid was dark brown, we doctored our tea: sugar for Mom, milk and sugar for me.

"What are you going to read?" she asked, as we eagerly headed, teacups in hand, to the living room like two kids skipping school.

"*Misty of Chincoteague*."

"Of course," she laughed, "I should have known. Another book about horses."

"What are you reading?" I asked. "Another romance?"

"Yes," she said, carefully hugging me with one arm. "We're a predictable pair, aren't we?"

Mom sat in her favorite, Early American rocker with the brown and gold flower print and ruffled skirt. With her cup of tea on the

Make Me-Time

round end table, she picked up the latest Harlequin novel she was reading, perched her elbows on the armrests, and crossed her ankles on the small, matching footstool.

After depositing my teacup on the coffee table, I dashed upstairs to my bedroom and grabbed my book off the nightstand.

I kicked off my shoes and stretched out on the dark-rust sofa. Ebony wandered into the living room and jumped onto my chest. She curled into a knot, closed her eyes, and began purring.

The house was quiet except for the grandfather clock ticking in the dining room and the soft rumbles coming from Ebony. Mom and I disappeared into our books.

When we heard a truck coming down the gravel road, we snapped our books shut and jumped to our feet.

Mom rushed to the window and peered through the curtains.

"Dad?" I asked.

She nodded and hurried to the kitchen while I put Ebony outside. I came back in and started setting the table as Mom pulled out pans for boiled potatoes and peas and threw thick slices of ham in a skillet.

I don't know if Dad ever suspected us of whiling away afternoons reading. All I know is that those were some of the most special times I spent with my mom.

She taught me important basics of life: how to keep house, cook, be responsible, and care for others. But she never once said to me, "Take time to enjoy those things you love." Instead, she put aside the dusting, forgot the laundry and ignored the vacuum sweeper a few hours a week to indulge in tea, books, and a purring cat.

Today, I have shelves stacked with books and a houseful of cats. The hot drink at my side when I read is freshly brewed coffee with sugar, no milk. I give my mom full credit for the growing and keeping of these passions. She knew the things we have to do in life change through the years, but the things we love only grow more precious to us.

— Teresa Hoy —

Farmer's Hours

*It's not selfish to love yourself, take care of yourself,
and to make your happiness a priority. It's necessary.*
~Mandy Hale

"I just finished *The Girl on the Train*," Melissa said during our warm-up.

"Oh, I've read that!" Carla said. "What did you think?"

"I liked it," Melissa said. "It's intense, but I liked the psychology in it."

Kristen chimed in, "I haven't read that one yet."

"Oh, I've seen the movie preview," I said. "Not sure it's my genre."

It was a little after 5:00 in the morning, and we were warming up for our CrossFit workout. The 5:15 class has a small but dedicated group of regulars, and these women have become good friends over the years. We discuss books, work, spouses, and kids, along with how sore we are, how much we hate the assault bike, and how yesterday's workout went. We've become a tight-knit group and banter on a group text when outside the gym (including Caley, who's been out with a shoulder injury for several months).

I set my alarm for 4:40 a.m. every weekday so I can go. As a stay-at-home mom to five-and-a-half-year-old twins, a four-year-old and a two-year-old, my me time happens before dawn, before they're awake, before I'm fully awake. And it's wonderful.

On my twenty-minute drive, I listen to music without interruption, questions or requests. I contemplate the day ahead. Once there,

I get to interact with adults! We joke around and laugh a lot. I have fun! That kind of time is precious and invigorating. Almost as much as the workout.

When COVID-19 hit our state, our gym shut down for nearly five months, but we continued to work out on Zoom together. It did wonders for my mental and physical health.

I started these early morning workouts before having kids and intended to keep it up after having them, so I had to make it a priority. During the newborn/early-morning-feeding phases, that sometimes meant waking up at 4:00 a.m. and then staying up to go to the gym. Sometimes, I'd dash out after having heard a child wake up. But I left without guilt, knowing said child would crawl into bed with my husband and fall back to sleep. Occasionally, I would have to remind myself that I am a mother, not a martyr.

I knew I had to continue taking care of myself. And I wanted to. I'd seen the toll that not taking care of yourself takes on a person. Growing up, I saw my mother put everyone else in our house — me, my two brothers, my dad, her elderly mother, our dogs — ahead of herself. She did not complain, but it clearly took a toll on her. My mom, still young, would have trouble sleeping. She often got migraines that, ironically, necessitated she take a break and lie down. But I didn't want to have to reach a breaking point before taking a break. I had to change my mindset and realize self-care is not selfish.

That regular quiet and thoughtful time to myself is key to my wellbeing and ability to take care of my family. I will sacrifice a few hours of sleep for this alone time because I am more alert, perky, and happy having done so.

— Kristiana Pastir —

Put On Your Oxygen Mask First

Self-compassion is simply giving the same kindness to ourselves that we would give to others.
~Christopher Germer

I sat in the parking lot of Rhode Island Hospital. Alone in the privacy of my car, I sobbed. It was 8:30 a.m., and I was already exhausted. I had gotten up at 5:00 a.m. and rushed out the door to drive a half-hour to get my father ready to go to dialysis, which was another forty minutes away. This was a typical morning for me. But this morning, in my haste, I had misjudged the threshold in the hospital lobby and had dumped my father out of his wheelchair in front of the elevator. I felt both helpless and hopeless.

As I sat crying, my cell phone rang. The number on the display indicated it was a newer friend whom I didn't know very well. Despite my hesitation, I decided to answer the phone. I tried to compose myself, but she could tell. "What's wrong?" she asked.

Perhaps because my new friend was a retired nurse, she knew people and could sense the strain in my voice. In response to her question, I began to sob again. "I just dumped my father like a sack of potatoes out in front of the elevators in the lobby of the hospital," I said.

"Well, at least you were in the right place for that," she said.

My tears changed to laughter.

"You know, Deb, you're lucky nothing worse happened," she said.

"What do you mean?" I asked.

"Well, you're running your family business, taking care of a family, taking care of a mother who has dementia, shuttling her and your father, who is in renal failure, back and forth from medical appointments, and managing their affairs and your own. Don't you think that's a lot?"

She was right. I was tired and felt like I was running on empty.

"And what are you doing for you?"

"There's no way I have time for me," I said.

"Deb, there's no way you *don't* have time for you. Think of yourself as being in a plane, and it's going down. You have a lot of people depending on you, but the one person who must come first to get you through all this is you. Put on your oxygen mask first, Deb, before you help others," she said.

"I guess I don't know how to do that," I said.

"What kind of help are you getting?" she asked.

"What do you mean?" I asked.

"Do you get homecare or have someone coming in to help make meals?"

"No, my parents would never go for that," I said.

"Since you have all the responsibility, you should be the decision-maker. Make it clear that if you go down, so will they, and they may then end up in the nursing home. So what kind of things are you doing for you?" she asked.

"I don't have time for that," I repeated.

"If you don't start building in a half-hour to an hour each day to either exercise or go have a coffee with friends or something fun, you're going to get sick. You must build that in," she said.

Slowly, I let her words sink in. Within the next few weeks, I put a plan into action that would allow me to take breaks. Even though it has been years since I've been in touch with this woman, I still remember her words as if they were just spoken. Even though my circumstances have changed, whenever I find myself or a friend running out of gas, I stop and say, "Put on your oxygen mask first."

— Deborah Henderson Roberts —

Already Possessing the Answers

We all have within us a deep wisdom,
but sometimes we don't know we have it.
~Shakti Gawain

"No matter how hard I try, I just can't seem to keep up," Julie confessed, and then she began to cry. "I'm exhausted, physically and mentally. Charlie was up most of the night last night. There are piles of laundry all over my house. I haven't showered in days. And I can't remember the last time I looked into my kids' eyes — really looked." Her voice trailed off as tears streamed down her face.

I passed Julie the box of tissues. I had explained earlier that night, before the retreat's Faith Sharing segment, that several groups had dubbed the box of tissues the "Talking Stick." Inevitably, when it came time to share, the tears came, too. Julie had refused the box, saying she wasn't one to cry. But she accepted the tissues now with gratitude.

This was the fifteenth retreat I had run for mothers of young children. I could count on just one hand the number of moms who hadn't cried when it was their time to share. Goodness knows, I wasn't one of them. I don't cry often, but I've cried more in motherhood than in my entire life combined.

Five years before, I had done just that for an entire week. My kids were then eight, six and two. They were typically good kids, and I did an okay job as a mom, but neither applied that week. Their mistakes aligned with my moodiness. It was like the perfect storm. I felt like a complete failure as a mother and as a person. I wanted to run away from my life forever!

That Saturday, all those years ago, my husband saw the desperate state I was in. "Go," he said. "Just go out, anywhere, for as long as you need. I'll hold down the fort here." He didn't need to say it twice. I grabbed my journal, Bible and car keys, and ran out the door.

I ended up at a retreat center twenty-five minutes from my home. It wasn't that I had decided to go there; it was more like I was led. I only went inside the building to ask permission to be on the grounds. Then I spent the rest of my time there wandering around in all of God's beauty.

I walked the outdoor labyrinth, weaving in and out of the pattern, just like my thoughts. I meandered down the hiking trails, barely noticing the lush trees and plants everywhere. My final destination was the outdoor chapel at the water's edge. As I sat facing the cross, with Lake Cochichewick as the backdrop, I cried, journaled and prayed. Then I cried, journaled, and prayed some more.

I felt like a pressure cooker whose release valve had finally been opened. For three solid hours, I sat on that bench and let all those feelings of frustration, desperation, confusion, and disappointment pour out of me.

When I walked back to my car, I was shocked to find I felt as light and free as a bird. I couldn't wait to go back to my life as a mom, despite having literally run from it just hours before.

Driving home, it occurred to me that every mother out there needs what I had just experienced. But motherhood can be so busy; most moms don't have the time or the energy to plan that getaway. That's when I realized I wanted to be the one to create that for them. So began my MOSAIC of Faith ministry.

Over time, MOSAIC of Faith has branched out in many different directions. But the evening retreats for mothers are definitely the most empowering branch. The secret to their success is the Faith Sharing.

After I provide the content for the evening, as well as a guided meditation to de-stress the moms, I send them all off to their own rooms to reflect. When they return, we Faith Share: Each mom shares her thoughts and feelings *uninterrupted*. When do we moms and women ever get to talk uninterrupted?

Women *always* interrupt each other. We do so usually with the best of intentions: to affirm, to give advice, to share our similar stories as a way to prove we've been there and understand. But when we interrupt, we derail the talker in her journey toward discovery.

I truly believe we already possess most of the answers we need deep within ourselves. But life's busyness and noise drown out those whispers. If and when we are fortunate enough to find some peace and quiet, we're so beaten down that we lack the self-confidence to believe the answers we hear.

That's why it's so important to speak those answers out loud. Talking, uninterrupted, lets us flush out the strong emotions. In doing so, we become more objective; we see things more clearly. Suddenly, everything makes sense. Not only do we see the solutions to our problems, but we see why we had the problems in the first place. Best of all, we recognize and appreciate both the problems and the solutions as necessary aspects of our own journey.

Things were no different for Julie. As she continued to share, uninterrupted, her tears grew fewer, and her vision grew sharper. With no help from us, except for our sincere acceptance and deep listening, Julie stumbled upon idea after idea for how she could approach her daily life differently. With every thought she gave voice to, her voice grew stronger and more self-assured. Soon, the tears in her eyes were replaced with glimmers of hope and confidence.

Later, as we were gathering our things to leave, Julie came over and gave me a hug. As she pulled away, she said, "You know, I really had no idea all those awful emotions were inside of me. I knew I was struggling, but I didn't know I was struggling that much. Thank you for creating the space for me to figure it all out, face it, and get rid of it. I'm leaving here tonight believing I can really do this mom thing now, and actually be good at it. Thank you for helping me to see that."

"You're welcome, Julie," I said, with all sincerity. "Thanks for digging so deep and trusting me with everything. It was an absolute honor to witness you finding the answers you already possessed deep within."

— Claire McGarry —

Ode to a Quiet Bathroom

Not merely an absence of noise, Real Silence begins when a reasonable being withdraws from the noise in order to find peace and order in his inner sanctuary.
~Peter Minard

This year I'll turn forty. I'm just waiting for my husband to ask me what I want for my birthday. I've got my answer all prepared. It's probably not what he expects though. In the years before kids, he'd have gotten off easy with jewelry or clothes, dinner out and a gift certificate to a day spa. But after ten years and three kids, my idea of the perfect birthday gift has evolved. What I want this year, what I really want, is four hours alone and uninterrupted in my own bathroom. Just peace and quiet and porcelain. I suppose that makes me a cheap date but, after ten years of doing whatever I've got to do in the bathroom with an audience, four hours of bathroom solitude sounds better than anything he could buy me.

My birthday fantasy looks like this — me loitering in the tub with my eyes closed. Around me are no action figures, no stick-on alphabet letters, no naked Barbies. (Talk about depressing. The last thing I need, when I'm bent over shaving my legs, is a naked Barbie smirking up at me.) I want no little urchins there to offer commentary on my breasts or belly or buttocks or anything else. I don't want to hear that

I'm getting fat but "Don't worry, Mommy, you look good that way."

I want to shave my legs without delivering a safety lecture about my razor. I don't want to share my shaving cream with anyone no matter how much fun it is. I want to fog up the mirror without having to peek around the curtain and answer, "What letter is this, Mommy?" I want the curtain to stay shut — not be fanned open every few seconds leaving me to explain once again the mechanics of a shower curtain keeping the water OFF the floor.

I want the water as hot as I can stand it and not to hear that anyone is taking up all the room. I want all the room. I don't once want to hear, "Oops! Guess I forgot to tinkle before I got in the tub." I want to stretch out my legs without it being seen as an invitation for a pony ride. I want to step from the tub without hearing, "Boy, the water goes way down when you get out, Mommy!" and to towel off without having to teach an anatomy lesson entitled, "Why Mommy looks different than Daddy."

And while I'm at it, I want to do what I need to on the toilet without spectators. Not to have to remember who tore off the toilet paper for me the last time so I'm sure everyone gets their turn. I want to pick up a magazine, read an article from start to finish, and actually comprehend what I'm reading. I want to close the door and not have little notes slid underneath with my name on them or tiny fingers wiggling up at me.

Then I want to paint my nails — only mine — no one else's. Not to have the "But, sweetie, nail polish is for girls and mommies." I want to give myself a pedicure, a facial, and touch up my roots without once stopping to yell, "I'm in the bathroom. No, I can't come to you. You come to me."

I don't really care where my husband takes the kids. I just want four unbroken hours to luxuriate in my own bathroom alone! Maybe I'll remind him while he's sitting in the McDonald's play yard staring at his watch that he's turning fifty this year and I'm toying with the idea of declaring the remote control off limits to anyone but Daddy for one long, glorious afternoon. Consider the possibilities.

— Mimi Greenwood Knight —

The Young and the Rested

It is so liberating to really know what I want,
what truly makes me happy, what I will not tolerate.
I have learned that it is no one else's job
to take care of me but me.
~Beyoncé Knowles

Napping is new to me. I'm usually the mover, the shaker, the restless soul who can't stay still. Now I retreat to my room for midday naps and press pause on the COVID-19 and Black Lives Matter posts that infiltrate my newsfeed. If I'm going to make it through a global health crisis and achieve social justice for all, I need my rest. Rest is a form of resistance and I am a well-rested revolutionary ready to take on the world.

I used to stuff my thumbs into the crowded pockets of my jeans to keep them from twiddling. I'd think of errands to run, like picking up odds and ends from the dollar store, or take on new hobbies like letter writing and yoga — anything to help me escape the boredom of a blank agenda.

Then, the pandemic hit, followed by store closures and shelter-in-place orders that forced me to spend more time with myself. I thought of creative things to do — virtual karaoke parties with family and friends, scavenger hunts in the garden, photography assignments — but they were quickly replaced by meaningless meetings and Zoom calls as I navigated the waters of working from home.

When my self-assigned lunch break finally arrives, I look for the two-year-old first. "You want to go to the park?" I ask eagerly, competing with Elmo and Big Bird for his attention.

"Not today, Mommy!" he responds with such clarity. But I refuse to be deterred and move on to the seven-year-old. "How about a walk in the park?" I ask enthusiastically.

"I'm busy," she responds curtly as she retreats to designing clothes out of old T-shirts for her dolls. Finally, I approach my husband, my last chance for lunchtime companionship. He is finishing up a work proposal as I softly massage his shoulders.

"Huh?" he responds, barely looking up from the dim glow of his laptop.

"Wanna go on a romantic walk around the neighborhood?" I whisper in my most seductive afternoon voice.

"And who's going to watch the kids?" he retorts, deflating my blissful balloon of daily adventures.

"I'm taking a nap!" I announce and stomp straight into the bedroom. I snuggle under the covers fully clothed and frustrated. The curve of my growing belly pushes against my pillow. The kids knock on the door not even five minutes into my nap, making false claims of starvation and bloody boo-boos. Luckily, I remember to lock the door to protect myself from their terrorist attacks. "Tell Daddy!" I bellow groggily.

My eyes close and I float between dreams of day cruises to the Bahamas and starring as the lead actress in a daytime soap opera. It's like binge watching my favorite TV shows, but far less strain on the eyes.

My alarm pressures me to wake up at the twenty-minute mark. At first, I resist and then I give in, remembering the series of scheduled meetings and deadlines before the end of my work-at-home day. The only escape I have besides grocery store runs and the occasional take-out order are my trips to the doctor. My OB/GYN reports that I am now in the second trimester and stresses the importance of eating balanced meals and getting daily exercise. "It's recommended that you get at least thirty minutes of exercise a day. Is this something you have been doing?" she asks as if reading from a script.

Make Me-Time

"Yes," I lie with a smile. It's hard for me to lie without smiling, but luckily, she can't see it from behind my mask.

"Great to hear. What is your preferred form of exercise?"

"Na... natal... prenatal yoga."

I correct my course quickly. Sometimes it's hard to commit to a lie. I mean it isn't a complete lie since I did do yoga throughout my last two pregnancies. This one was just proving to be different. A surprise baby during a pandemic doesn't always allow for business as usual. I greet the alien figure on my sonogram photo and pack it neatly into my purse, making my way back into the world. I would usually treat myself to ice cream or a Target run, but this time I just want to go home. Not to take a walk or join an imaginary yoga class, but to engage in my new favorite form of exercise. My nap lasts two solid hours and I cherish every moment.

—Aja Moore-Ramos—

Chapter 2

Take Back Your Power

Choosing People Who Choose You

Surround yourself with those who only lift you higher.
~Oprah Winfrey

"I'm sorry, it's just going to be too tight for me. Let's plan for next week :)" I sighed as I put down my phone after reading Joseph's text. We'd made plans a week ago to hang out, but now he was putting me off at the last minute. Again. And we hadn't seen each other for over a month.

The relationship began about eight months prior with shared interests in bettering ourselves and encouraging each other in our careers. It was an instant connection. We started hanging out once every couple of weeks, then about once a week. I loved spending time with someone who shared the same ideas as me and was so easy to talk to.

But then something happened. Quite frankly I don't know what it was, but our relationship changed. He stopped answering texts right away. Sometimes, I'd wait three or four days to hear back from him. Other times, he'd completely ignore me. At first, I was worried about him.

"Haven't heard from you in a while. Are you okay?" I'd text.

A few days later, he'd reply, "Yep! Just busy."

Gosh, too busy to send back a three-second message? Now that's busy.

After a few of these exchanges, I started to feel like something was wrong with me. Was I boring? Stinky breath? Did I inadvertently say something that offended him? Or was he just not that into me? Ouch, the thought of that stung.

So when he texted out of the blue, saying we really needed to catch up and he was excited to see me, I was happy but guarded. How would our interaction be? Would we just pick up where we left off? That seemed... awkward. The more I thought about it, the more I realized that things had always been one-sided, with me putting in more effort. That didn't sit well.

So the ball was in my court. Well, actually, the ball had always been in my court, but I had bought the lie that I had no power in my relationships. That deception is difficult to reverse. The truth is that I do have rights. The relationship doesn't exist for me to please Joseph and make sure he's always satisfied with our interactions. I matter, too.

With this last text message, I had a choice. I could turn the proverbial cheek and dismiss my feelings of being undervalued. Or I could say something that, although true, might end the relationship for good. It was a tough call. I really liked Joseph.

I deliberated. I assessed and then reassessed. I tried out possible messages. "Okay, no problem! See you next week!" "Whenever you have time, let me know!" Nothing felt right. They all felt like violations of me, as if I'd be demeaning myself if I sent them.

I thought hard about the message I really wanted to convey. What was my heart yearning to tell Joseph? Here's what I finally decided on: "No worries. And no thanks for next week. I'm choosing people who choose me." Send.

I vacillated between mental high-fives to myself and head slaps. Then, before I could lose my nerve, I did something even more drastic. I decided, I mean *decided*, that I was worth more than how he had treated me. Therefore, I wasn't going to waste another moment of my time, mental energy, or emotions second-guessing my decision. I didn't even wait to read Joseph's reply. I deleted his number and blocked him on all social media.

Harsh, I know. But I had to make a clean break.

Now I'm choosing people who choose me. And Joseph, quite frankly, had been choosing Joseph all along.

— Elizabeth Yeter —

The White Couch

*You don't need to live to fulfill others' expectations.
Live for yourself, love yourself and do not
let them tell you that it is selfish.*
~Mridula Singh

There's nothing sensible about a white leather couch, which is exactly why I purchased one. This luxury item was worlds away from my humble beginnings.

In graduate school, I'd bought ugly lime-colored chairs from Goodwill. When I got my doctorate, I upgraded to blue velour couches from Goodwill for my West Hollywood apartment.

Eventually, I found myself in New York City. To my surprise, I moved in with a boyfriend after several months of dating. We started out with his hand-me-down couch that had traveled with him throughout his moves across the country. We added a cheap red fabric futon for the numerous guests who visited us in our prime midtown Manhattan location. The home was furnished according to his taste and that of his godfather. I didn't have any say.

One of the first things I did after buying a home for our West Coast relocation was purchase a couch. I sought my now fiancé's approval. We opted for a dark brown leather L-shaped couch. It looked like every other trendy but conservative couch we saw in our friends' apartments. It made sense. This couch showed the world we had "made it" and could now join everyone else in the game of life, the "adult version." I charged the couch on a credit card, along with numerous other

Take Back Your Power | 29

purchases. My partner was between jobs after a stint in rehab and was caring for his mother, who was dying from cancer. I couldn't save her and didn't know how to be there for him, but I could get this couch.

The couch moved with us to Hawaii the following year. Then we upgraded to Honolulu high-rise living. We had the life that tourists could only have a week at a time, but we were miserable. His mother died, and all of my clients were active-duty Marines with PTSD. He was depressed, and I was burnt out.

We sold the leather couch and that helped pay for our move back to the mainland. This led to more moves, lower-paid jobs, and couches that were once again cheap. Along the way, my fiancé became my husband. We may not have carried a couch with us, but we carried the baggage of his grief over both of his parents' deaths and the numerous other challenges he faced with jobs, and physical and emotional issues.

Eventually, I found myself in England. I was able to slowly pay off the credit-card debts from all our moves and our faux lavish lifestyle.

The time came to upgrade our couch. We outdid ourselves by getting a more extravagant brown leather Chesterfield couch, with an accompanying accent chair. It was so fancy that it took ten weeks to be made and delivered. Once again, we had reclaimed what we had lost — an ideal brown leather couch fit for accomplished, stable adults. This time, I paid for the couch and chair in cash.

And this couch was fine — until it wasn't. One year after attaining this furniture, my husband landed a dream job back in America. He would finally be an executive chef for an elite restaurant and get all the acclaim he deserved. As he was prepping for his move back, I had the realization that the marriage was no longer working for me. The signs were there on the couch all along. When we sat on it, our only cuddling was with our two dogs.

One Sunday afternoon, I walked into a furniture store alone. Fabric couches wouldn't work, what with the dogs' constant shedding. I tried out another Chesterfield brown leather armchair, but it wasn't comfortable. There was an ugly sienna armchair that was quite cheap and comfy, but I realized it didn't suit me.

I felt like Goldilocks searching for the perfect chair.

Then I saw it—an L-shaped white leather couch. It was quite beautiful and modern, but I realized I shouldn't even look in that direction. The only places where this kind of couch was seen were nightclubs in Miami or Los Angeles. It wasn't practical; it wouldn't work for writing. I continued to search the store, trying to find anything else as compelling. But the bright white couch was so alluring.

I circled the store like a hawk, looking for something other than that white couch. As I passed the brown leather section, I thought back to all those beautiful, but masculine, brown couches in our past. If my husband had been there with me, he would have talked me out of the white couch. He would have said, "It doesn't make sense. It's going to stain. It doesn't go with anything. It's not us." I would have agreed quietly and ordered another brown leather couch.

But this time, he wasn't there. In fact, nobody was there to talk me into something more sensible. I had gotten a slight raise earlier in the week and was moving once again. I thought to myself, *I deserve that white leather couch, even if it doesn't make sense.*

I bought it.

The next day, I showed a colleague a photo of my spontaneous purchase. At first glance, he said, "It's so you!" I was shocked by his response. *This is me? How could he see this in me, when all I ever saw were brown leather couches and Goodwill hand-me-downs?* Perhaps more surprises will be revealed. In my new life as the owner of a very impractical white leather L-shaped couch.

— Dr. Tricia Wolanin —

The Ring of Hope

Hope is grief's best music.
~Author Unknown

A rusted metal chair was on the front porch of what would soon be my new home. It looked just as fragile as the splintered wood of the deck on which it sat. It was early on a Sunday morning when I found myself perched on that chair, hours before heading to church. I clutched a cup of coffee that I had brought from the large and beautiful suburban home that I was leaving behind. Everything that had felt comfortable and secure was gone.

Even though the sun was bright that early spring day, my spirit was dark and dull. Hot tears flowed down my cheeks and I wondered how I would find the strength to accomplish the tasks I had to do that morning.

The discovery that our family finances had eroded was shocking. My husband was leaving and I had to find a new home for my teenage daughter and me. In spite of her desperate pleading, we had no choice but to move. We had to pack up almost two decades of belongings and start over. The worn out, garbage-filled townhouse was the only place I could afford. I could not envision it ever becoming a home.

There was crayon on the walls, a hole in the ceiling from a leaky bathtub, and garbage everywhere. This abandoned townhouse was like the mirror image of my broken marriage.

As I sat on the deck that first morning, crying, I was surprised to hear the sound of church bells. They were playing a familiar hymn. I lifted my head. And after a few stanzas, I found myself crying harder and choking out the words "great is Thy faithfulness." When the song ended, somewhere deep in my heart I heard another sound—the whisper of God saying, "Be at peace. I moved into this neighborhood long before you did."

For the first time in many months I felt a flicker of hope. God's reminder that He was near made me feel less alone. The bells rang out His presence and their timing had been perfect. With just enough energy to lift myself from the chair, I put down my coffee cup and weakly smiled at the heavens.

Wearily I opened the front door and began the process of cleaning and reconstructing. The project was enormous. It required a complete demolition and took a small army of deeply caring volunteers to tear down and then rebuild the terribly neglected structure.

In a strange way, the townhouse and I became one. There was tremendous pain in the things torn from my life; what I had believed to be a happy family, a beautiful home, a solid future, dreams and plans, extended family and friendships. But it took a surprisingly short amount of time to remove that which no longer had value, what was destroyed beyond repair, and to clean out the shell before deciding how to rebuild.

Countless hours were poured into the endeavor, and with it, slowly, came the hope that my daughter and I could create a home. For months I painted, laid tile, managed the installation of a hundred details and bore the stress of creating something out of little.

It seemed like a small miracle when the renovation was completed in three short months. When we had settled in, one precious friend, herself cruelly familiar with loss and pain, shared with me that massage had been a therapy for her in managing stress. As a generous housewarming gift, she gave me a certificate for a massage with the man who had helped her so much.

It took me several months to find the courage to make the appointment. It had been a long time since I had been touched in any way by a man; and even though I knew he was a professional, I was anxious.

His practice was in the lower level of a home office building. It was cozy and quiet. He was gentle and kind, but my nerves were still uneasy.

After allowing me a chance to get settled under the warm flannel blanket, he entered the room where I lay face down on the massage table. The lights were low and soft music played. He warmed some oil and began to work on the knots that seemed to have settled permanently in my neck and shoulders.

Sensing my edginess, he asked easy questions and I chattered in response.

"What brought you to my practice?" he asked simply.

I answered that our mutual friend had offered his service as a gift.

"Ah, that is a good friend," he replied.

His response opened the door for me to tell him how difficult life had been, the physical strain I had carried in renovating my townhouse, and the anguish I had experienced over the loss of my marriage, my home, and my dreams.

Then I told him the story of the church bells. The long, firm strokes of his palms on my shoulders paused and then he stepped away from the table. Although I could not see him, I knew he was still in the room and I guessed that he was changing the music, or getting more oil or warming some towels.

But the minutes went by and I heard him softly apologize, his voice cracking. What he said brought us both to tears and will forever remind me that God has a plan and a purpose for everything in our lives.

"My mother," he said haltingly, "was the secretary for many years at the church that rang those bells. When my brother and I were younger we would often climb the big trees on the property while she was at work.

"One day," he went on slowly, "my brother had climbed high, too high. He lost his balance and to steady himself he accidentally touched the nearby electrical wires and was killed instantly." The air was still and silent between us before he finished.

Somehow I knew how he would finish the story and we were both crying as he said, "My parents donated those bells in honor of his life. It will mean so much to my mother to know how God spoke to you through their song."

Even though I didn't get to see the smile on his mother's face when she learned that her gift had given me so much hope, I have imagined it many times. It is a sweet reminder to me that there are lovely things that can grow from tragedy and that church bells can ring a message of hope through a world of pain.

— Diane Lowe MacLachlan —

A Little Housekeeping

Real friends are those who, when you've made a fool of yourself, don't feel that you've done a permanent job.
~Erwin T. Randall

"You're just a number, and it's just a job for them," announced my best friend. "My advice to you is to keep quiet and smile."

"What?" I asked. "Are you telling me this to make me feel better or worse?"

My friend, Linda, had come all the way from California to take care of our little family in Lancaster, Pennsylvania, while I underwent radiation treatment for breast cancer. I appreciated her help — especially with our boys (ages nine and fourteen) — but some of the things she said absolutely unnerved me.

I had radiation treatments five days a week, and Linda accompanied me every day. That Friday, the "light bulb" went out in the radiation machine. It would take a week for a new bulb to arrive, which would put me back a week and a half on scheduled treatments because of the Memorial Day weekend. I made it known to the receptionist that it simply wasn't acceptable. "Don't you keep extra 'light bulbs' around just in case one goes out?" I asked, rather annoyed.

The receptionist informed me that it wasn't any ordinary "light bulb," and it cost a lot of money. They were doing their best to get one to the radiation center as soon as possible, but I needed to be patient.

It was cloudy outside and threatening to rain. My gloomy mood spilled over to all the staff and my best friend, who kept informing me how out of line I was.

As I sat on the sofa surrounded by travel magazines, I let my friend undo the damage I had caused with my not-so-polite behavior. I was within earshot of everything Linda said as she scheduled my next appointment, including the fact that I was "emotionally unstable."

Linda and I had been best friends since fourth grade, and we had weathered a lot of storms together, but cancer was putting our friendship to the test. Something about facing your own mortality makes you question a lot of things—including the friends you have in your life. For the most part, Linda was a stormy kind of person. She had a way of putting me in my place and treating me as if I were a child. The "hurricane force winds" that blew inside the house even had my husband and boys wondering if it was a good idea to have Linda around.

Normally, I was the stable one and hardly ever made a fuss, even when Linda was at her worst. She was, for the most part, the drama queen. She was also homecoming queen in high school and could talk me into almost anything—including trying out for sign carrier in the band (next to the majorettes). I learned my routine, put Vaseline on my teeth to keep my smile shining, and outperformed even my own expectations during tryouts. I made the cut, but I didn't like being in the limelight. It was Linda who enjoyed that.

I was working full-time and radiating on my lunch break (except on Fridays when I finished work at noon). On the one day I thought we could have a semi-normal day, it was ruined by my outburst at the treatment center. Would our relationship ever be the same? Worse yet, even though she'd been right in her assessment of my behavior, did I want Linda in my life? As we drove home from radiation oncology, I had a heart-to-heart with Linda. "This isn't easy, but I feel like I have to say something," I said tentatively. "Breast cancer at forty has taken me by storm. I'm vulnerable right now, and you can't blurt out everything that's on your mind."

Linda stared at me and replied, "You are so ungrateful. I gave up my life for a week to take care of your family, and this is the thanks I get?"

I pulled off to the side of the road and explained, "My life has been turned upside down, and I'm re-evaluating everything — my job, my friends, and what I want to do with the rest of my life."

It was a quiet ride back to the house after that. It had rained, but now the sun was out and we saw a beautiful rainbow; normally, I'd have stopped to take a picture, but I didn't have the strength.

Linda was leaving the next day, and I had hoped for a better ending, but she went up to the guest room, and I ended up fixing dinner. I tapped lightly on the bedroom door and whispered, "Dinner is ready. Would you like some?"

I got the silent treatment, so I let her be. The next day, as I drove Linda to the airport I apologized and let her know how much I appreciated her help during my final week of radiation.

In typical Linda fashion, she gathered up her things while I parked curbside under the departure sign. She didn't say a word, got out, and slammed the car door behind her. That was the last time I saw Linda.

It's been almost twenty-four years since that spring day in 1996, and I've learned a lot about myself through cancer. It changes you. You figure out what's important in your life and what's not. You set boundaries, and you protect your heart from unhealthy relationships. I had to let go of all the "Lindas" in my life.

Little did I know that my "friendship housekeeping" would come in handy for my second breast-cancer diagnosis three years ago. I was older, wiser, and much more prepared than I was the first time. I learned the secret: Always stay close to people who make you feel like sunshine, and you'll weather any storm that life brings your way.

— Connie K. Pombo —

Buying a Ticket to Life

*Sadness flies on the wings of the morning and
out of the heart of darkness comes the light.*
~Jean Giraudoux

That October morning, I awoke with a very uneasy feeling and I had no idea why. As the day went on, I continued to feel something gnawing at me. I kept checking my calendar to see if there was some place I needed to be or something I needed to do. It's always possible I'd forgotten an appointment, but nothing came to mind. No matter what I did, I couldn't shake the ominous feeling. Finally, as evening approached, it hit me — this was the tenth anniversary of the day my ex-husband and I faced our marital problems and separated. I thought I would never forget the date my life unraveled, but to my amazement, I had.

The memories of when my life consisted of lying in bed and crying tears of rejection and pain came flooding back. I remembered feeling paralyzed by fear, not knowing if my future would involve marriage or divorce.

Little did I know then, that now I would have tears of utter joy and thankfulness rolling down my cheeks for the amazing journey I took to reach the destination that awaited me.

There were some tears of sadness for the death of my marriage. I think it is always heartbreaking when two people love each other but somehow lose each other in the process of living. I am happy to report we remain friends. I'm proud of both of us; we agree that we did a terrific job of destroying our marriage, but we are great at divorce. We kept the wonderful memories of those years, which thankfully are many — and let go of all hurt and pain we inflicted upon each other.

I never want to completely forget that horrendous time because I now cherish every pain-free day, which is an everyday event.

When I was newly divorced, I found life scary and intimidating. At first, I felt I was being punished, but in reality I was given the opportunity to find myself and create a new life. I had no idea where it would take me, but I was ready to take the leap. Although I was frightened to travel in a new direction, it was also exciting to ponder my options. I didn't know exactly what I wanted, but I knew what I didn't want: the old me. I was not the same person I had misplaced all those years ago. Prior to this time, my epitaph could have read, "She died without ever having lived." Thankfully, that would no longer be the case. I was now strong and embraced the courage I never knew I had.

I remembered a very old joke about a man who prays to God every week to win the lottery, to no avail. Then one day when he makes his usual prayer, God answers him and says, "I'd love to help you win the lottery, but you've got to help me out and buy a ticket."

I chose to buy a ticket to life.

I've enjoyed all my adventures, the places I've seen and the people I've met.

Sometimes I feel as though I'm living life backwards. Most people become independent, start their careers and create the life they want in their twenties. I never stood on my own two feet until I was forty-seven. I moved out of my parent's house the day I got married. I also quit working at age thirty-three and enjoyed all the benefits of retirement at an early age.

When my marriage ended, I grew up and became an adult. Buying a house all by myself gave me a feeling of real independence. Starting a writing career at the age of fifty has opened up a whole new world. Most importantly, I have had the courage to unlock my heart, allowed myself to fall in love again and to be happy in a relationship. Some people never experience giving and receiving love. I've been blessed to have that blissful feeling twice in my life.

If I had it all to do over, I wouldn't change a thing. I would go through that agony again in a second to be where I am today, crying tears of joy.

I'm so glad I bought a ticket to life.

— Tena Beth Thompson —

The Power of a Word

Words create worlds.
~Pierre du Plessis

I am a hair puller. I have trichotillomania, an impulsive control disorder where I pull out my hair. I remember being teased about my bald spot in eighth grade, when I was thirteen — which didn't help, considering that one of the causes of the disorder is poor self-image.

I learned to brush my hair so it wasn't as noticeable, but I was never able to completely cover my thin hair on top. I learned to cut my own hair so I could avoid salons. It was easy with my natural curly hair. The curls cover up uneven edges.

I tried to stop many times, but failed. That changed when I read about a study that showed the phrase "I don't" provided more empowerment than "I can't." For example, it would be more effective to say "I don't eat cake" than to say "I can't eat that cake."

After thirty-seven years with the disorder, I saw the possibility of a solution. What if I told myself, "I *don't* pull my hair anymore" instead of "I *can't* stop pulling hair?"

It's a completely different mentality. It gave me control over the impulse immediately. I could see a change in my hair in about three weeks.

It has been three-and-a-half months, and my hair is getting thicker every week. I still have the urge, but I remind myself *I don't do that anymore*. Who knew one little word—"don't"—could change a lifetime of impulsive behavior?

— Sandy Newman —

There's a Limit

*Being able to say "No" is a necessary
ingredient in a healthy lifestyle.
~David W. Earle*

A real Good Samaritan. That was me. Need a ride to the doctor? I'll be glad to take you. Does your dog need to be walked while you're on vacation? No problem. Would you like someone to talk to about your troubles? I'm here for you.

I thought of myself as the true definition of a friend and was more than happy to put the needs of others before my own. After all, what are friends for?

Judging by how often my phone rang, it seemed that my reputation as a ready, willing, and able helper was common knowledge among those in my circle. Relatives, co-workers, neighbors, and even casual acquaintances all seemed to have my number—literally and figuratively speaking. I didn't mind, really, if I had to put some of my own responsibilities and needs on hold. It felt good to do good for others. Besides, it was the right thing to do. And I was okay with that until one afternoon when I received a call from an acquaintance of my dad's.

This man I barely knew phoned to inform me that I was to chauffeur him to a medical appointment he had made for the following Tuesday. I sighed and checked my calendar. Then I told him as nicely as possible that I couldn't help him that day. I had a morning appointment with my brother, an afternoon business meeting, and then I needed to stop at the pharmacy for a friend who was recuperating from knee surgery, followed by a stop at the supermarket to buy milk and bread for her and her children. If I was lucky, in between I might find a few minutes to wait in the drive-thru line at some fast food joint and eat lunch in my car. "No," I told him, "I just can't do it." His reaction wasn't very kind and the conversation ended with the threat of some really bad karma on my part for not helping an elderly fellow in need.

That phone call was my turning point.

I took a closer look at my calendar. I was averaging fourteen good deeds a month. That meant that almost every other day I was running somewhere for someone. Clearly, some things in my life had to change. I stepped away from the calendar, eyes finally opened, and took a closer look at myself. Dark circles shadowed my eyes. Well, I'd known for a while I didn't feel like my usual energetic self. Instead, I felt weary and worn, and sometimes, resentful too. Really resentful. Like the time I got not one but two late-night distress calls in the same week and the time I realized I was "picking up a few groceries" for someone who could have just as easily shopped for her own provisions. Obviously, my Good Samaritan routine was wearing on me.

Yes, it was time for a change. By being overly generous with my time I was not honoring my own needs or myself. Instead, my schedule had put me on a hamster wheel where I ran circles for the benefit of others. And was it really for their benefit? I started to wonder. Or, was I actually doing those I sought to help a disservice by allowing them to become dependent upon my kindness and not allowing them to learn to care for themselves? It was time for me to change. But how?

I brought my concerns to my friend Lucille, another busy woman. With a job, a husband, three kids, two grandchildren, and an aging father who needed her, I knew she had a lot to do every day. Yet, she somehow managed to maintain balance in her life. Despite the fact that she worked full-time, her house appeared well cared for, she had time to socialize, and in most cases, got a good night's rest — things that were lacking in my own life. How did she manage all that? I asked her.

She gave me her secret in one word: limits. You have to set limits, she told me. Don't run every time someone calls. Instead, ask the person some key questions: *Is this an emergency? Is someone else available to help you? Is this something that can wait?* And, the question I knew I should have been considering all along: *Is this something you could do for yourself?* "Certainly," Lucille said, "if someone is in a bind, by all means help them. But don't become a doormat. Set limits."

Now I consider those logical questions before jumping to another's aid and the benefits have been great. Thanks to paring down the favors I do for others I have more energy, sleep better at night, and even gained enough free time to pursue a hobby or two. Though I was fearful that cutting back on my kindness would have been met with disapproval from my crowd, those friends, relatives, and acquaintances quickly lost their sense of entitlement and started showing some real appreciation for my help when I chose to give it. Now, sometimes, they even help *me* when I'm in a bind. And that, perhaps, may be the greatest benefit of all.

—Monica A. Andermann—

17

Your Marriage Is Killing You

Life's problems wouldn't be called "hurdles" if there weren't a way to get over them.
~Author Unknown

In April 2000 I became very sick. I thought I had the flu, but there were other symptoms that led me to believe it was something more. I wasn't one to visit the doctor. While my three children had health insurance, my husband and I did not. Besides, I was super mom and could conquer any illness that came my way.

I was thirty-two at the time, working a full-time job and going to school at night. To say I was doing it all was an understatement. I was the breadwinner for our family.

After a battery of tests the doctors diagnosed me with Crohn's disease. When I went to the doctor's office for the test results he looked me square in the eyes and said, "You need to make some major lifestyle changes."

I nodded, waiting for him to tell me what needed to be changed.

"Your diet will have to change. You need to stay away from fried food, spicy food and chocolate, to name a few."

"Okay," I said. "It'll be difficult, but I can learn to eat better."

"It's really important, Tina. Your health requires the change."

I sat on the edge of the chair, worried about what else was going to change for me.

"And the other things?" I asked.

"Stress. You need to get your stress levels under control. I realize you want to go to school, work and care for your children, but something has to give. You can't do it all."

"Do you really think I have to give up school?" I'd finally just gotten to go back after having children at a young age.

"Yes, and I need to know how your marriage is."

I shrugged. "It's like all marriages. We have our good and bad times."

I refused to tell him that my husband was abusive and we fought all the time.

"Just try to keep the fights to a minimum please. Low-key is your goal."

"I understand." I wasn't sure how I could manage that, but I'd tell my husband what the doctor said.

I left the doctor's office in shock. My life really had to change.

It didn't. By July I was in the hospital. I needed intense treatment, blood transfusions and pain meds. What I also needed was rest and relaxation, but that wasn't to be. My husband called and harassed me every day. He said I would lose my children because I was sick and in the hospital. He didn't like having to take care of the children even if I was at death's door.

His calls would last five hours at a time. Nurses would come in and check on me, only to leave shaking their heads.

"Please, I need rest and I want to see my children," I'd beg. He refused to bring my children to see me. It was his way of punishing me for being sick.

Twenty days passed and I felt Crohn's was a death sentence. My health was terrible and I feared losing my children and my home. On the twentieth day, my doctor walked in and looked down at me lying there weak and worn. He touched my hand and I could see he was pensive.

"I don't normally stick my nose in something that isn't my business, but I feel I must. Your marriage is killing you and if you don't get out of it, it will."

I was stunned. At first I didn't know how to respond.

"Thank you," I said. "It's something to think about."

Think about it was all I did. It was the doctor's words that made me change. I fought to get better. I spent twenty-seven days in the hospital that time, and once I got out it took another four months to get back on my feet and back to work.

When I went back to work I had a plan. I was going to sock away cash in a secret savings account and when it was time I'd leave my husband.

It took almost a year, but one day while in the middle of a fight I'd had enough. I ran and ran and I didn't look back.

I left my marriage that day. To this day I still recall that conversation with my doctor. Most people would find a disease like Crohn's a life sentence. There is no cure, just ways to control it. I see it as a lifesaver. If I hadn't been diagnosed I probably would still be stuck in an abusive marriage. Instead I'm now married to a wonderful man who would never dream of harming me. For that I'm truly blessed.

I took a potential death sentence and turned my life around for the better.

— Tina O'Reilly —

Chapter 3

Get Outside in Nature

A Motorcycle and the Open Road

*Remember that happiness is a way
of travel — not a destination.*
~Roy M. Goodman

I feel guilty for saying this, but I'm happiest when I'm astride my bike. I experience a primitive joy when I ride. It's a feeling that can't be replicated, a sheer pleasure of gunning the throttle and stringing together a dozen or so smooth turns. Even after years of motorcycle insanity, I still chuckle to myself on the twisty stuff.

There's something about experiencing a meandering road, free and uncaged. You can smell nature when you're on a bike, and feel temperatures fluctuate as you pass through shadowy areas. In a car, you're inside a compartment. Watching the scenery through a windshield is like watching TV. You're a passive observer, and everything moves by you unexcitingly, a frame at a time. On a motorcycle, the frame is gone. You are in total contact with your surroundings.

Riding a bike makes me feel young again. Powering into a corner, hugging the turns, sinking into the dips, and powering out are more natural than wrestling an automobile around a bend. The power, the sound, the feel, the acceleration and exhilaration, the sense of control and the freedom — these are just a few of the physical sensations of being one with your machine.

Stress relief! There's that, too. Not that I have as much stress as I did as a younger man. But when I'm on my bike, there isn't anything else on my mind. Riding is meditation, a place where all worldly concerns melt away, and there's just the open road. Being faster than others is not important. I'm not a reckless rider by any stretch. I roll with sufficient pace to make it an enjoyable experience. It may take longer for me to reach my destination, but that's cool. Other motorists are fleeting guests in my world. Slower vehicles are gently and smoothly passed. Faster vehicles zip by, hungrier to reach their destinations.

In my senior years, I've come to enjoy the solitary nature of riding, the oneness of the world. Even when I ride with a group, I'm on my own without a care in the world, living in the moment.

The freedom to explore is another good reason to ride. I've ridden down dirt roads and along narrow highways that I would have never discovered on four wheels.

The sensation of power is an awesome feeling. I enjoy the challenge of trying to perfect my riding skills. I feel like a different person on my bike. My helmet, riding gear, and the adrenaline rush make me feel like a superhero. The bone-numbing cold, the wildlife I see and avoid hitting, the mind-blowing effort that goes into complex overpasses, the simple beauty of a slightly cloudy mid-spring day — it's all there. The only thing really making conscious noise is my brain. No radio, no books on tape, no hands-free conference calls, just me. Whenever I travel on my bike, I enjoy getting there. It's not that I don't feel upset or sad before I kick it down into gear, but those emotions drop away, because I'm doing something that requires a great deal of concentration.

Motorcycle riding has made me a more deliberate person, too. You can only carry so much aboard a motorcycle. Excess baggage is left at home, figuratively and literally. Differentiating between necessity and desire has become much clearer to me.

For this old man, bikes are what make life interesting. They keep things simple and in perspective. A lot of people allow fear to control their lives and stop them from doing the exciting things they enjoy. I'm not one of them. People love to give excuses and call their apprehension something else, but they don't know what they're missing. Motorcycling has changed my life and made it so much better. Tomorrow, I will ride.

— Timothy Martin —

Cabin Life

*Deny yourself the connection to the wild places
that your soul craves and the fire inside
you will slowly turn to ash.*
~Creek Stewart

When I was a child, I had a teacher who played the sounds of the forest during our nap time. It was relaxing to hear bubbling brooks, light breezes in the trees, and wildlife calls.

Many years later I adopted my first dog, a German Shepherd coyote mix who came from the woods. Because my townhome was not ideal for him, I searched for a place I could bring him that suited him better. I found a rental cabin in the Blue Ridge Mountains.

Baxter and I spent many seasons exploring the surrounding woods, admiring the wildflowers and watching clouds of ladybugs swarming like tiny tornadoes as they passed us on our trek. I learned to identify tree frogs, golden flies, and peacocks from their sounds.

Baxter was a wild one, but also fiercely protective. He always stayed close by, and I never had a flutter of fearfulness with him there.

He was from those woods. He was part of that wildlife. Before coming to live with me, he'd been hit by a truck. A Good Samaritan rescued him from certain death. No one would adopt him due to his injury and wild nature. Then we met and became best friends. But deep down, I always knew he belonged to these woods, more to the woods than to me.

Eventually, he and I brought our other dog on vacation with us, a yellow Lab that I often called My Sunshine Girl. Her favorite pastime was sitting on the screened-in porch snoozing while I spent the day nearby on a swing reading. Once, I found a copy of *The Phantom of the Opera*, and I read it from dawn to dusk as I lay on that swing lazily, completely content with my life under blue skies.

I've been to that cabin as thunderstorms threatened. I've stayed there on moonless nights when it was so dark that you couldn't see your own hand directly in front of your face. I have woken up there as early morning mist has risen from the depths of these mountains like hallowed spirits. There have been bone-chilling days when I sipped piping-hot coffee while watching the sun come up over the horizon. I have decorated a Christmas tree while nibbling on homemade treats and listening to holiday music before watching a classic Christmas movie.

I have taken hours-long bubble baths in sweet silence there, spending some quality time with my own thoughts. There have been days I cooked like a pro and then sampled my efforts while happily sipping on a favorite glass of wine or, even better, a glass of sweet orchard cider. Later, there would be a good movie to watch while cuddled up under several blankets, sometimes sitting beside a roaring fire that I proudly started myself with kindling I'd collected and the logs that were piled up outside for guest use. At night, I'd fall asleep with the stars so clearly visible overhead in that dark mountain sky. Sleeping well is never a problem there.

I have visited this cabin in good times and bad. It's been a sanctuary when I've needed it, like when Grandpa Ben passed away. I've been to these woods seeking refuge from exhaustion and sudden illness, to recover and rest. I've come to celebrate milestones in my life and to have a porch party with friends. Other times, I've gone there to mourn the passing of a friend. I recall sitting on the porch that Baxter and I shared for so many seasons, reading *Chicken Soup for the Pet Lover's Soul* with tears streaming down my face since I had just released his ashes in his favorite place. And yet there was a smile on my face.

Sometimes, when I return to the cabin now, I am overwhelmed by too many memories, but then I imagine the familiar pitter patter of

Get Outside in Nature

his paws and I realize he'll always be there with me. This is our place, available when I need it.

The cabin is my church, my sanctuary. and my escape. When I leave the cabin, it often rains, just lightly, as if the woods are sad that I have to go. But as I look over my shoulder, at what's fading from view behind me, I always whisper, "I'll be back," because this is where my heart is, and this is where my spirit feels most free, at Mile Marker 13, Highway 5, in Northwest Georgia.

— Tamra Anne Bolles —

Forever Changed

We live in a wonderful world that is full of beauty, charm and adventure. There is no end to the adventures we can have if only we seek them with our eyes open.
~Jawaharial Nehru

Resting on my swing, rocking back and forth, I close my eyes and enjoy the sounds of autumn — the cool wind, the leaves rustling as they fall to the forest's floor. The caw of a crow, the coo of some doves, and the rat-a-tat-tat of a woodpecker add to the sensory experience.

Several years ago, I retired after more than three decades in a stressful and exhausting job in a city of millions of people. Back then, if I closed my eyes, I would hear the racket of traffic, sirens and the chatter of people around me all the time.

I was a shift manager in passenger service for an enormous airline in the busiest terminal in one of the largest airports in the world. And if that wasn't rough enough, I was the guy everyone called to deal with the loudest passengers with the biggest problems. I wore stress like a suit and then internalized it into an ever-churning stomachache. Oh, I got good at handling it, but I was tired and longed for escape.

So, I left and moved from a tiny apartment at the bottom of a stack of other tiny apartments. Everyone told me I wouldn't leave the big city, or I wouldn't last long before coming back.

They were wrong. I now live in a house in the middle of a forest.

My closest neighbor is over half a mile away. I live five miles from a small town and thirty miles from a small city. When I close my eyes now, there are no bustling people, cars clanking or any of the manmade noises that polluted my existence.

I'm home, where after basking in the surrounding sounds, I can open my eyes and spot a spectacular cardinal in a tree forty feet away or watch a bunny nibbling grass under a gardenia bush a few steps beyond my patio's edge.

Several times a day, I go outside to immerse myself in the great outdoors, with my dogs Thunder and Trixie accompanying me. With me on my swing and my dogs on their cots, we marvel at the grand performance of Mother Nature.

Seasons change, temperatures rise and fall, and witnessing it fulfills my love of the phenomena of our natural world. Every hour of every day is a wondrous adventure when spent amongst this scenery within my reach.

To spy a little green lizard change his colors as he halts his scurry, pauses on a different colored surface and then blends his hue is amazing. To see my dogs go crazy at the sight of a wild turkey—one who's unconcerned about their excited barking behind our fence—fulfills me.

Sometimes, the slightest hint of skunk swirls in the air as he hides just beyond the forest's boundary. Recently, I witnessed a possum trot out of the woods' undergrowth a few feet into view and then head back to cover. After a few seconds, a second possum followed the exact track of the first.

My house sits on a hill with a pond at the bottom of a slope. It's a whole different ecosystem from my forest but just as relaxing and fascinating to observe. Clinging willows and silver maples satisfy their thirst, cattails sprout right out of the water, and prairie cordgrass stabilizes the wet bank. An abundance of critters also depends on the giving waters of the pond. Gray and white cranes frequent the spot as they fish for their lunch. Deer stop by for a drink. Ducks visit every year as they pass through, escaping the harsh winter of the North and then returning for spring's awakening.

Focusing on the pond and its surroundings allays my tension and deepens my understanding that man's touch need not be on everything. Since moving to my forest, my blood pressure has stabilized in a healthy range. I've lost weight, and I am no longer subject to an addictive personality and immediate gratification. Spiritually, the woods have found me, and I breathe in a life of calm and satisfaction.

I've never slept better or felt more rested. I focus on what's in front of me with little interest in the distractions that kept me off balance in the past.

Thoreau's quest in living next to Walden Pond was to live deliberately and simplify his life. Living in the forest, my goal was to escape the rat race. But a funny thing happened on this journey: I found a beautiful world of unspoiled landscape, and I am forever changed by it.

— Jonney Scoggin —

The Best View

*I took a walk in the woods and
came out taller than the trees.*
~Henry David Thoreau

Every room was occupied. The kids were home from school, each ensconced in their room, trying to focus on their online lessons. My mother-in-law was staying for the first three weeks of our national COVID-19-induced lockdown. The dogs flopped in either the lounge or on the veranda. And my husband was working in a room in the vacant house next door, shouting over the wall if he needed anything.

For someone used to hours of peace and quiet, and the space to potter at will every morning, this was a challenge. I had no sooner cleaned all the kitchen counters and popped the stray cups in the dishwasher than another dirty dish would appear. The milk seemed to be more out of the fridge than in, snacks were in constant demand, and doors clattered and rattled.

Just as I sat down to get my own work done, someone would request help or attention. Add to that the stress and anxiety experienced every time I read the news or watched updates on TV. Coronavirus numbers were climbing; deaths were rising. The world was suffering.

I was overwhelmed. I needed to do something, go somewhere. A place with a distant horizon, a wide-open sky and a gentle breeze. My garden. My retreat. My spacious place.

I live in Durban, on the east coast of South Africa, in a home overlooking the warm Indian Ocean. Palm trees wave their branches in the salty sea air, and yellow-billed kites play in the thermals. Pods of dolphins surf the waves below, and whales breach and smack their tails with glorious delight. Little wonder that there, under the palm tree, was my favourite place to rest, recover and recharge.

It was time to head there now. I brewed a cup of strong, black coffee, aromatic and earthy, grabbed the brightly coloured cap I'd bought in Mozambique a few months earlier, and tucked a comfy cushion under my arm. I closed the back door firmly behind me and took the few steps down to the pool area of the garden. Sheltered from the wind and drenched in warm, end-of-summer sunshine, my plastic pool lounger awaited.

I stretched out on the lounger, grateful for the feeling of finally being on my own. I sipped the coffee, gazing over the rim of the cup at the ocean stretched in front of me, blue and peaceful. As I drank, savouring the bitter taste, I began to engage my other senses, taking time to tune in to the sights and sounds around me. Putting down the emptied cup, I began to deliberately notice the ebb and flow of the waves below me, observing the dark of the rocks under the surface. I watched numerous swallows rise and dip in search of food and tried to see the insects that were the object of their desire. I listened to the layers of sound — first, the loud crash and suck of the rolling breakers, then the closest of the birds until gradually I could discern the rustle of the leaves in the tree below me.

I took a deep breath in, one of those stuttering breaths taken by a child at the end of a torrent of tears. I hadn't been crying but must have been more tense and on-edge than I thought, holding my breath tight in my lungs, raising my shoulders nearly to my ears. I took another breath, less shaky this time, and felt my diaphragm stretch and suck air deep within. Exhaling slowly and steadily, my shoulders fell and softened. I settled a little more deeply into my seat.

This practice of observing the wonder of God's creation, of truly looking and noticing, has become a vital aspect of my self-care journey. In doing so, I hear again His whispers, feel His love, enjoy His presence. I am reminded that He is God, and I am not. As such, I don't need to be weighed down with the burdens of the world. He opens the windows of my soul, and the claustrophobic stuffiness is expelled by the fresh wind of His Spirit.

I gathered my coffee cup and cushion and returned to my over-full house. But this time, as I walked through the door, it was different. Or, rather, I was. Now there was space.

—Anna Jensen—

Three O'Clock on Phantom Lake

I could never stay long enough on the shore;
the tang of the untainted, fresh, and free sea
air was like a cool, quieting thought.
~Helen Keller

This time,
I don't give the drain rack a second glance.
Someone else can stack the glasses and
Slide the cutting board back into its narrow cubby.
The plate with eggs baked on by the microwave
Can sit and soak.
I'm out the back door.
The shed smells of mildew from
The left-in-the-rain lifejackets;
Remembered and stowed in September.
And who took apart these paddles?
Just because it's November doesn't mean
I'm in for the season.
It's worth it, these pesky preparations,
To skim along the still waters
And push away the lake fog
with the blunt, blue nose
Of my little kayak.

Let the bills wait.
Leave the cellphone on the kitchen counter.
There will be time enough to grade papers tomorrow.
Here is my peace.
Just me and the sky and this boat.
And sometimes the dog.

— Ilana Long —

Kleenex Capers

*The only real mistake is the one from
which we learn nothing.*
~John Powell

One, two, three, four. My head nods to the annoying rhythm of the sounds. They're worse than nails on a chalkboard! I feel the muscles in my shoulders tighten and realize I'm holding my breath. Who would have thought that the sound of Kleenex being pulled from the box could be so incredibly nerve-wracking!

At first, I thought she was using the tissues to wipe her nose, until I took a moment to sit and watch closely as she pulled out one at a time, unfolded it, and carefully added it to the growing stack on her lap. When the stack finally reached the correct height, she took the top one into her hands, meticulously folded it into a perfect square and gently placed it in the small wicker wastebasket on the floor next to her recliner. She continued until the pile on her lap was gone and then began the process all over again. One, two, three, four.

Repetitive actions are the most frustrating part of Mom's cognitive-behavior issues and make my job as her caregiver more stressful than all her physical needs combined. I've tried a variety of methods to wean her from the tissue routine without success. It's possible to distract her for a while, but she goes right back to it.

My one attempt to talk with her about it didn't go over well. Thinking I was upset because she was using too many tissues, Mom reached for her purse and tried to give me money to pay for them. It made me feel so sad that I've never been able to broach the subject again.

Probably the only real harm in this repetitive activity is that it causes me anxiety. However, going through a large box of tissues every day is also a waste of money and resources.

I don't mean to sound so self-centered, especially with everything my mother is having to endure, but I do believe there is truth in what I've read about the importance of relieving caregiver stress and fatigue. Our doctor also cautions me that if I don't stay healthy, my mother's health suffers as well.

So, I hatched a plan to reduce my stress caused by this particular behavior. I decided to salvage the unused tissues from Mom's wastebasket. Perhaps, if I could recycle them, my anxiety level would drop.

I squatted down behind Mom's chair, reached around and grabbed a handful of the neatly folded tissues from the basket. I ran to the laundry room with my booty and opened each tissue, laid it flat on top of the previous one, forming a nice little pile on the ironing board.

I did this several times a day. Watching my stack grow over the weeks was extremely gratifying. I felt so much better until the day my daughter came to visit and went to look for something in the laundry room.

"Mom!" she shrieked. "What is this huge stack of tissues doing on the ironing board?"

Grasping at the chance for a little humor to soften the situation, I yelled back, "Isn't it nice that I've finally found a use for the ironing board?"

When I walked in to explain what I was doing with a nearly two-feet-high pile of tissues, I wasn't prepared for her response. "Mom, don't you see you're doing exactly the same thing Granny does? I'm afraid that I'm going to be caring for both of you before long!"

That jolted me right back to reality. Jacqui was right! I decided it was time to bite the bullet — forget about Granny's tissues and find something that works to safely relieve my anxiety.

In my search for a solution, it came to mind that I hadn't been going on long walks like I used to. Perhaps that was one reason I had been feeling more anxious and fatigued. I didn't like leaving Mom alone these days while I walked several miles from the house, but we had the perfect place to walk on our own acreage.

With camera in hand, I ventured to the pond one sunny fall afternoon. It was much more peaceful than I had remembered — a nature reserve, a sanctuary for my troubled spirit. The birds were chirping in unison from their perches on tree limbs, while the geese and ducks floated together on the pond. Heart-shaped, mating dragonflies fluttered among the reeds of pond grass and cattails. I got lost in the sounds of nature as I snapped beautiful photos of the natural habitat.

I strolled back across the field to the house feeling refreshed with the warm sunshine on my face. I hadn't felt this peaceful in a long time. I vowed that I would walk to the pond at least once and maybe twice each day.

I have managed to keep that promise to myself, and I have gotten much better at dealing with Mom's repetitive behaviors. I no longer collect the tissues she discards. I have come to the conclusion that the excessive tissue use is her way of coping with anxiety. Perhaps it is both mentally and physically therapeutic for her. I have also made an attempt to get her outside every day. There is nothing more rewarding than sharing Mother Nature's therapeutic beauty with those I love.

— Connie Kaseweter Pullen —

The Solitary Cottage

*An inability to stay quiet is one of the
most conspicuous failings of mankind.*
~Walter Bagehot

"Oops, sorry." Those two simple, solitary, apologetic words once got me kicked out of an outdoors game that I like to play at our cottage. The game is called "The Silent Hike" and it is based on the premise that nature and silence go together. It is played on a series of groomed trails that have been blazed in a forest across the road from the log cottage that my wife Kris and I had built on a lakeside lot two hours north of our Toronto-area home in 1992.

Everyone who plays the game must adhere to one simple rule: You must not talk at any time during the one-hour hike. Not. One. Word.

On one occasion several years ago, on a warm July afternoon, I stood at the edge of the forest and explained the rules to a group of six gamers who included Kris, her brother Bob, his now-deceased wife Ann, and their two preteen sons, Andrew and John.

"You must be quiet as a mouse," I explained. "Even if you see a bear, you must keep your trap shut," I joked. "Utter a sound and you're out of the game. The winner is anyone who can complete the hike in complete and golden silence."

For the first twenty minutes, we tramped through the woods as "noiseless as fear in a wide wilderness," to quote John Keats. I took up a rear position and was thoroughly enjoying the serenity of the hike through the woods. We all became immersed in the tranquility of this walk with nature, where the only audible noise, other than the gurgling sound of the babbling brooks we crossed, was the rustle of snapping twigs under our feet. I was paying close attention to the stillness of the event when at one point, while lost in my thoughts, I came up too close to Ann and accidentally stepped on the heel of her hiking boot. "Oops, sorry," I said, automatically. "That's okay," she whispered, politely.

Well, you'd think we just killed Bambi! Everyone stopped and pointed at us, noiselessly but accusingly, and indicated in no uncertain terms that we were out of the game. Since I had created the rule, I had little choice but to suck up my punishment. We all trooped onward.

Now that I had been banished, I played devil's advocate. When I spotted a tiny snake slithering through the grass, I yelled out: "Hey, John, I'll give you $10 if you can tell me what kind of snake this is." John didn't bite. Neither did the snake. Later, I called out to the tight-lipped adolescents. "Kris and I have two extra tickets to a couple of Toronto Blue Jays games next week. Would you two like to come?" Both boys nodded their heads excitedly and in silent unison. "Which game would you like to see? Wednesday's game against the Yankees or Saturday afternoon against the Red Sox?" The expression in their bulging eyes was painful to watch. "Speak now or forever hold your peace," I teased. "Let me know now or we'll take your mom and dad instead."

Bob thought I was being a tad unfair and he let his feelings be known when he uttered a sympathetic "Awww." Both boys jumped up and down and, still under the gag order, demonstrated a universal sign that their father was toast by drawing their forefinger across their throat.

"Ha," laughed my wife.

And another one bit the dust!

To their everlasting credit, and despite the best efforts of four scheming adults, the two youths completed the journey without so much as a peep. Later that evening, Kris and I hosted an Awards Barbeque to honour the winners. Everyone got a chuckle when they saw the booty bag of prizes which included aptly named chocolate bars and candy, namely Turtles, Snickers and Smarties. I had tried to find a Noisette bar — delicious caramelized hazelnuts buried in milk chocolate — but they are available only in the U.S.

The Silent Hike is just one of many quiet activities that Kris and I enjoy at the cottage. I can easily spend a speechless summer afternoon chopping wood for the fireplace while she enjoys the sweet serenity of reading a novel on our deck that overlooks the still and deep waters of Lake Manitouwabing

Whenever I feel like exercising at this soul-satisfying place, which is surrounded by tall pines and maples, I put on my running shoes and run up and down the wooden stairs that lead from the cottage to the lake. When my father Wally died a year after the cottage was built, I had the staircase built in his honour. There are fifty steps, and at Step #25 I placed a gold-plated plaque that reads: "Wally's Stairway to Heaven." If I'm going down for a swim or coming up from a canoe ride, I know I'm halfway there when I stop at Step #25 and whisper a silent prayer. Often, the prayer is one of gratitude for owning such a place of splendid isolation. We feel extremely fortunate, especially when we learned that only seven percent of Canadians own a cottage. Our secluded spot is indeed a treasure. Even a poor little rich girl like the late Diana, Princess of Wales — who seemed to have it all — once lamented: "I've got to have a place where I can find peace of mind."

During snowy winter weekends, at our four-season cottage, we are reminded of the phrase that "serenity is not freedom from the storm, but peace amid the storm."

As much as we love the stillness at our lakeside retreat, we decided to put the cottage up for sale this year. We got a bug. The travel bug! We want to explore more of the world before we get fitted for the "Forever Box." But no matter where we travel and whomever we meet, having owned a cottage will give us lots to talk about.

— Dennis McCloskey —

Tiny Sanctuary

*I go to nature to be soothed and healed,
and to have my senses put in order.*
~John Burroughs

I stared at the trailhead knowing exactly what I wanted from my hike before I embarked. I wanted a beautiful challenge, the sort of hiking experience that was brutal on the muscles yet breathtaking in its beauty. I needed steep elevations winding through forested area so canopied by trees that it changed the light of the blazing summer sun. I needed a cold creek to temper the Texas heat, for the humidity to drape itself over me. I needed to sweat out the sadness, worry, stress-eating, secret crying, and sleepless nights that come with mothering a child who is on the autism spectrum.

"Why don't you take a long break for yourself and go on a real hike, like the Appalachian Trail or camp at Big Bend?" a friend asked me when I told her about my plan.

"Because that's not how motherhood works," I said.

I needed a quick dose of peace, a trail that could be hiked in the few hours my son spent in his new autism therapy clinic 16 miles up the road. It was less romantic than sleeping beneath the stars, but healing for both of us would have to be done in smaller increments.

It had been two years since I last hiked the River Place Nature Trail, but it remained my favorite in Austin, a city full of beautiful nature preserves. I considered hiking all of them on my son's therapy days, feeling productive by covering the most territory, but healing doesn't work that way. I needed to be nurtured by the familiar, to walk the same paths each time and get lost in the sort of meditative trance that comes with repetition. Only this trail, an oasis protected and maintained by volunteers from the surrounding neighborhood, would do. Perhaps the love the trail received from its caretakers would soothe me, too.

I knew we couldn't undo the autism, and there are so many beautiful things about his unusual mind that we wouldn't want to. His autism affords him a near-photographic memory, a love of math I cannot comprehend, and an ability to create art with advanced perspective. We do, however, want a life for him with fewer stresses or dangers caused by autism triggers and sensory overstimulation. Like all parents, we want our child to have a life filled with love, independence and self-created happiness.

I looked back down the street and said, "I love you," sending the words out over the wind to my boy on this important day. While he took his first steps toward a different life, I moved forward and took the first steps toward mine.

The first hike was brutal and beautiful. Accidentally, I took the longest part of the trail. It boasted the highest elevation change in the Austin area — 1,700 feet in just a few miles. I needed breaks, several of them. Despite the heat and my dangerously high heart rate from the climb, I felt relief by wading in a stream so clear and cold that I was certain it had been consecrated. I half-expected a vision of a saint to appear.

Instead, I saw a cardinal. It perched for a moment on a large rock facing me, its deep red color a complement to the rich greens that surrounded us. I looked up and saw its partner on a branch, less red but still beautiful. Cardinals are rather common in Austin, but the birds still felt like little guardians along the path, rooting me on as I persevered. They are said to symbolize wisdom and living life with confidence and grace. They were the sort of cheerleaders I needed.

As I approached the end of my hike, I noticed the smooth and heavy rocking chairs that awaited hikers at the end of their journeys. I drank my last drops of water as I allowed the heavy motion of the rocking chairs to soothe my tired body. A breeze picked up from the nearby pond, cooling me off as I rocked back and forth, the trail nurturing me to the very end. Then I took a deep breath and went to pick up my son.

He looked forward to his therapy sessions each week, evolving in a way that gave him visible confidence and happiness. My slivers of time in this tiny sanctuary did the same for me. It wasn't a grandiose journey, but it was ours. At the end of each day, my boy ran toward me, undeterred by my sweat and disheveled hair, with smiles and hugs and some new project to show me. I always waited with my arms open, ready to embrace him with love, joy and the newfound sensation of hope.

— Tanya Estes —

Gone Too Soon

Sisters make the best friends in the world.
~Marilyn Monroe

"Hey, Kat!" I said cheerfully as I answered my phone. It was around 2:00 P.M. on a weekday in September. My sister's voice sounded pained, almost inaudible as she whispered, "I am in the emergency room with a terrible pain in my side." I could tell she was holding back tears as she said, "They ran some tests, and they think I have cancer." Paralyzed by her words, all I managed to say was, "Katherine, I am on the way."

Engulfed in fear, I drove to the hospital to be with my sister. On the drive to the hospital, I kept thinking, *You didn't come this far just to get this far.* After a marriage that didn't work and with many trials to follow, Katherine had flourished and made a beautiful life for herself.

Being only twenty months apart, Katherine and I grew up doing everything together. Our personalities couldn't have been more opposite, but our souls couldn't have been more alike. Katherine was fearless and full of life, while I was cautious and reserved. Katherine always did the courageous things, and I did the worrying. I told her when to be quiet, and she told me when to speak up. She was the yin to my yang, and I to hers. Katherine's gentle, kind heart was always a soft place for my secrets to be understood, kept, and protected.

When I walked in, Katherine looked up at me with tears in her eyes. She looked so fragile and childlike in her hospital gown, covered

74 | Get Outside in Nature

in blankets. Speechless, I hugged my sister. The white room looked harsh beneath the fluorescent lights. It was unfriendly, cold, and smelled sterile. Machines beeped, and tubes ran from her arms. My vibrant sister didn't belong here. It wasn't long before the doctor entered the room. I saw the concern in her eyes as she explained that more testing would be done, and we would have the results in a couple of days.

Two days later, on Katherine's thirty-fourth birthday, in a hospital room filled with balloons, flowers, friends, and family, we received confirmation that Katherine had stage IV colon cancer. It was advanced and inoperable. As the doctor spoke words like "extremely uncommon" and "very unfortunate," the devastation in the room was palpable. Katherine had three children who needed her, whom she loved more than anything in the whole world. How could this be? Just three days ago, Katherine seemed to be the picture of health, doing yoga and working two full-time jobs as a counselor. Now, she was a terminal cancer patient.

Katherine started chemo to slow the cancer's progress, and we desperately clung to our hope for a miracle. It was our only lifeline as we boarded this sinking ship. Chemo was a true test of Katherine's physical, emotional, and spiritual endurance, and she fought with all her might. She fought for a future with her children

As we sat in the waiting room before each doctor's appointment, Katherine closed her eyes and sat in silence. I stared at her in awe as peace emanated from her. With each appointment came a discouraging report. "What will we try next?" Katherine asked. "I have to try everything. For my kids." We were running out of options, but Katherine refused to give up.

As the cancer got worse, Katherine knew it was time to fully live each day, so we made a little bucket list. Katherine had been dreaming of going to a beach with turquoise water, so we traveled to Turks and Caicos. We rode horses through the ocean, relaxed on the beach in the day, and sat beneath the stars at night. Katherine had always been religious, but she embarked on a deeper spiritual journey that gave her much comfort and light, especially in her most difficult days. Most amazingly, Katherine wrote letters to her children to be given to them in the future. I watched her cry as she thought about all the moments she would miss: first day of high school, marriage, the birth of their first child, and so many more.

I witnessed the supernatural strength it took to find the words she would never get to speak to her children but could say through the letters. This was, perhaps, the hardest thing Katherine had done in her life, but it was worth it to her because, through the letters, she would, in a sense, be with her children.

Katherine focused on what a blessing each day was. To Katherine, her doctors, nurses, family, friends, and prayer warriors were "angels" whom she believed had been placed in her life. We all felt the power of this divine orchestration of angels who blessed Katherine as her life came to an end.

Katherine's "angels" made her cottage in the woods a place of comfort and joy. Lights were strung over the back patio of her cottage, gardens with her favorite flowers were planted, and her porch was filled with potted plants. Her "angels" made sure that the inside of her home always had burning candles and fresh flowers, two of her very favorite things. The cottage had a magical essence and looked like a scene from a fairy tale. Katherine enjoyed her time with her children here and the peace that nature provided her.

I spent many precious nights with Katherine in her final months. We often sat on her back porch, a fire blazing in her fire pit, as we visited beneath the canopy of twinkling lights. We listened to music and talked about life. Fireflies sparkled in the night, and coyotes howled from deep in the woods as we laughed about stories from our past and cried as we mourned that these would be the last of our memories together. Katherine cried as she told me she wished she could bring me with her, and I cried as I told her I wished I could keep her here to grow old with me.

Katherine's health declined quickly. Her body became weak and feeble, but she was more beautiful than ever. Katherine's strength, faith, and courage gave her a veil of supernatural peace and grace. She was truly majestic. Katherine died peacefully on May 7th, about seven months after her diagnosis, much sooner than anyone anticipated. All our hopes and prayers for a miracle weren't enough to keep my sister here — not when God had other plans.

I miss my sister terribly, and the void in my heart is indescribable. I find myself seeking peace in nature now, just as Katherine did. Through nature, I feel my sister's presence.

— Rachel Chustz —

Chapter 4

"No" Is a Complete Sentence

The Strength of No

*I encourage people to remember that "no"
is a complete sentence.*
~Gavin de Becker

All my life I heard yes, yes, yes. Any time a patient needed my dad he would go to his optometrist office no matter what time of the day it was. He would make sure breakfast was always made for my brother and me, but he would leave the house immediately to take care of whoever had called him. If a volunteer organization needed him, he was there. Any time they would ask him to help with something, it was "How high do I need to jump?"

Dad was a huge role model for me. He appeared to always be fulfilled and happy. So I tried to do the same thing, "be everything to everyone."

Amazing, right?

The part I never saw was what I witnessed when he was on his deathbed, truly exhausted. Because he had always said yes to everyone except himself. He had been sick for fifteen years but never told us, pretending that everything was fine.

My dad's need for love and acceptance from the external world was so strong that it drained him in many areas of his life. As much as he loved my mom, she wanted to support him and not deny him his wish to be the "ultimate giver." She was always the strong woman, and she never spoke up about how he was living his life. She just wore this mask and took it. So that was another thing I modeled — being strong. Give and be strong.

As an adult, I continued the cycle — giving and giving, even to people who did not appreciate my giving.

Why did I do it? What made me say yes all the time?

And what did saying no really mean to me?

It took some time to figure it out.

All my life I have been a pleaser. I love to make people happy. I used to do ANYTHING and EVERYTHING for ANYONE who needed me! That is what life is about, right? At least that's what I thought when I modeled myself after my generous, loving, altruistic father, who pleased everyone at the expense of his own health and happiness.

I remember the day... the day I finally said "No." That was the day I grew up. A little girl trapped in a forty-five-year-old body became a woman who truly understood her worth that day. I could still help people and have purpose and do what I was here to do in the world, but not at my personal expense or the expense of my children.

Here's what was happening in my life the day I grew up. I had just gone through a divorce, my kids' dad had moved to California from Las Vegas where we lived, I was driving my kids to three different schools every day, and sometimes I had more month than money. I was working hard to support us, but not at the expense of my kids. I was committed to being there for them no matter what.

I was stretched thin!

So that day, I was working at my desk, going on conference call after conference call, attending meeting after meeting. I was rocking it! Then I looked over at my phone and a longtime friend was calling. We talked for about fifteen minutes, just small talk, and I could sense she was getting ready for "the ask." And there it was: "Oh and by the way... do you know someone who can help me with this or can you help me plan this..."

I remember catching myself... the old me, the one who was a pleaser no matter how much extra work it was for me, or how much it would distract me from my mission. I would always just do what I was asked. But this time I took a deep breath and said, "I'm sorry but I just have to say no. I need to focus on my kids and my work."

I felt this sense of power like never before. I didn't worry about whether she would get upset. Instead, I really looked at my values and what was most important was for me to thrive and for my kids to thrive.

That day I got clear. Really clear. I learned that being a martyr is not good at all, and it is NOT what we are supposed to do. In the end, it benefits no one.

Honestly, that was the best call of my life. Ever since, I have set boundaries for what I will and won't do, and also for what I will stand for and not sell out to.

Now I make sure to take care of the relationships that matter to me, and that means keeping myself in top form. Watching the most successful people in the world, I noticed there were certain things that they did, one being to stick to the routines that worked for them. So every Sunday night at six, no matter where I am in the world, I sit myself down and plan my week. I look at what needs to happen that week and what resources I need to access to make that happen.

And every morning, I wake up and I say, "Today is going to be the BEST day of my life." It might sound silly, but it really works and it sets me up for the day.

I also make sure that I stay true to my ideals and that I work with people I respect.

I'm creating a new role model for my children, building on what I learned from my father, but taking it up one more level to make sure that my priority remains myself and my children. It's like they say on the airplane — "put your oxygen mask on first." You can't give what you don't have.

— Loren Slocum Lahav —

Silencing the "Should" Monster

Half of the troubles of this life can be traced to saying yes too quickly and not saying no soon enough.
~Josh Billings

Women have it tough. Maybe it's biological. Perhaps it's just plain insanity. But women, in general, have this deep desire to be everything to everyone all the time. We want to be the fantastic wife, amazing mother, loving daughter, caring sister, dependable employee, and supportive friend. The list is endless and exhausting. Every single day, I am surrounded by amazingly smart, strong, and independent women who are "shoulding" themselves to death.

Let me explain.

We think we should be Superwoman. We should keep a sparkling clean house and cook dinner for our families every night. We should plan themed birthday parties for our kids with twenty of their closest friends. We should be community volunteers throughout the week and bring homemade dishes to church functions on Sunday. We should pick out the perfect baby/birthday/graduation/wedding gift and then attend all those events with smiles on our faces. And we should do it all without asking for help from anyone.

Is that realistic? Absolutely not.

But more importantly, it's unhealthy.

Unrealistic expectations on our energy, time, and emotions can lead to anxiety, depression, guilt, and low self-esteem. Frazzled isn't just a state of mind. It's a reality. And it's a reality that leaves us feeling physically exhausted, mentally drained, and emotionally unfulfilled.

As wives, mothers, daughters, and employees, we fight the "should" monster every day. Of course, there will always be things that must be done. But what about the things we don't have to do? I don't always have to do the grocery shopping. My husband can help with that. I don't always have to go to the funeral of an acquaintance. I can send a card or flowers instead. I don't have to pick out the perfect birthday gift for a niece or nephew because kids love gift cards too. I don't have to bake a homemade dish for a church dinner when something from the grocery's deli will be just as appreciated.

We have to learn to give ourselves a break.

And, if we don't want to do something? It's absolutely okay to say no.

Let me repeat that. It's absolutely okay to say no. In fact, it's a necessity, because the truth is we can't do it all. We can't. Not if we want to keep our sanity.

I went through a period a few years ago where I was dealing with anxiety issues, and a lot of it was caused by the fact that I was spreading myself too thin. I was always the dependable one. The reliable one. The first to volunteer for anything.

Why? Because I "should."

While dealing with my anxiety, I spent some time with a therapist who asked me a question that still resonates with me to this day. During one of our sessions, I mentioned that I was dreading a particular event. She wondered why I was going if I felt this way.

My answer? "Because I should."

My therapist looked at me and very simply asked, "Why should you do something you don't want to do?"

I explained that while I didn't want to go, I felt that it was expected of me. She said, "That's why you're dealing with anxiety. You're trying to make everyone else happy. What about you? Are you happy? You can't be, because you're trying to juggle all the things you have to do with the things you feel like you should do. You have to start being a little selfish with your time. You have to learn to say no."

I honestly couldn't imagine such a thing. But I gave it a shot. I started saying no when it was possible, and you know what? The world didn't spin off its axis.

Now, I do my best to silence the "should" monster by doing the things I want to do and politely declining the rest. I delegate as much as I can (my husband honestly loves grocery shopping). I volunteer for things because I want to and not because I feel obligated.

It's not always easy, and I still struggle with feeling selfish from time to time, but I'm a happier, calmer person.

And that's the way it should be.

— Sydney Logan —

Finding Me

*Know, first, who you are; and
then adorn yourself accordingly.*
~Epictetus

I've been a lot of different people in my life. Not very many of them were really me.

Because I was such an insecure child, I became both a straight-A student and a sullen argumentative "hippie" to impress my parents and my peers at the same time. It was a pretty big task. All that skipping school to be with the cool kids made for some very long nights of make-up work to keep up my straight A's. I did it, though. I'm sure there are still teachers out there who think I was the perfect student, and students that think I was the perfect radical. The real me was neither of those things.

Once I started dating, things got even worse. Like a chameleon in a rapidly changing environment, my personality would transform to fit whatever man I happened to be dating at the time. In the span of a couple of years, I went from being an overzealous religious fanatic while dating a good Catholic man, to a bar-hopping, beer-drinking groupie when I dated a local musician. Other versions of "me" included the reluctant beach bunny who suffered through the humiliation of displaying my skinny, scrawny bikinied body at the beach to be with my surfing boyfriend. Or the hermit who quit my job and moved away from my family to try to find the right place where my unsociable boyfriend-du-jour could feel comfortable in isolation. Then I was the

"No" Is a Complete Sentence | 85

New Ager, who ate tofu and bean sprouts and thought I was actually going to pass out and die while I tried to reach enlightenment by sitting through the searing heat of a sweat lodge. I tried not to think about the sweaty naked guy sitting right next to me with his sweaty naked bottom on the sweaty, naked ground.

I've worn high heels and hot pants and push-up bras and dressed like Madonna and dressed like the Madonna and all just to please somebody else. I was not me for so long that I eventually began to forget who the real me was. And the really sad thing was that I thought I had to do those things to fit in and be accepted. And the even sadder thing is, that when you do that, you either have to choose to not be yourself for the rest of your life, or you need to face the inevitable place in any relationship where you do decide to be yourself, and your mate or friends are sitting there wondering what in the heck happened to the girl they fell in love with.

I was actually over forty before I realized what a mistake I was making with my life. I went to a guy's house for a date and he didn't like the way I was dressed and he actually took me by the hand and led me to the store to have me buy different clothes that he approved of. It's funny how we sometimes need Life to give us a little slap in the face like that to make us realize what we are doing to ourselves. The guy might have even loved me for myself if I had given him the chance. But it was easier for me to become myself again while I was by myself again, so I left him at the store and went home and began the difficult process of trying to find "me" inside all the layers that I had put around myself to please others.

I'm still working on the process of being comfortable being me. Writing helps. Oddly enough, although I'm sometimes reluctant to show the real me to individuals, it isn't that difficult for me to write my innermost thoughts and deep secrets and life experiences and have them published in newspapers and magazines for the whole world to read. So that's what I do. I write about life and the things I have learned that have helped me to find my way and I hope that some of the things I've learned in life help other people to find their own way, too.

Because it really seems like once I began to live my life my own way, then everything I always wanted in life and asked for in life began to come to me. It's almost like Fate was looking for me all the time with a big sack full of goodies. It just didn't recognize me in those high heels and hot pants.

— Betsy S. Franz —

The Power of "No"

The most common way people give up their power is by thinking they don't have any.
~Alice Walker

As a child, I couldn't wait to be grown. I saw "getting to twenty-one" as freedom, unbounded by anybody's rules. Life would be a wonderful marathon of doing whatever I wanted, when I wanted, and how I wanted.

The reality? Winter, spring, summer, fall. No matter what the weather, I had to get up five days a week and go to work. The big reward was supposed to be payday, but payday often meant paying bills with only a few dollars left for a new pair of shoes or something special for dinner.

A few things changed in my life around the age of forty: my 20/20 vision began to slip, my low blood pressure began to rise, and I discovered the power of "No." What is the power of "No?" It's turning down requests that require you to "go that extra mile," requests that are just not a good fit for you. The first time I said "no" I was shocked, and so was the other person, who'd never heard me say "no" before. But guess what? We survived it.

Time passed and I found myself saying "no" to someone else, a big someone — my mainstream publisher. I turned down the deal they offered me and walked away with no book contract, publishing house or agent in sight. It was a crazy move in some folk's eyes, but my spirit said it was the only move to make. "No" had now become a part of my vocabulary.

It was scary and it left me with deep anxiety. Some of my fellow authors marveled at my bravery. After all, this was a major publishing house and I wasn't that big of an author yet. I hadn't gotten close to making the New York Times Bestsellers list. But I left anyway, and a year later, I had a new agent, a new publishing house, a twenty-eight-city book tour and a six-figure book deal. For me, that illustrated the power of "No."

Since that time I've used the power of "No" often. I've abandoned lucrative business arrangements because I realized proceeding wasn't in my best interest. I've turned down business contracts for the same reason. At the end of the day, "No" protects me and I've come to respect its call when I feel it. But the most interesting example happened just recently. I told myself "no."

I'm an independent author now and there are times when I work seven days a week, hardly taking any time off. I had a major literary event coming up and I had been working hard on it for months. One day something said: *Don't do any work today.* Of course, my business mind immediately ran down the list of things that needed to be done and balked at the very idea. But that voice inside me was insistent. *Take some time off. No work today. No work tomorrow and no work the next day.* Three days of no work? That was crazy.

I was saying "no" to myself and it felt very strange. But the little voice wouldn't go away, so I yielded, striking a bargain where I would compromise by relaxing for a few hours in front of the TV. I popped some popcorn, eased into my recliner and watched a few shows. Afterward, I got back on my computer and tried to do some work. I couldn't.

The next day it was the same thing — I didn't feel like working at all, so I didn't. By day three I knew exactly what I was doing, I was giving myself a "stay-cation" — away from work. I enjoyed it fully, but more important, I was giving my mind, body and spirit a much needed and long overdue break. I was recharging myself.

I didn't understand that part until after five days of no work, I got back to work and it flowed real smooth. Things that had perplexed me suddenly made all the sense in the world. Glitches that I was

"No" Is a Complete Sentence

having with my website totally disappeared, and uploading my video on YouTube was a piece of cake. Not only that, new and fresh ideas started coming to me in a steady stream and the writing for my next book was effortless. It was then that I knew that as a result of walking away from work, telling my own self "no," the heavens had opened on all my creative fronts.

— Margaret Johnson-Hodge —

Time to Say Goodbye

*No person is your friend who demands your silence,
or denies your right to grow.*
~Alice Walker

I'd just returned from our regular monthly lunch date. As usual, my friend and I had exchanged the latest news, relished the gossip about other friends' breakups, and laughed until our make-up ran. But driving home, I began to feel as I had the last several times.

It started like a wisp, a feather across my mind, and quickly heightened. What irked me so much?

I went to my journal. It always gave me answers.

Warming up, I started writing about the basics to help get me started — the phone call for a day that fit both our schedules, the big discussion the night before. "What do you feel like? Chinese? Italian? Decadent Deli?" Giggling, we chose Decadent — two kids skipping healthy diet school.

Then I described the restaurant. Arriving first, I had time to look around. The booth was roomy, upholstery past its prime. On the table sat the perennial bowl of sour pickles, with little pieces of garlic bobbing in the brine. The plastic-covered menu, three feet tall, promised anything your heart desired. Smiling hello, the gravel-voiced waitress asked if I were alone. From her collar hung a giant wilting cloth gardenia.

Continuing to write, I felt a small nervousness, an excitement that always told me I was getting closer to the truth.

As I studied the menu, my friend rushed in, breathless and flushed. We screamed and hugged. She slid into the booth opposite me and immediately started talking.

"The traffic! This idiot in front of me for six miles! Couldn't make up his mind. Where did he learn to drive, Jupiter? Kept weaving in and out, the jerk!"

I wondered why she didn't pass him or take another route.

She kept talking, interrupted only by the waitress taking our orders for overstuffed pastrami sandwiches and diet sodas.

I kept writing, trusting the moving pen. Reliving our visit, I found, as always, the answers coming.

She lived, I saw, in a state of chronic indignation. Everything—from the curl of the napkins to the highway driver to how others raised children—was cause for her righteous anger.

As she talked, the frown between her eyebrows deepened, and her lips moved like a sped-up cartoon. Her outrage was punctuated by hand motions that alternately clutched the air and flattened in open-palmed incredulity at humankind's folly.

She jumped from one thing to another with quirky logic: shopping on the Internet revealed the stupidity of retailers. Restaurant pasta less than al dente was a sin punishable by leaving the waiter two quarters. The supermarket checkers' sluggishness proved the regression of human evolution and threatened our entire civilization.

After almost an hour, she wound down, sandwich untouched. Now, I thought, I could talk, finally sharing meaningful bits of my life and the news about mutual friends. That was when I knew she would listen and nod in understanding. And we'd laugh with full abandon like we used to.

But instead our conversation reminded her to deplore something else. And she was off again, eyes popping, voice strident in irate virtue.

In the past, sometimes I'd sympathized with her constant diatribes and even joined in. But then I'd come home with a headache, and, despite my lunch indulgence, not at all nourished. Today, I now saw, was no different.

When it was time to leave, we kissed and promised to call.

As I kept writing, the picture grew clearer. I'd really known for a long time but didn't want to admit it. She'd been a friend so many years, and we used to have such fun. But the truths scribbled out in my journal couldn't be denied.

It was time to say goodbye.

— Noelle Sterne —

Recharging Batteries

*Sometimes, asking for help is the bravest
move you can make.*
~Author Unknown

Ten minutes to go and I can lock the shop's door behind me. There are still a few customers who can't decide what to buy, who test this perfume and then that one. One lady tests all the lipsticks on the shelf. Her friend is busy with the sunglasses. They must be tourists with lots of time on their hands. I have a fake smile glued on my face as I wait behind the counter for them to make up their minds. They walk out without buying anything. Now it is ten minutes past 5:00. They have wasted my time.

Sometimes I wonder if this is really what life is about. Working from 8:00 a.m to 5:00 p.m., I catch just a glimpse of the sunrise on my way to work every morning. I wish I could stand on that hill and wait for the sun to rise. To feel that isolation and listen to the birds welcoming a new day. It feels like life is slipping through my fingers without enjoying the little things in life that would make me happy.

Going home after a day's work isn't much relief. At home, a family is waiting for my attention. While preparing dinner, I put the laundry in the washing machine and take care of the pets. After dinner, it's time to wash the dishes while the rest of the family relaxes with their own activities. I wish I could do that.

My feet are tired. My body is tired. My soul is tired. I can't go on like this. It's my own fault that I don't make time for myself. I spoiled my family over the years by doing everything by myself. No time for a walk with the dog, no time to read a book, no time to just sit on my own and stare at nothing.

Even on weekends, I get up early to clean the house properly and do the shopping, while the family sleeps in. Only on Sundays do I make time for an afternoon nap, but that is sleep, not me time. I'm not doing something interesting or enjoyable when I catch up on sleep.

Why are women like this? I am one of those women who thinks my way is the best way. If I give a family member a chore to help with, I want it done *now*, not later, so I step in and do it myself. My frustration must be a pain for everybody around me.

I need serious time for myself, time to recharge my batteries and do things that will make me a better person. I'm an outdoor person, but I spend most of my time indoors.

A family meeting is the first step. During the meeting, I explain why I am grumpy and ask them what they think would solve the problem. Everyone gets a turn to come up with ideas for how they could help me achieve my goal to have at least one hour per day to do what I like.

"Hiring someone is not an option," I tell them. I don't want a stranger to invade my privacy. The family is open to practical solutions. "What about having everyone be responsible for cleaning their own room?" I suggest. "And what about taking turns to cook, do laundry and clean up after dinner?" Their reaction is quite positive. I create a chart with the days of the week and the chores, with the name of the responsible family member each day. There are four of us and five weekdays, so I offer to do each chore twice in the five days. I don't mind. I can already see that I will get an hour to myself every day after work.

A month has passed since the new rules in the house began. The plan is working perfectly with a few hiccups now and then but nothing serious. I am impressed by how willing my family is to make life easier for me. It gives us more time to spend together, chatting and laughing. I no longer feel like I am living a rat race.

For a month now, I have been able to put on my walking shoes after work, walk the seven kilometers up the hill with my dog and watch the sunset. On weekends, I admire the sunrise and sunset. Now I have something to look forward to when I close up the shop at 5:00 p.m — or a little after. Now, I don't mind if customers are lingering in the shop when it's time to lock the door and go home. My smile is no longer fake. My boss, Gloria, noticed that I look younger and healthier and have lost that extra bit of weight that was bothering me.

My soul benefits the most during the time I can spend on my own on the hill. Later in the evening, I've got time to do some reading and, lately, try out some writing. My body is recharged from the exercise, and my mind is relaxed from the alone time. The rhythm of nature energizes me. Now I look forward to each day, knowing that I'll have the time I need to recharge my battery. All I had to do was make it a priority and ask for the help I deserved.

—Jonet Neethling—

The Day I Banished Busy-ness

*The difference between successful people and really
successful people is that really successful people
say no to almost everything.*
~William Hague

I will never forget the moment I banished my busy-ness. We were living in Sydney, Australia, at the time. It was a difficult place to live on just my husband's income, so I was working almost full-time at a location that took one agonizing hour to reach during rush hour.

My husband often traveled for work. Our two children were at school, and our daughter had a number of after-school activities throughout the week. The household chores were a constant demand on my time, and I had decided that my identity was not going to be limited by the roles of mother, wife and housekeeper. Therefore, I played several sports, sang in a choir and attended a weekly theater class. I was also producing a television pilot and hosting the occasional speaking gig about well-being.

Life was full. Life was fast. And, supposedly, life was fulfilling.

The idea of taking a vacation emerged slowly. I was often too busy to pay full attention to my thoughts, and deep reflection was reserved for my random, hurried meditations. So, it was some weeks before I realized that a simple yearning had crept into my awareness, which came in the form of one static image: the view of my own toes, sprinkled with sand, raised to a vertical position with a peaceful ocean view beyond them.

Eventually, the yearning transformed into action, and a family vacation was booked: five days and nights on Green Island, in the tropical waters of the Great Barrier Reef. Green Island is tiny. It boasts a dash of native forest, a handful of resort chalets, a crocodile park, stunning snorkeling spots just off the beach, hundreds of sea turtles and free sunset cocktails on the sand every evening. And for five glorious days, it hosted my toes — often in a very grateful, vertical position.

What the island doesn't have is crowds, cellphone coverage or Internet connection… and I must admit that the fear of being bored flashed across my mind when we arrived. When you're used to living life at breakneck speed, rest doesn't always feel like relief. Sometimes, it feels like a torturous nothingness.

Strangely, I didn't feel the change happening. I knew I was slower; I knew I was enjoying having nowhere to be. And I was surprised at how little I yearned for the quick-fire stimulation of my phone and the Internet. But, when we left the island at the conclusion of our stay, I didn't truly realize all the things I wasn't.

I wasn't running logistical algorithms though my mind, mentally juggling people, locations and activities at warp speed. I wasn't stiff in my shoulders or feeling vice-like tension in my neck. I wasn't breathing in quick, shallow gulps; the gripping pressure of stress in my chest had disappeared. I wasn't desperate to get online and check the news, flick through Facebook, check the latest listings… anything, anything, to feed the constant, frantic pace of my mind. I wasn't snappy or impatient, snarling at others (internally or verbally) to hurry up, get out of my way and, for goodness' sake, DO. NOT. SLOW. ME. DOWN!

I didn't notice these things had gone, but as we boarded the plane to return to Sydney, I noticed them returning. Steadily. Insidiously. Emphatically.

As we flew farther south, I became increasingly aware of what needed to happen in the week ahead. My husband was flying to the U.S. the next day. I had the usual activities to coordinate — my daughter's and mine — plus a speaking gig booked for that week. I would have to arrange a babysitter and make sure that I had two nights' worth of dinner prepared. I would have to cook those meals somewhere between my sports and my son's dentist appointment because there was no way I could get that done between my daughter's activities and mine. My husband's best shirts were in the ironing pile; I would find them as soon as we got home, after I had taken out the garbage. He would have to iron them himself when he arrived at his hotel.

As my mind flew into its familiar frenzy, my body began to tense up again. In less than an hour, the stillness and relaxation of five days were rendered completely useless. It was then, suddenly and sincerely, that a powerful intention rushed through my body: STOP! NO! I WILL NOT DO THIS TO MYSELF!

A few hours prior, I had been relaxing, toes vertical, in the warm sands of Green Island... and my body remembered what that felt like. I wanted it back badly. And I didn't believe that I should have to live in this horrible, overwhelming, exhausting, adrenaline-fueled state of mania anymore.

The changes started as soon as we got home. I cancelled my speaking gig. "So sorry, but this week is not the best timing for me." I gave my daughter the chance to choose the one activity she loved the most, and I wrote an e-mail removing her from the others. Then, I did the same for me. I looked up a sports team that played weekends and I dropped my weekday events. At my first day of work, I approached my boss to discuss how I could work friendlier hours, both to free some time and miss a lot of the rush-hour traffic.

I began to say "no." A lot. I began to notice the state of my body, and to pay attention to tension and unease. I started stopping off at a small forest near our home, just for five minutes every day on the way home from work. Five minutes where I would just sit, breathe, and acknowledge that the world could function without me for those few brief moments.

I learned how to turn my commute — those long minutes in stalled traffic — into a celebration of solitude. That's when I would sing my favorite songs, shed any private tears, ponder unsolved challenges, or work through any unprocessed emotions.

I learned that doing something for me, as an intelligent and empowered woman, can be as simple as paying attention to my truest needs. I learned to prioritize what was most important to me and vital to the well-being of my family. And I decided not to stress over what we could be missing out on if we didn't follow through on an activity or opportunity. I learned how to lovingly offend people, on occasion, if a scheduled event was looming large and causing me, or my family, stress about how to make it happen.

There would still be those times that were too busy. I figured out how to get through those, too. After my husband's longer work trips, school holiday madness, or our relocation back to Singapore, I made sure I had time to unwind, refresh and drain the stress from my body. Now I give myself a gift whenever my body tells me it's necessary — the chance to view my toes, weary and grateful, in some secluded hideaway, and in a definitively vertical position.

— Kim Forrester —

No

*Sometimes the most important thing in a whole day
is the rest we take between two deep breaths.*
~Etty Hillesum

It was a warm winter day and I remember wearing a short-sleeved red checkered blouse with my favorite blue skirt. Suddenly though, I felt a chill and I froze.

It was at a community meeting of women. I was comfortable as we visited and shared stories. And then, it happened. The hostess handed us each a paper and pencil and asked us to write down our New Year's resolution.

My pencil wouldn't write. Those around me smiled and wrote non-stop. I knew my friend to my left was writing about the new diet she was going to go on the first of the year. My friend to the right had to be writing about making more money in her job, as that was always her primary focus. Someone across the room was chuckling out loud as she described the man of her dreams who she was determined to find in the coming year.

I was blank. Blank and confused. I thought about my everyday life. I am content. Sometimes I am really tired and often wish there were more minutes in a day. But, don't most of us think those things? I am happy in my relationships. I love my job and my family and friends. I work out and feel fit. I volunteer in the schools, in the community and for many organizations. I am always there when someone needs me for carpool, an emergency, or to run an errand. Wow! What to do?

Others were folding their resolutions in half once and then again. The crackly sound of the paper folding annoyed me as my page was still empty. Everyone smiled as they placed their well-chosen words into a basket. Then they discussed openly and happily how the new year would change them. "For the better" was the agreement by all and a toast was made with sparkling cider. I wanted to be in on the toast.

My face turning red to match my shirt, I knew I had to write something. This same group of women vowed to look at these resolutions at the same party, same place, same time... next year. So in a rush I wrote something down, folded it and folded it again, and put it in the basket.

"Say no." That was all I inscribed on my resolution.

That was the best resolution I have ever made. And, I kept it! I realized on that warm winter day that I had become too busy doing for everyone else. I believe in volunteering and reaching out to help others. That is a gift I love to give. However, listening to the giggles and busy chatter about other women's daily lives, I heard the word "No" in my mind. I realized that I had stopped reading books, watching my favorite shows on television, baking fresh bread, or sitting on the couch relaxing. I resolved that I could still give to others, lead my busy fulfilling life, and also save time for me.

Each woman left with a colorful sparkly hat to wear on New Year's Eve and a hug for happiness in the New Year. I left feeling heavy, and wondering what they would think of me in one year when the paper with my brief words was unfolded.

On the way home, enjoying the birds singing and observing the colorful trees lining the street, I realized that it didn't matter. What mattered was, for once, me taking care of me. I even said it out loud, "I need to take care of me!" I never told anyone this before, but that New Year's resolution began even before the hands on the clock ever got to midnight for the New Year. When I got home, I brewed a cup of my favorite herbal tea, turned on the television, and turned on the answering machine.

I learned something that December day. Writing my resolution truly opened my eyes. I actually asked myself questions out loud:

"Where had I been? What was I thinking?" I reflected back on being a child and always hearing my grandparents saying, "Life is too short." They are no longer here to know the impact they made on my most meaningful New Year's resolution. I never knew a New Year's resolution could work out and come true. Mine did, I think about it every year.

— Gail Small —

Saying "Yes" to Myself

Sometimes, we have to say no so we have more time to say yes.
~Suzette Hinton

"Will you do a favor for me?" someone would ask.

"Of course, I will. What do you need?" I would always answer, agreeing to do the favor before I even asked what it was.

I would never have dreamed of saying "no" to anyone. If anyone asked me to do anything, I'd do it. Saying "no" was never an option. I wanted to be a good person. I wanted to help people. I wanted people to like me. I wanted people to love me.

I was a good, obedient child and grew up to be a responsible adult. I married a dependable, hard-working man whom everyone said was perfect for me.

I had four children, and I was always the "room mother," helping with class parties and taking cookies to every school event. I helped with the Girl Scouts, Boy Scouts, charities and fundraisers. Nothing was too much trouble.

After my children grew up and left home, and my husband passed away, people thought I needed things to do to fill what they felt was my empty life. I volunteered at the hospital and a nursing home, and

I taught a Sunday School class.

I was free labor. I'd drive people to the airport and go back and pick them up when they returned from their vacations. Your mother-in-law needs a ride to the airport at three o'clock in the morning? Sure, no problem.

I was spending time and money I couldn't spare, and I often didn't get thanked. I didn't do things to be "thanked," but I would have appreciated some sort of acknowledgment. I was "busy" being "busy." I was exhausted, but I was afraid to say "no" because I thought people wouldn't like me anymore.

I had to have back surgery, and I told everyone I would be confined to my home for at least a month while I recovered. No one offered to drive me to the hospital or drive me home. I didn't want to inconvenience anyone, so I took a cab. No one visited me in the hospital, and no one brought any meals to me after I got home.

No one called to ask if I had enough groceries or if I needed a prescription filled or if I would like some company.

I'd always filled out certificates of appreciation for people who contributed to the zoo, and when the man in charge of the zoo called and asked if I could prepare 100 certificates, I told him "no." I wasn't well, I explained, and I would not be doing the certificates in the future. He'd have to find someone else. He was shocked.

"Do it for the animals," he said. He offered to drop off the certificates at my house where I could fill them out. He'd come back and pick them up. He couldn't believe it when I said "no."

A lady at church asked if she could drop off her cat for me to take care of for a week while she took her family to Disneyland. I explained I'd had back surgery, and I couldn't take care of her cat. "But you always take care of Fluffy!" she said. "He's really no trouble at all."

The truth was Fluffy was a lot of trouble. I had taken care of him twice while she'd gone on vacation, and he'd gotten hair on everything, climbed my drapes and pulled them down, and didn't always use his litter box. I told her I was sure she'd find someone else to take care of Fluffy, but I couldn't do it anymore.

The church secretary called, not to ask how I was feeling, but to ask when I could start teaching the Sunday School class again. I told her someone else would have to take over. She asked if I had any notes for the classes, and I said "no." I thought whoever took over the class would want to teach it their own way, and I was sure they'd do a great job.

I have the right to say "no," without an apology, explanation or guilt. The world didn't end when I started say it, and much to my surprise, things got done without my help. Other people stepped in and did the things I used to do.

People say I am not the same person since I had my back surgery. They are right; I'm not the same person. I was laid up for a month with a painful back, and during that time I found my spine.

People haven't really missed "me"; they have missed the services I provided. I had allowed people to use me, thinking they would like me, but when I needed help, no one was there.

I don't volunteer for anything anymore. I spend my time doing things I never seemed to have time to do before. I'm taking an art class. I go for walks in the park. My time is my own.

It's hard to say "no" when I've been a "yes" person all my life, but I feel powerful for the first time. I don't have to make up excuses or lies or explain or apologize. "No" is a complete sentence.

My time is the most precious thing I own, and for years I let people steal it from me. I don't blame them; I blame myself. I was a doormat, and I let people walk all over me. I was trying to earn friendship.

Some people might say I've gotten "hard," but that isn't true. I've just gotten strong. I don't like people less; I like myself more.

I saw a bumper sticker on a car that said, "I don't regret the things I've done wrong as much as I regret the things I did right for the wrong people."

Saying "no" to other people is saying "yes" to myself.

I feel so free!

— Holly English —

Just Say No — and Sometimes Yes

Learn to say "no" to the good so you can say "yes" to the best.
~John C. Maxwell

The phone rang. It was the president of the library board of trustees. Three months previously I'd resigned from that board; it wasn't a good fit for me. I did remain on a non-board committee, as I believed in the mission, but the process had frustrated me and eaten up more time than I anticipated when I joined.

"Good morning. How are you?" His cheeriness put me on guard. Something was up. "Janet is stepping down as chair of the public relations committee and I hoped you would be willing to take over. It requires, you know, writing letters and refining talking points for speaking to groups and since you've done a lot of public speaking and you write..."

"No. No, I'm sorry I can't do it."

Wow! I'd said that?

After a few pleasantries and best wishes for him to find a new committee chair, we said goodbye.

I poured a cup of coffee and sat at the kitchen table to watch the blue jays bully the other birds for space at the feeders.

I felt light, free, amazed at myself. I'd just said "No" with no explanation. I gave him no opening for discussion. No exaggerated excuses about other responsibilities, problems, too many commitments, not being up to the challenge. Not even, "I'll think about it," while gathering the courage to call back and say no. Just "No." And surprisingly, I didn't feel guilty about it. I could have done the job. My calendar had lots of space. I had the credentials and experience in both writing and public speaking.

But I was done with all that. After more than twenty years on the local animal shelter board, twenty-eight years as a 4-H leader, an officer in the Cancer Society and garden club and other organizations, I needed my life back. Now retired, I dreamed of uninterrupted time to tackle writing a novel, to try pastel painting, and to experience other new things. It was time to stop saying "as soon as…."

One by one I had resigned from each responsibility as my term finished, or when someone else could step up in my place. The next years would be mine. I wanted to write, to learn to paint, to take classes instead of teaching them, to try yoga, to spend some days doing nothing.

I wrote it on the refrigerator memo board. "Choose wisely. 'As soon as' is here."

I don't plan on being a hermit. And I will take on short-term volunteer tasks, such as manning a yard sale booth for three hours, or giving one lecture on canine behavior, or spending one morning weeding the county courthouse flowerbeds. Saying no to the big obligations and recurring commitments will let me look forward to the things I choose to do, instead of resenting the time it takes to dress, drive, and attend yet another meeting of an organization.

I realize that sometimes I did choose to do the things that were on my calendar, to rise through the ranks, to take responsibilities that ate up more time than I believed they would. The trouble is, many times when you assume the mantle people expect you will continue to wear it year after year.

From now on I will be chary of chairmanships. Bored with boards. I don't want to be in charge of, president of, chair of, leader of… anything. Been there, done that, successfully, if I do say so myself. I will now be a happy occasional soldier instead of a general.

I will be gleeful when I awake to nothing more pressing than brushing the dog or hanging laundry out in the sun, and reminding myself that "as soon as" is right now.

When the phone rings, as it will, asking if I can edit one letter or arrange one luncheon for a visiting author, I will probably say, "Yes, I'll do it. Just this once."

— Ann Vitale —

Chapter 5

Love Who You Are

Goals for Growing Older

*If you want to be happy, set a goal that commands
your thoughts, liberates your energy
and inspires your hopes.*
~Andrew Carnegie

I'm running half-way across Canada — some 2,200 miles — for my seventy-fifth birthday. It's a long way, for sure, but I have two years to get there. And if my knees hold up, it'll be a great way to celebrate this milestone birthday.

To be more precise, this cross-country jog will be mostly around my neighbourhood in Ottawa. It is the distance by air to Vancouver on the west coast that a friend and I are doing. That's 3,550 kilometers (in Canada we use metric) but it's far no matter how you measure it.

If we reach our goal, my friend Louise Rachlis, whose birthday is just a month before mine, and I will get on a plane and actually fly to Vancouver the year we turn seventy-five. We want to run in one of the BMO Vancouver Marathon weekend races in May. Likely that'll be the eight-kilometer (five-mile) race and not the marathon distance.

We may not win medals, but for sure we'll have cake at the finish line.

I should be clear that neither of us is an elite runner, nor do we love the sport the way good runners do. Although it has its moments, sometimes it's a hard, slow slog.

Love Who You Are

We've modified some rules to help account for this. We can count the distances of longer, fast walks. But the walk has to last for at least thirty minutes and get your blood pumping. So we can't count steps at the shopping mall, dog walking or strolls to the corner store.

So far, I'm finding that averaging three miles a day, nearly ninety miles a month is very hard for a natural couch potato like me.

Still, the point is to do something that's really challenging so we can revel in our accomplishment as we hit our birthday goal.

This build-up to big birthdays represents an enormous change for me. I used to hate birthdays, especially those milestone ones. Even when I turned thirty, I remember feeling low because I wasn't married yet. At forty, I was married with kids but hated that milestone because I no longer felt young.

Turning fifty was the worst—I was divorced, had moved to a new city where I had few friends and was struggling to raise three children on my own, after returning to work. That birthday two friends took me to lunch at a fancy hotel. I am still grateful for that act of kindness, which helped me though a particularly dark day.

Perhaps it was the memory of that awful birthday that helped shape a change in attitude as I approached my sixtieth birthday. But I also have to credit Louise, who suggested setting goals to mark milestone birthdays.

"That way you are looking forward to something, not dreading it," she pointed out. It was wise advice.

By setting goals that expand my world or demand new skills, I can feel myself growing, not shrinking, as I hit those special birthdays.

For my sixtieth, I got it into my head that I should do an Olympic distance triathlon. This was no small feat for me. The race involved swimming 1500 meters (close to a mile), biking forty kilometers (twenty-five miles) and running ten kilometers (six miles).

I had not been athletic in my younger years—I took up running and open lake swimming in my fifties. So, as my goal began to take shape, I took both spinning and swimming classes from a triathlete training club. I also signed up for a weight loss program and dropped thirty-five pounds.

Love Who You Are

It was exhilarating to cross the finish line with an enthusiastic group of friends cheering loudly. After more than four hours on the course, I was last among the ninety-five competitors. But I was the oldest woman competing, so that made me first in my age category.

Ever since that day, I've looked at birthdays as a reason to celebrate. Milestone birthdays, especially, are a call for trying something different.

For my sixty-fifth birthday, I went with a friend to Disney World to run in the Princess Half Marathon, the longest distance I had ever done. I wore a T-shirt that said: "Never Too Old To Be A Princess — Running for my 65th."

I got many birthday wishes and one "Happy Birthday" serenade as other runners passed me. There were also several inspiring moments when women ran up to me to say they had passed that sixty-fifth milestone some years before and were still going strong. I loved that.

Approaching seventy was a different journey. Again, Louise had a role to play in this. We were talking about the benefits of learning something new to keep our minds sharp and attitudes young.

So, we promised each other we would do seven activities that would take us out of our "comfort zone" during the year we turned seventy. (In truth I jumped the gun and did two of them in the months leading up to our milestone year but I counted them anyway.)

Louise and I did only one of our goals together. We signed up for a tap-dancing class for older adults. It was fun and excellent brain-body training. But it was tough for both of us first-time tappers. Louise finished two fourteen-week sessions, but I only made it through one and a half. After missing a few weeks, I found it too hard to catch up, so I bailed out. Kudos to Louise, who danced right to the end and continued the following year.

Another time, I agreed to let a friend introduce me to a guy she thought I'd like. Going out on a date for the first time in decades took me way out of my comfort zone. But it was fun and good for my self-esteem, even though we parted ways after a few dates.

In the year before my seventieth, I took a trip to India to practice yoga and meditation at ashrams. The next year I went to China, where I climbed on the Great Wall and hiked in the awesome Yellow Mountains.

Love Who You Are

My other projects involved going to a paint night at a bar, when I've always been embarrassed by my lack of artistic ability; collecting donations for the Salvation Army, when I hate to ask for anything from others; and finally, solving an issue that weighed on my conscience for more than a decade. I had inherited a valuable set of antique silverware from a dear friend and mentor, but I never used it. I put off the inevitable for years, but finally sold the set at auction and donated the proceeds to cancer research.

I know that I'm fortunate to have already celebrated so many birthdays in good health and good spirits, so whether I succeed in running to Vancouver or not, I am grateful for the opportunity to try.

One thing I've learned in taking up these challenges to mark my milestone birthdays, is that there are lots of possibilities for new adventures and achievements, even as we grow older.

And that's a gift worth celebrating every day of every year.

— Kristin Goff —

You Are More than the Way You Look

*To accept ourselves as we are means to value our
imperfections as much as our perfections.*
~Sandra Bierig

"What was the date of your last period?" This is a question women are often asked throughout their lives. Most women answer nonchalantly as if they were answering the question, "What did you have for breakfast this morning?" For me, that question would cause my head to bow in shame.

I hated going to the doctor's office for that reason alone. I had no idea about the date of my last period. I had gone almost nine years without a period. After my response, the doctors would always ask the same questions. Without fail, they would cock their head to one side and give me a look of pity. As a twenty-eight-year-old woman, I had given up hope that there was going to be a period in my future unless I did the one thing I couldn't do.

Most women would love to stop running. For many, running is far from enjoyable. For me, though, stopping wasn't that easy. I was a professional runner, an Olympic hopeful for Great Britain. To stop running would take away my career and definition of who I was. The years of hard training would be lost, potentially forever. I would be wasting my talent and throwing away my biggest strength. So I buried my head in the sand and got on with my training.

There was more to my missing menstrual cycle than just running. Sure, running ninety miles a week is very hard on the body, but my disordered eating and careful restriction of calories were endangering my long-term health. A distorted view of myself (even though I looked like everyone else who stood at the starting line), along with desperation to look like other elite runners (which led to an obsession over my weight), and my continued yearly weight loss were the cause.

With a history of eating disorders in my family, I knew how devastating this could be. I could eat, but it was at meticulously planned times. On the days I ran over fifteen miles, I could eat whatever I wanted. But on the days I had "only" run an hour, I ate exceptionally clean. Except for the evenings! My sweet tooth, driven by insufficient calories, would grind down my willpower enough that I would binge on sugar.

I continued like this for many years, getting faster and faster as a runner, but hearing that voice inside transitioning from a whisper to a yell. Something was wrong, and I knew it. I needed to get my health back from medical malnutrition. I just couldn't see a way out without giving up the sport that I loved, which had brought me so much.

One day, it wasn't the sport I loved; it was the sport I despised. That day, it became a chore. All the joy was gone. I had accomplished my lifetime goal of running for Great Britain and Northern Ireland in a World Championship. A few weeks later, I smashed my personal best in the marathon to run a 2:37. It was then that I noticed the narrative in my head had changed. It became all about the finish line. I was now addicted to the success, the glory, the hands-in-the-air moments. Training was just about surviving. The screams from inside to take care of my health became so loud that I could barely take it anymore. Every day, I thought about quitting. About the same time, my sister brought a beautiful baby girl into the world. My niece Charlotte filled my mind. Running didn't seem to matter anymore. "Done, done, done," I repeated in my head.

One day, I snapped. I really was done. I didn't know if I would ever run again. All I knew was that I was going to be the best damn period-get-backer there ever was, and I was going to do *everything* I could to get my health back.

I confronted the demons telling me that my weight was what defined me. I ate whatever I wanted, whenever I wanted, and I gained weight quickly. I, who had never taken more than a four-week break from running or more than two weeks from training altogether, didn't once consider running for the next ten weeks. I rested, did acupuncture, and journaled a lot.

For the first time in a long time, I could feel myself recovering, gaining health, feeling alive again, with my soul nourished.

I decided to share my story publicly. I would educate those around me about amenorrhea. I would show other women that they were not broken, and certainly not alone. I wanted to become a beacon of hope for women. I wanted them to know that there was another side to this life, that the way you look does not define who you are. If an elite runner at the peak of her career could stop running and get her health back through fueling her body correctly, surely they could, too. My story went viral. It seemed that more women had been struggling with this than I realized. Tens of thousands of women reached out to me, thanking me for being vulnerable and sharing my story.

Within ten weeks, I was pregnant. I could barely believe it. I crumpled to the floor of the bathroom as my husband Steve and I stared at the pregnancy test in disbelief. It had worked. It had all been worth it. I always knew I wanted to be a mother, and now I finally felt ready. Suddenly, this was the most important thing I had ever done in my life. My running accomplishments seemed so trivial. My body was functioning normally, and I was about to bring life into this world.

This little person inside my belly would learn all the lessons about how she should perceive herself from me. I *had* to make a mental and physical change about the way I viewed myself. There would be no more self-degradation, judgment, or shaming myself for my decisions. I had done a lot of work to get to this point, but I still had a long way to go (and still do).

The day she was born, my world changed forever. I felt more proud of my body than I ever had in my life. My love for my daughter grew with each passing day, and now as I watch her explore her world, find her confidence, and discover who she is, I have to fight the urge to help her and solve all her problems for her. I know that doing that only makes it harder for her to believe in who she is and what she can do. For now, I try to be a good role model and show her I make mistakes, too — and that's okay.

I determined from the moment my baby was born that I would be real with others and myself. I would speak my truth, and I would show her that I am beautiful, wonderful, and perfectly imperfect, as is she.

— Tina Muir —

The No-Share Zone

*Don't wreck a sublime chocolate experience
by feeling guilty.
~Lora Brody*

I am a disciplined person, especially when it comes to food. I watch what I eat. I regularly consume admirable quantities of fruits and vegetables. I strictly monitor my intake of sweets, resisting that deep craving to sink into the blissful blur of sugary extremes. I do not keep cookies, candy or cakes in the house. I rarely allow myself to order dessert in a restaurant. If I must have chocolate, I make sure I have to walk to the store (preferably through rain or snow) to get my candy fix.

But my discipline disappears when it comes to the Personal Box of Chocolates.

When such a gift comes into my life, I abandon all pretense of sensible eating and sink into that rare environment that many adults silently yearn for — the No-Share Zone.

This is what happened when a dear friend handed me a wrapped birthday present.

"Don't leave this sitting out in the heat," she said and I knew it contained chocolate. That night, I tore into the wrappings, then reverently removed the plastic that protected a small Whitman's Sampler.

I eased off the lid and smiled when I saw eight pieces of cozily cradled candies.

That small box of chocolate transported me to that mystical Zone, where politeness yielded to the primal and I embraced a supremely selfish, divinely decadent indulgence of the highest order. I was home alone. I was going to eat what I wanted, how I wanted, and I was not going to consider any other human being in the process.

Lavishly, I bit into two chocolates, the caramel and the coconut. I loved the insolence of only partially eating each one.

Then I reviewed the remaining chocolates, thinking about the order I might sample them in. I had no thoughts of calories or restraint — I had only the pure joy of possession.

Normally, of course, I loved to share. Had someone been around, I might have pleasantly offered her a chocolate. Had my friend given me a larger box, I would have saved it for a party or meeting. But she wisely fulfilled the secret wish of the chocolate-obsessed: permission to graze, glory, gorge and revel in sweet sensation.

When I was growing up, the Whitman box came into our household once a year, a symbol of romance from my father to my mother. My mother, normally a very sharing person, kept tight rein on the Sampler. Her face looked almost pained as she offered my brother and me one chocolate each. I remember studying the map of those chocolates more carefully that I ever studied any atlas. Nuts, chews, creams, caramels — making the right choice was crucial. After that one luscious candy, the box would disappear, hidden somewhere in my mother's bedroom.

At the time I thought my mother was selfish and unfair. But now, I understood and applauded her. Like so many moms, I realized how much she had to share, all day, every day. I imagined how utterly luxurious she must have felt, surveying her box of chocolates, sampling, tasting, and savoring, without worry that anyone would interfere.

Like my mother before me, my candy box allowed me to simply care for myself. The bliss of the No-Share Zone, that lovely luxury of not worrying about even one other person, renewed and delighted me.

My small Sampler was an invitation to be frivolous and beautifully indulgent. I took a bite of a nut bar and let the flavors flow through my mouth. For this moment, I was feeding only myself and that made the chocolate even sweeter.

—Deborah Shouse—

Defending Our Children

When you are a mother, you are never really alone in your thoughts. A mother always has to think twice, once for herself and once for her child.
~Sophia Loren

My husband and I had finally decided to be licensed for foster care. Our children were young at the time, and they were excited to get involved in caring for a little brother or sister. The children we cared for were never much older than three months, almost exclusively female, and African American.

Providing foster care was a fun, rewarding and exhausting ministry. Everyone in the family was involved, pitching in where they could. It truly was an enjoyable experience. There was only one big issue. My father-in-law.

Our first long-term placement was three-month-old Evelyn, who lived with us for two years. She was an even-tempered, fun-loving little girl.

My husband's father was an eighty-year-old immigrant from the "old country." Having suffered a stroke before my husband was born, his body was paralyzed on the left side. My father-in-law didn't like Evelyn because she was African American.

When taking a family picture, he'd make sure she was positioned behind someone. While she sat uncomprehendingly in her high chair, he would point his finger at her and request that she "Go back to Africa."

Mercifully, my children were too young to know what he was saying. My mother-in-law would glare and tell him to stop. But that only worked for a while. It would start all over again at the next visit.

I would leave those weekly dinners with a mix of anger and sadness. This was my child he was talking to. How could he do that? My husband wouldn't address the issue. "That's just him," he'd say. "He doesn't know any better."

After living with us for two years, Evelyn was adopted by her maternal grandmother.

Time passed, and we were ready to accept another long-term placement. I told my husband that I'd have to call his father first. His remarks and attitude would no longer be tolerated. The words were bad enough, but now my children were older, and they would understand his hurtful comments.

If he couldn't change, we would stop visiting. He wasn't going to be a reason to stop fostering, but he'd sure be a reason to stop putting a helpless child in his line of fire. I had to speak up.

I practiced my lines for days. It felt like weeks. The day of the call, I paced around the house waiting for more courage. I muttered to myself, "Come on now! It's just a phone call. What's the worst that can happen? What if he gets so mad, he refuses to speak to me again?"

All of this internal chatter wasn't helping. I was getting short of breath, which happens when I get nervous. Shaking my hands, trying in vain to flip away those nerves, I finally called.

My mother-in-law answered the phone, and we exchanged pleasantries. I asked to speak to my father-in-law. "Oh!" she responded. I never called to talk exclusively to him, so I knew she'd be surprised. Now he was on the phone.

Oh boy. My words came out very slowly at first. My stomach was flipping. "Hi!" I started out brightly. I should get an Academy Award for acting. I was feeling anything but bright.

"Remember how we were foster parents a few years ago?" No response. I plunged ahead. "I know how you treated our daughter last

Love Who You Are

time. You said some mean things, and it really upset me."

It felt like I'd popped the cork from a shaken bottle of champagne. Finally released from my mind, the words now tumbled over each other in the race to be expressed.

"We are going to be taking another placement soon, and I wanted you to know that I can't accept that kind of attitude toward any child we are caring for."

Continued silence on the other end of the phone. Now for the really scary part. "If you feel that you can't change, we won't be visiting you while we are caring for this child."

And I was done. I felt like I was suspended in midair. Or waiting for the ax to fall. Now what?

Silence.

After a few seconds, which felt like years, he told me he didn't understand what I was talking about. While he did have a thick accent, I knew he had heard and understood me. I asked for my mother-in-law, and I explained the situation to her. I was a complete sweaty mess at this point.

She told me that she would speak to him as soon as we got off the phone.

Click.

Oh my Lord, call the paramedics. How I hated this. I try to avoid confrontation, and apparently my father-in-law does too. We never spoke of it again. We never had to.

I don't think he had ever been approached this way by any of his immediate family, and the experience probably shocked him. Maybe he was as surprised as my husband that he was capable of changing his behavior.

He accepted our next daughter. Not with open arms, but with tolerance. He would offer her little treats at the dinner table, and praise her block-building skills. It was a transforming moment for me to see him change so radically. Actually, it was probably more transforming for him.

We went on to care for ten more children, and with each one, he became more and more at ease. Seeing him finally singing "Happy

Birthday" to our foster children, I knew his heart had changed.

This whole episode showed me how important it is to stand up for what is right, with or without fear. It taught me that sometimes you just have to take the lead, bite the bullet, grab the bull by the horns… pick your favorite cliché.

In spite of my anxiety, I had to do the right thing and speak up. You know what else I learned? That words can change the world, one person at a time.

—Ceil Ryan D'Acquisto—

Like Daughter, Like Mother

*One woman filled with self-love and self-acceptance is
a model more super than any cover girl.*
~Amy Leigh Mercree

She was unlike anyone I had ever seen. I watched her while lying on the beach in Hollywood, Florida. And I didn't know what illuminated her more — her wind-blown, tightly spiraled curls or her radiant happiness.

But what struck me — even more than her presence — was the fact that I was able to conflate the two.

Some background: I was thirty-three years old, and I literally had no idea how to style or maintain my natural hair. I had spent my life trying desperately to make my curly hair something it wasn't, and I worshipped my flatiron like it was my religion.

I would sooner gouge out my eye with the nearest blunt object than be seen in public with my hair in its natural state. But there I was, mesmerized by a complete stranger with the kind of hair I had previously despised.

I wanted to talk to her.

Looking back, I now see that my desire to approach her was driven less by curiosity and more by a primal need for understanding.

When the man she was sitting with rose from his Adirondack chair and walked off, I made my way to her and asked blatantly, "How do you wear your hair like that?"

As soon as the words escaped my lips, I cringed. I knew she didn't do anything to her hair — my question wasn't literal, no. What I really wanted to know was how she was able to experience such apparent joy in the wake of vulnerability. I likened wearing my hair curly in real life to one of those bad dreams when you're inexplicably walking down the street naked and embarrassed, and everyone's laughing at you.

But, somehow, she had deciphered my intended context. She chuckled and responded, "How do I *not* wear my hair like this? These curls are mine. And I love them. How can I deny who I am?"

I heard her words, but I still didn't understand. I unleashed on her my feelings about hair, identity, and unrealistic beauty ideals — topics better suited for a therapist's couch. Again, I asked, "But how do you do it?"

"Oh, honey, you just do!" the woman said, laughing. She was so carefree. "Embrace your curls. Don't think about it. Just do it. It's a heck of a lot easier than you think. One day, it will be clear, and you will understand," she said.

That was in September 2010.

Fast-forward to a Saturday in November 2015.

Despite my best intentions to evade the massive raincloud looming over the parking lot, an all-out monsoon had broken out by the time I had exited the market with my two small kids in tow. (Scotty was four then, and Kennedy was two.) I sprinted to my minivan, soaking my hair and nearly pulling a hamstring in the process. Then I drove home as fast as I legally could and immediately commenced flatironing my hair in my bathroom. Only after I had finished did I realize that I had neglected to put the kids' frozen treats — a hard-earned reward for good behavior — in the freezer.

The bag was a pile of mush on the kitchen counter.

Frustration and shame washed over me.

I couldn't function like this anymore.

One might dismiss my mishap as simply what women do in the name of beauty. But the lengths I have gone to — to make my curly hair straight — are no laughing matter.

There is nothing funny about spending my entire life shunning my natural hair texture. And there's certainly nothing pleasurable about enduring scalp burns — and the subsequent scabbing — that result from the use of chemical hair straighteners, which I had put up with for years.

To be clear, straight hair isn't the enemy; it's lovely, in fact.

The problem, though, is when the pursuit of straight hair rules your life. There is a difference between straightening your hair because you want to, and doing it because you feel it's mandatory or, worse yet, you know no alternative.

From the time I was knee-high to a grasshopper, Sunday afternoons were spent sitting still as my mother blow-dried and then braided my hair. When I hit the teenage years, I wanted my hair even straighter, so she used a hot pressing comb, too. And, before long, that didn't get my hair straight enough — enter chemical relaxers.

As the late poet Maya Angelou stated so beautifully, "When you know better, do better." But there were few alternatives back then. In the eighties and nineties, drugstores didn't have entire aisles dedicated to serving the natural-hair community — there *was* no natural-hair community. YouTube didn't exist, and no one had any idea what a hair tutorial vlog was.

But the birth of my daughter sparked a change in direction for me.

Kennedy was born with thick, dark, perfectly clumped spiral curls, and from day one I instilled in her that her curls were beautiful. And she agreed. I prided myself in caring for — and never straightening — her curls, despite my need to straighten mine incessantly.

And herein lies the problem.

When I straightened my strands during my lengthy blowout sessions, I noticed how Kennedy studied my every move. I could see the wheels in her head beginning to churn: *If you think my curls are so pretty, why do you straighten yours?* The day Kennedy would call me hypocritical was heading toward me like a freight train.

The image of the gorgeous woman on the beach began appearing in my head more frequently, poking my conscience; her words were more poignant than ever.

I decided, at age thirty-eight, that I would stop straightening my hair.

But imagine the horror I experienced when I washed my hair... and it wouldn't curl.

Come to find, all the years of applying excessive direct heat in the form of blow dryers and flatirons had permanently altered my curl pattern.

Instead of "big chopping" — cutting off all my hair at once — I chose to trim my hair over the course of several months until the last of my damaged ends were cut off on my fortieth birthday.

Although I've been on this journey for nearly three years now, I feel in some ways that I've only just begun. But, make no mistake, the woman on the beach was right: That day had come, it is now clear, and I do understand.

Here's what I've since learned: I should have done this sooner, and that chance encounter on a Florida beach many years ago was a clarion call.

And here's what I'm most grateful for: In an effort to teach my young daughter to love her wildly curly hair, I've finally learned to do the same.

— Courtney Conover —

My Picture-Perfect New Year's Resolution

A happy person is not a person in a certain set of circumstances, but rather a person with a certain set of attitudes.
~Hugh Downs

I never make resolutions. Every December 31st, at the stroke of midnight, my mind usually wanders from the resolution-making task at hand and is more concerned with why I'm not at a fabulous confetti-filled party somewhere, wearing a cocktail dress, and talking to a dashing gentleman (who might even have an accent). I mean, will all of my photo albums consist of consecutive New Year's Eves with me in my sweats, covered in cat hair, eating leftovers, with a distant glimmer of hope in my eye? Seriously? All I want is one, just one; fantastic picture to hang on my wall so all the world can see what an exciting and enviable life I lead — is that too much to ask? Not that I have anything against Dick Clark. He's a great date, and he always shows up.

One year, all of this sullen introspection got me to thinking about expectations. Why did I feel the pressure to have a picture-perfect New Year's Eve? Why did I care if people thought my life was exciting? Probably the same reason I felt like I should be settled in a career and married with three kids already. Throughout most of my life, I had deviated from the norm; somehow, I still felt it necessary to make apologies and excuses for my decisions.

But, why? Where was this desperate need to please coming from? I had traveled the world, owned my own business, bought my first home, and started fulfilling my dream of writing all before the age of twenty-five. So what did I have to apologize for? Well, as previously stated, I was still single and indecisive about my career, which for a woman of my age was not considered "the norm." (Dear me, whatever shall they say at the class reunion?)

Then, suddenly, as I was about to ring in the new year by doing a load of laundry, an epiphany shone down from the heavens. It was a lightning bolt of realization. For my very first resolution, I was going to resolve not to care. Not to care about anyone's expectations but my own and to make no apologies for it. After all, I had gone wherever the road had taken me, and it had taken me to a lot of fabulous places—places I never would have been able to go if I had "settled down" already. Not to mention, I'd probably be starring in *Desperate Housewives* or making an appearance on *Divorce Court*.

And as far as my career went, being indecisive was just being honest. I couldn't change who I was just because I didn't fit into the social norm. At least I wasn't going to watch my life go by as I punched the clock at a job I hated, in order to climb a very shaky and uninteresting corporate ladder. No thanks! If I didn't try out my options, I would never discover my passions. And don't we all want to do something we feel passionate about?

Of course, these were all great thoughts, but actually incorporating them into my everyday thinking process would be a whole other story.... So, was I able to rise to the challenge of my very first resolution?

Well, let's just say that I have made the choice to be okay. Okay with my single-hood and my ever-changing career path, and okay that others might not be okay with it. I think that is the most important ingredient. And every New Year's Eve, I make sure to clear my schedule, dress up in my ugliest sweats, eat some delicious leftovers, and relax with my cat. Then as I tune in to watch the rest of the world create a

Love Who You Are

picture-perfect New Year's, I glance at the photos on my own wall and think, "What a beautiful year it has been."

— Britteny Elrick —

Un-Resolved

The person who views himself at fifty the same as he did at twenty has wasted thirty years of his life.
~Muhammad Ali

Age sixty-three: Birthday resolutions: I will lose weight. I will exercise until my muscles are firm and my pot belly disappears. I will look like I did back when I weighed 100 pounds soaking wet and ate anything I wanted.

I knew it was possible. I knew it was easy. I'd done it before. Why not again?

So I joined a gym and went faithfully three days a week.

First came the equipment room. It was filled with tanned, well-muscled men, toned women dressed in miniature Spandex clothing. I heard the clank of metal against metal, but the only piece of equipment I recognized was the treadmill. Cautiously pushing the start button, I began walking. Nothing to it. But after a few days, boredom turned my brain to the consistency of spoiled peaches. I tried reading while walking, but the print in the magazines bounced with every step and I got so dizzy I was afraid I'd go flying off the end and land ungracefully in a sweatpants and T-shirt heap against the wall.

Maybe, I decided, classes would be better. Yoga. I became very good at lying on my back on my purple mat, palms up, relaxing. In fact, I was an excellent relaxer. It was all those other poses that made me decide I wasn't yoga material after all. The day I crouched on the floor, looked out from under my leg, and vaguely tried to put my foot

Love Who You Are | 133

somewhere over my shoulder, I knew it was time to move on.

I'd never tried belly dancing. It looked like fun. How hard could it be? I bought a pale blue scarf with hundreds of little coins sewn on it and tied it around my waist. The metal coins jingled happily as I positioned myself in the second row. The music played. I swayed. And then I watched the teacher's firm hips gyrate in directions my hips would never go. Not in a million years. I tried. The jingling, pale blue scarf I'd been so proud of slid slowly to the floor as I shimmied. It went in the car's trunk with my yoga mat.

Line dancing? I couldn't remember the steps if there were more than four. Cardio? My face turned red and I was left gasping for air.

Did my muscles become firm with all of this effort? They did not. They screamed and cramped if I so much as approached the gym, and revolted by keeping me awake at night.

I didn't lose weight, either. In fact, I gained two pounds.

And that's when I saw myself reflected in the window of the No-Longer-Petite Store, over near the mall. Windows don't lie. "No matter what you do, woman," it said, "you'll never look like you did forty years ago. Get real. Check it out. Hair turning gray. Sensible shoes. Square body. Think you're going to look twenty again? It ain't gonna happen."

And that's when the happy truth hit me like a runaway skateboard. I'm at a different stage in my life now. Oh, I can exercise for my health, but nothing will ever give me back the body of my youth. And if I'm able to diet, I still won't end up looking like a thin and sleek magazine model babe; I'll just be a bony old lady.

Me? An old lady? Hey, that's what I am! The thought was liberating. I smiled. I wanted to dance right there on the sidewalk, and even took a few quick steps.

I was finally free to be me. To do what I wanted. To forget about what people expected. And guess what? I realized I was already a terrific old lady. I had smile crinkles surrounding my eyes. I welcomed any adventure that might come my way. And I was equipped with enough padding to make a comfortable lap for grandchildren to climb into.

Age sixty-three and a half: Un-birthday resolution: I'll be what I am, live in the moment, and enjoy the ride. After all, that's what life's all about!

—Michele Ivy Davis—

Running for My Life

It's the fire in my eyes, and the flash of my teeth.
The swing in my waist, and the joy in my feet.
I'm a woman phenomenally.
~Maya Angelou

A plaque with the silhouette of a city skyline hangs proudly on a wall in my house. Six medals dangle from its hooks, each with a different size, shape, color, and meaning. The one in the middle, though, is my favorite — its thick red ribbon holds a pendant of a buffalo, with the words "Buffalo Half Marathon" and "FINISHER" embossed on it.

Every time the medal catches my eye, I smile and feel unstoppable.

My body and I have known each other for twenty-five years, but we just recently fell in love. Growing up, I was never much of an athlete. While I dabbled with sports and exercise, I had little natural talent and enjoyed junk food far too much.

My family kept sweets, snacks, and soda on hand at all times, and maintained a weekly tradition of indulging at the local pizzeria. As a result, I developed an unhealthy relationship with food. I oscillated back and forth between binging and starving, being sedentary and exercising on an empty stomach.

These habits caught up to me after graduating from college. I'd reached my heaviest weight and my lowest self-confidence. Entering graduate school, I was depressed and resigned to unhealthiness.

My mother had been diagnosed with diabetes several years prior, and each time I watched her test her blood sugar, my stomach grew queasy. Was I looking at my future? I knew something had to change, I just didn't know how to do it. When I looked in the mirror, my stomach would seize at the sight of my thick waistline, thunderous thighs, and jiggly arms. It was like looking in the mirror at a repulsive stranger whom I had no intention of getting to know.

Learning to love yourself in a society that tells you what you are supposed to be is one of the hardest tasks women face, but it is also one of the most urgent jobs we have, especially as women of the next generation. Looking back at pictures from my teens and college years, I realize that I had never actually been overweight. Hating my body, however, had been a theme in my life from a very young age.

During their adolescence, nearly every woman in my family struggled with an eating disorder, but no one talked about it. My mother and I eventually shared our stories, and as it turned out, they were hauntingly similar, as were my grandmother's and my sister's. I felt a sense of reassurance knowing that it wasn't just me who struggled. We were a community of women, and someone had to take the first steps.

So, I did. Little by little, I started working out here and making a healthy choice there. When I was feeling exceptionally ambitious, I would lace up my sneakers and jog around the block. The next week, I'd jog a little farther, and the next, I'd run.

At first, a little voice in my head whined and told me I couldn't do it. But the longer we ran together, the more we got to truly know one another.

I eventually learned that the little voice didn't really believe I couldn't do it; she was just afraid of failing and falling into old habits. Deep down, she wanted this as much as I did.

After a long talk with a close friend of ours, that little voice and I decided to tackle a seemingly insane task: running a half marathon. As we embarked on a training routine, she would chime in with her fits of self-doubt, and I would gently talk her off the ledge with chants of "Just a little bit farther!" or "Trust me, we can do this!"

Occasionally, she would call me that ugly three-letter "f" word, even though our waistline was shrinking and our legs were getting leaner and more muscular. I learned to silence her with — of all things — a cookie, because I discovered that depriving her of cravings only made her grow cranky and tiresome. The key was to supplement those treats with whole grains, fruits, and vegetables and to pay close attention to how much I was consuming. Diet is crucial when running thirty-plus miles a week. To work in unison and to make the training program work, that little voice and I needed balance.

Those grueling miles and long weeks of training helped me understand the importance of listening to my body. When my mind told me to stop, it could usually be attributed to doubt, fear, and insecurity. When my body told me to stop, however, it acted as a warning signal against injury, undernourishment, and overexertion.

Before running, I ignored the whispers that came from my body, but once I started running regularly, I listened for them with the attentiveness of a mother awaiting her baby's cry. Sometimes I would disregard them, knowing that my mind was trying to speak for my body, but other times, I would respect my body's wishes and cut back on my mileage or eat a little extra.

I completed my training, and one warm day in May, I crossed the finish line in front of hundreds of spectators, alongside one of my dearest and most encouraging friends. When a happy stranger knighted me with my shiny buffalo, I was exhausted, but my mind was calmer than it had ever been before. After victory photos and post-race snacks, my friend looked at me and smiled.

"You look super athletic, by the way. You've lost weight."

I returned his smile. Covered in layers of sweaty clothing, wearing my first medal, I realized how little those words meant. Together, my body, mind, and spirit stood united and strong; stronger than they had ever been before. To me, that was more beautiful than any compliment.

Now, whenever I feel my confidence waning, I look at my first medal, lace up my sneakers, and remind myself that I run this life.

— Jenna Schifferle —

Lord, Make Me a Babe

An empty lantern provides no light. Self-care is the fuel that allows your light to shine brightly.
~Author Unknown

I recently found out that my soon-to-be-ex-husband is dating someone. He and I were sitting outside of our son's classroom door at the middle school, waiting for our parent–teacher conference. At school events where parents are present, it's easy to spot the divorced parents. They look kind of stiff and surly. Generally, they are not talking to each other. They can be spotted at soccer games, too. One doesn't need a graduate degree in psychotherapy, which I happen to have, to figure out which couples are together now only by the necessity of parenthood.

Down the school hallway, a lady I did not recognize flounced by. "Hii-yii," she sang out in a lilting, singsong voice. She was not talking to me. The soon-to-be-ex turned beet red. Like a character straight out of a time-machine movie, I instantly morphed into a high school junior.

Harry's teacher came to the door and invited us in. Thankfully, I morphed back into my middle-aged-parent self. The focus shifted to Harry, our adolescent, soon-to-be-from-a-broken-home son. I survived the conference and walked to my car alone afterward.

As soon as I got home, I picked up the phone and called the soon-to-be-ex. "Are you dating?" I asked.

Love Who You Are

"Howdja know?" He never did know when to lie.

I don't know why, but it hit me like a kick in the stomach. Truly, this was the end to an eighteen-year marriage, where no one on the face of the earth could have tried harder than I did to save it. Several years earlier, my girlfriends had an intervention with me. "Linda," they said at a lunch meeting, "you're in an emotionally abusive marriage."

"I know," I said, "but it's still better than the alternative." The alternative is what I am now facing: the Big D. I still can't bring myself to say it.

So, there is no use crying over spilt milk or going into the maudlin details. Like the flaming co-dependent that I am, I tried to move heaven and earth to save my marriage. In fact, to borrow a phrase from a twelve-step program, I used to refer to it as rearranging the chairs on the deck of the *Titanic*. With icebergs rearing their ugly heads in the distance, I did everything I could and more.

And now, I am facing the D-word. He filed. Not only that, but now the other D-word is being thrown out there. He is *dating* someone. After eighteen years, he is not dating me.

So, if I explain that I woke up one morning several days ago with butt-kicking depression, one would understand why. This depression was like moving slowly underwater with a boulder on my back. I wanted to break into tears at the drop of a hat. I rehearsed calling a psychiatrist friend and telling her that it was time to sign me up for antidepressants. Through some serious hard times, I have resisted that option.

Friday morning, I trudged off to work. Keeping cash flow was a necessity at my stage of life. I sat down in my office. My client came in. I noticed a change from her previous appearance. She looked terrific! Her hair was natural and pulled back, instead of heavy and long. Her eyes looked wide open. This woman really knew how to put on make-up. Instead of winter brown and black, she was wearing pink and white with matching pink socks. She was getting enough sleep, and it showed in her complexion.

I marveled at the difference in her, especially the make-up. Then it hit me like a voice from God, like a bolt of lightning, like a revelation from above in a low, thunderous voice: "Linda, you can do this, too."

"What, God?" I asked the voice in my head, meanwhile listening empathetically to my client. (Only really experienced psychotherapists can listen to God and their clients at the same time.)

"You can do this, too." It was God's voice again.

Finally, the revelation came through loud and clear: "You can become a babe."

"A babe," I gasped internally. "But, Lord, what about the flab under my arms and my thighs?" No use arguing with God. The revelation was unequivocal. The still, small voice had delivered the message loud and clear. My calling, at this juncture, was to become a babe — a fifty-six-year-old babe.

Who am I to argue with God? My course is set. Whatever it takes — a trainer-diet-make-up consultant. I know what I've got to do.

My final court date is several months away, and what sweeter justice than to show up in divorce court having morphed into a veritable babe. Not for him, but for me, and for my girlfriends who will be cheering me on every inch of the way.

So, I'm on my way to Babedom. And you know what else? My depression mysteriously evaporated. Poof. Like the parting of the Red Sea. I am a woman with a mission.

Whenever I begin to mourn the past or even ponder the thought of my soon-to-be-ex with someone else, I say this little prayer, "Lord, make me a babe."

It's working. I'm looking better already.

— Linda Hoff Irvin —

Chapter 6

Treat Yourself

Just Socks

The cars we drive say a lot about us.
~Alexandra Paul

My husband Gary is known in our community for his photography skills, so it isn't unusual for him to get a phone call from someone who wants a special picture taken. That is exactly what happened one June day a few years ago.

"Jim asked me to take a couple of photos of something he wants to sell online," Gary announced as he headed to the door, camera in hand.

"What?" I asked.

Gary shrugged. "He didn't say. I'll find out when I get there."

An hour later, my husband returned with love shining in his eyes. Not for me. No, the love was for the red 1990 Mazda Miata that Jim wanted to sell. "I'm thinking of buying it," Gary said.

If he had announced that he was going to fly to the moon, I wouldn't have been more surprised. Us? Buy a sports car? What was he thinking? We're in our seventies. Seventy-somethings do not buy sports cars on the spur of the moment, if at all. I had to talk some sense into him.

In all fairness, I should explain that owning a Miata had been my husband's longtime dream. When our children were growing up and our daughter asked her dad what he wanted for Christmas or his birthday or Father's Day, his answer was always the same. "I want socks," he'd announce to the sighs and eye-rolling of our daughter.

Treat Yourself | 143

"But," he would quickly add, "the socks must be presented in a special way. They must be packed in the trunk of a Mazda." Needless to say, financial constraints made that wish impossible.

Flash forward to June 2013. "Jim said we can take the car for a test drive," Gary said. "Not today because it looks like rain and Jim never takes the car out in the rain, but tomorrow for sure if the weather is nice."

I prayed for rain the next day. My concern was not the cost of the car. It was whether I'd be able to get my senior body into and out of a sports car without doing physical damage to myself.

In spite of my prayers, the next day dawned sunny and fair, and Gary went to pick up the car. Hoping that my neighbours weren't looking out their windows, I managed to get myself into it, albeit somewhat clumsily. Seatbelts buckled, we took off.

As we headed up a never-yet-explored country road — paved, of course, because you don't drive a sports car on gravel or dirt roads — something magical happened. Low to the ground with the wind blowing in my hair, I felt as though I were one with the countryside. By the time we got back home, the love was shining in my eyes, too.

We bought the Miata that day. For the first time in his life, Gary ordered vanity plates: SOCKBOX.

We spent the next few months exploring the back roads and byways of the surrounding area, finding interesting shops, local produce stands and breathtaking scenery on roads we would likely never have taken in our regular vehicle.

That was not the only gift the Sockbox brought us. We discovered the Trillium Miata Club, based in southern Ontario. Their website included photos taken on tours, showing a group of proud Miata owners with their pride-and-joy vehicles. There were enough grey heads in the group that we knew we would fit in age-wise.

We signed up for Friday evening ice-cream tours, day trips and overnights throughout Ontario and Quebec and into the United States. The tours, organized by members, include winding, hilly roads and spectacular scenery. Overnight stays at hotels or motels include parties in rooms with wine, laughter and socializing. Joining the Trillium Miata

Club was a blessing, a big part of which are the many new friends we have made.

In 2016, we switched to a 2012 Miata, metallic red with a black racing stripe. It has all the bells and whistles because we want to go farther afield on longer trips.

Parting with the original Sockbox was sad, but the license plate on the new one remains the same. We will always be grateful to the amazing little sports car that brought the gift of new friends and adventures into our senior years.

— Marilyn Helmer —

In This Moment

*You've been criticizing yourself for years,
and it hasn't worked. Try approving
of yourself and see what happens.*
~Louise L. Hay

When I was fourteen, my first boyfriend called me pleasantly plump. He'd hug me and say, "There's just more to love on you."

When I was sixteen, my dad nicknamed me "Thunder Thighs."

Another boyfriend, when I was twenty-two, asked if I was pregnant because I'd gained so much weight.

Needless to say, their words made me feel unloved, judged and insecure.

So I would try to show my love for myself through food. I never attained satisfaction though, and the pounds piled on like a protective layer between the rest of the world and me.

My pride kept me trapped for years, hiding behind baggy tunics and stretchy pants. I'd tell myself, "I'm pretty cool, wearing fancy yoga pants every day." But who was I kidding? I hadn't done yoga in years. Stretchy pants were the only fabric I could squeeze into.

If only I could lose 10 pounds, I thought, *I'd be happy and my life would be great.* That 10 pounds turned into 20, 30, and then 50. For years I tried to change my body, forcing myself to endure uncomfortable diets and distasteful cleanses while suffocating in guilt because I couldn't keep the weight off or keep the cookie dough at bay. I'd squeeze my fat and cry, begging God to grant me a skinny body. But even when I did lose weight, I didn't feel comfortable in my own skin.

I pushed away men I was interested in because I was ashamed of my body. I passed up social engagements to protect myself from judgment and criticism of my weight.

My addiction to food was the problem, or so I thought. Why couldn't I be a normal person around food? Why did I shove food in my mouth when I wasn't even hungry? Why couldn't I put the peanut butter down?" I'd try to answer those questions every day, after each new food binge, but the answers eluded me.

For the past twenty-five years it's been me against my body — a painful, insecure, self-defeating battlefield.

A few months ago I said to a friend, "I weigh more than I ever have, I'm in the largest pants size of my life." The elastic was cutting into my stomach, but I was too stubborn to admit I needed a larger size.

A few days after that, I saw a quote that hit me to my core: "Accept what you can't change and change what you can't accept."

I realized that if I couldn't change myself, then maybe the real issue was one of self-acceptance. After years of sacrifice and suffering, my only other choice was to accept what I couldn't change. Gulp. Could I actually look in the mirror and like what I saw, even with stretch marks and 50 extra pounds cushioning my body? Could I completely love myself despite my body? From that day forward, I made this my full-time mission.

I started to approach food differently. Instead of saying I couldn't have something, I told myself I could eat whatever I wanted as long as I enjoyed it fully. This meant really tasting it — embracing the texture, the flavor, even taking in the smell. Instead of obsessing over what I ate or counting the calories in my chewing gum, I loosened the reins. I accepted that I really do love food, which led me to the real miracle — accepting myself.

Soon, I wasn't hiding or being ashamed of myself. I began to acknowledge that my body is a vessel for love and that I have a lot of love to give to the world. So the bigness I exhibit is a desire to be seen and give my heart to the world.

I began repeating the mantra, "I accept myself in this moment. I am right where I need to be. I am beautiful and full of life."

At first I didn't believe this, but in time I was able to retrain my brain to see the good. And as I embraced myself, I returned to my true self.

Once I admitted that I really like sugar and that eating it makes me happy, my cravings diminished. I stopped wanting it because I knew I could eat it whenever I wanted. My desire to shove cookie dough in my face has gone away. I replaced my years of resistance and pushing away the foods I loved with a more compassionate approach: consciousness.

Now I eat what I want when I want. I make healthy choices and feel more grounded. Accepting my desires has changed my life.

My shift was simple; I turned down my mind and tuned into my heart. Instead of trying to reach a predetermined idea of perfection, I turned inward. The result? Freedom and self-awareness. No more body hate and no more self-sabotaging thoughts.

With my obsessive food thoughts gone, my body is returning to a healthy weight.

All because I stopped fighting myself and embraced the real me, the one who loves life fully and enjoys each moment, even when… no, especially when… she's eating chocolate cake!

— Shannon Kaiser —

One Day

Taking time to rest, renew, and refresh yourself isn't wasted time. Recharge. Choose what energizes you.
~Melody Beattie, Journey to the Heart

When my husband asked me what I wanted for Mother's Day, I said sheepishly, "A night away. By myself. Oh, and I'll take the dog."

I felt guilty asking for a night away. After all, I was a new mom, blessed with a beautiful daughter, then five months old. I loved her to the moon and back. But I was tired, exhausted. I wanted to drive somewhere and spend the night, read and sleep with no interruptions.

My husband looked a bit surprised, but he assured me it would be okay. Even with his encouragement, I felt a pang of guilt when I looked into my baby's eyes. What had I heard about mothers and guilt? It comes to new mothers along with all the other gifts, wrapped in a pretty bow… the gift that keeps on giving.

To save money, I would be staying in a friend's cabin at a local ski resort. Beverly said it would be quiet since it was May, with no snow or skiers. That suited me just fine. Quiet. Peaceful. Bliss.

The next day, I packed and kissed my daughter and husband goodbye. My Golden Retriever, Kia, eagerly jumped into the hatchback.

"Bye," I said, waving. I pulled out of the driveway, trying not to look back at my daughter, who was starting to cry, holding out her arms to me. *Should I go back? No, keep going. She'll be fine for one night.*

Treat Yourself | 149

She'll be fine.

The day was overcast and hazy. As I drove, I yawned, willing myself to stay awake. Houses and neighborhoods yielded to evergreens and snow-capped mountains. The newly budded deciduous trees, a light green curtain, waved in the breeze.

At the resort, cabins on stilts looked strange without the snow. Beverly's cabin was not the quaint retreat I had imagined. In fact, it was old and needed a heavy dose of TLC. The paint was faded and peeling, and the stairs looked rickety, as if they might give way at any moment.

A musty smell greeted me as I entered, but everything looked clean. I put a sandwich (my dinner) in the fridge. I thought of taking a hot shower but found there was none, just an old bathtub with rust spots.

The cabin was dark, and the lighting was minimal. I hated when people used low-watt bulbs. Don't people read anymore? I noticed an axe propped in the corner, like something from a horror film. *They probably need it to chop firewood,* I thought, although I didn't see any wood. I made some hot cocoa, which smelled heavenly. As I turned to get my book, a mouse scurried across the floor.

I shrieked and jumped. *Oh, my gosh!* My heart was beating fast. I took a deep breath. I would tell Beverly she had a squatter.

"You stay away from us, Mr. Mouse, and we'll stay away from you." I looked at Kia. "Maybe we should go back home."

She barked. "What's that?" I asked. "Just deal with it?" She barked again.

"Okay, okay."

I fed Kia and ate my sandwich. Birds chirped outside the kitchen window. I started feeling better. Nature and a quiet place, no interruptions. I sat in a big chair and started reading but soon nodded off. I woke with a start. It wasn't that late, but I decided to go to bed.

I eyed that axe again. I picked it up and took it into the bedroom. I'd feel better knowing it was nearby.

Kia followed me and curled up next to the bed. I liked to sleep with two pillows. There was only a skimpy one on my bed, and I didn't see another pillow on the bed across from me. I changed into pajamas and found some towels to put under the pillow. Not great, but it would do for one night. The bed was lumpy, and I could feel springs poking my body. *Where did she get this thing?* Despite the bed and pillow, I fell asleep.

I dreamed about floating on a cloud that cradled and rocked me. Then I heard something strange. I opened my eyes. I sat up. *What in the world?* I heard what sounded like hundreds of mice running through the walls and in the attic. I jumped up. My foot caught in the blanket, and I fell. Kia pounced and barked.

I imagined mice crawling all over me. *Oh. Oh. Oh!* I made it up and turned on the light. I didn't see any mice in the room but still heard them moving wildly in the walls and attic. It was just a matter of time before they decided to invade the bedroom. *Hundreds of rodents… too much!*

"C'mon, Kia," I said. "We're getting out of here." I dressed as fast as I could and threw my things together.

Once I was on the highway, tears clouded my vision. *What a disaster. I can't even get one night away to myself. I might as well admit defeat and go home.*

Then, up ahead, I saw a hotel with a Vacancy sign lit up like a beacon. I hadn't wanted to spend money on a hotel, but it was just for one night… The car seemed to turn into the parking lot on its own.

Fortunately, the man at the hotel desk said they had pet-friendly rooms.

"And there's a complimentary breakfast buffet in the morning," he said.

"Breakfast buffet? What's in it?" I asked.

"Bacon and eggs, toast, hash browns…"

"What else?"

"French toast, waffles, pancakes, oatmeal, Danish, donuts, muffins, juices, coffee…"

As he rambled on, a smorgasbord danced in my head.

I went to my room. Spacious and nice. Big, comfy, king-sized bed, no lumps. Plenty of fluffy pillows. The sheets were pulled down, and two mints perched on the pillow. The bathroom was modern, with a large shower. I would get a good night's sleep, shower in the morning, and eat as much as I wanted for breakfast. No cooking. No cleaning up. Sweet. I deserved this one night. For sure. I turned off the light, and the guilt.

— Wendy Hairfield —

Permission to Joyride

Listen, are you breathing a little and calling it a life?
~Mary Oliver

With my head against the glass of our fifth-story hospital window, my gaze lingered on the row of red rental bikes across the street at our Ronald McDonald House. Once again we were sequestered post-operatively with our daughter at a children's hospital a thousand miles from home. And by day eight of our stay, my bike-riding daydreams were quite vivid.

As the parents of a child with complex medical needs, this life wasn't new to us. Our little patient had endured a complex, eight-hour, multi-surgeon operation. We'd been working through recovery with a pain pump, follow-up therapies, and an endless flow of medical professionals through our tiny fifth-floor room. The hardest challenge? She was under NPO (nil per os) orders: nothing by mouth — no food and no drinks. It had not been easy for her or me, her caretaker.

Then came a Sunday afternoon when the doctors had completed their rounds, our girl was finally comfortable and happy, and my mom was with us. It was a calm day of rest. So, as we clicked on *Frozen* for our eleventh viewing, I looked longingly again at those rental bikes shining in the summer sun. I'd left our daughter's bedside many times for naps or laundry, but could I leave her for a joyride?

Treat Yourself | 153

As I wondered if it might finally be possible to slip away, my familiar doubts arose. What if the surgeon came back? What if a nurse needed me? What if my daughter cried? What if they forgot to give her pain meds?

"Go," urged my mom.

"Go," urged everything in me.

So, I pushed aside those noisy doubts and my guilty-mom feelings. I walked through the hospital doors into the open air, bound for that row of bikes.

As I swiped my credit card and the bike unlocked, something in me unlocked as well. For two freeing hours, I pumped the pedals fast, and then I meandered slowly. My hair blew, and my heart pumped. My soul responded with a flood of emotions from elation to buried, angry tears, then back to grateful joy. I even stopped to take a few photos of a flower garden.

When I returned and locked my bike back into its spot, my ride was over, but new breath filled my lungs.

Back on the other side of the hospital glass, my girl smiled wide when I re-entered, happy to see me. And instead of clicking onto yet another movie, I decided it would be better to pull out our unused paints and turn on some music. Soul care was long overdue for her, too.

That joyride shifted my thinking. Yes, my priority is my family. Yes, life is hard, full, and even scary, but I'd gotten a good taste of the value of attending to the soul.

The reality is, I am a medical mom of four children. So, unfortunately, my "me time" has limited parameters. We've got long to-do lists and a full schedule. There are multiplication tables to memorize, dishes to scrub, book reports to complete, and Cub Scout meetings to attend.

But now I have a changed perspective and a tea towel in my kitchen that reminds me: "Do something each day that brings you joy."

When I care for my soul and take a little me time, it might feel unproductive, but it's also a gift to my whole family. A happy momma often results in a happy family. And, while I want my kids to know how to subtract and make a bed, I also want them to discover what makes them come alive. I want to help them increase their capacities to survive and thrive. If they see me take joyrides, maybe they will, too.

I wrote myself a permission slip to seize a little slice of joy that day in the pediatric hospital, and it has made all the difference.

After that Sunday bike ride, Monday inevitably came. The new day brought my girl discomfort and agitation. For hours, I tried to no avail to do everything I could think of, from holding her to distracting her with Snapchat filters.

Then I remembered my joyride. So, I dimmed the lights, pulled a chair and tray table close to her bed, and dumped out a 100-piece puzzle. I hummed as I sorted through the pieces. She was annoyed at first, but I kept humming and sorting. Then slowly, as I settled, so did she. I moved the tray closer, and her little hands went to work, helping me find all the blue-sky pieces.

As it turns out, when I took the time to attend to my soul, it helped my daughter settle hers as well.

— Rebecca Radicchi —

Hearts and Hurricanes

If you surrender to the wind, you can ride it.
~Toni Morrison

My husband and I are rookies when it comes to travel as a couple. We stay in the United States and have ventured to Mexico only recently.

In contrast, I grew up in a family where travel was one of the four food groups — good health demanded it. Summers were spent voyaging to Europe on the Queen Mary, picnicking in the English countryside and watching tremendous men throw logs the size of redwood trees at the Scottish Highland games. At six years old, I found nothing about this interesting, romantic or beautiful. I spent a lot of time just wanting a hot dog. The youngest of three children, I was squashed in the back seat between my brother and sister, feeling carsick and dreading the next castle. Inevitably I would feel lost in a large group of foreigners, listening to a French guide point to doorways and furniture in excited tones. Castles smelled like a mixture of my father's starchy shirts and musty closets. In between museums, my mother read to us from *Michelin* guidebooks as my father drove haltingly ahead on a different side of the road. Like the guides, she too would get very excited, interjecting, "Isn't that fascinating?" like a chorus hoping we'd sing along.

So now, decades later, I am trying to find my own sweet melody

Treat Yourself

in travel—as my husband and I venture away each year without children. Our recent trip to the California wine country began with yellow sticky notes decorating the kitchen counter, as my son and daughter would be left in the care of a dear friend. The notes were yellow reminders about two tennis lessons, one dentist appointment, my son's volunteer work with developmentally disabled adults, two Halloween parties, one school field trip, garbage pick-up and plant watering. Puppy care, bunny care and fish feeding had their own full page. The puppy goes to Canine Campovers and I had to remind my friend she gets car sick so to avoid stop and go traffic.

My careful note taking occurred before a couple of last-minute emergencies threatened to scuttle our vacation plans. A Florida hurricane hit my son's university and my father-in-law had triple bypass surgery.

Suddenly my organized sticky notes provided no comfort, no direction. When I was making reservations at our Mendocino bed and breakfast, I hadn't taken into account old hearts and young hurricanes. Our family looked like the route map in an airline magazine—my son was driving north, my father-in-law was ailing in the south and we were considering going west.

My father advised, "Go west, your son will be fine."

My mother said, "Stay home, you should be there."

My husband was pondering traveling to a southern ICU, and I was left with a lot of cross-outs on sticky notes. My heart told me we needed to get away. I'd recently had a dream in which my husband and I stopped in the kitchen to talk to each other! Obviously our lives were moving too quickly. As I zipped my suitcase, guilt was stuffed in the corners next to a good novel and my running shoes. We were going anyway, with charged cell phones, Internet access and the hope our self-care wouldn't impinge on dying hurricane winds and recovering hearts.

We landed on a rainy San Francisco runway. The Hertz lady said we needed a six-cylinder engine for the curvy wine-country roads. I was more concerned about the color of the car and was just happy to be standing next to my husband with no one asking me for anything. We weaved our way up north on Highway 1, listening to a radio station that played old songs from when we were in ninth grade.

After stopping in Santa Rosa for tofu and vegetables, a shared glass of wine, a shared cup of decaf coffee, and a shared chocolate chip cookie, we were feeling like adolescents again. Without children, we were free to be children. The Mendocino coast brings together the redwood forests, rocky cliffs and a quiet blue ocean. The stillness of the forest on morning runs matched an inner stillness allowed by our solitude. In our regular life, my husband and I have gotten used to running separately. Young children demanded "revolving door" running. My husband would return through the front door and I'd head out the back. He usually did the early run just because he felt more comfortable with a headlamp — but no revolving doors in Mendocino.

Daily calls back to the "real world" kept us informed about heart and hurricane realities. Power to the university campus was restored; my father-in-law's pacemaker at full charge.

There are no sticky notes on vacation, and stepping out of a morning shower has no deadline. We hit more coffee shops and bakeries than wineries. Heading home, our suitcase zipped more easily because we had no guilt stuffed in corners. Everyone survived. And I am reminded of the importance of making the pace slower — it strengthens the heart in a marriage. So tomorrow when the winds blow again, we're that much stronger to take care and hold tight. And someday, we might even make it to a French castle.

— Priscilla Dann-Courtney —

Every Day a Friday

Monday is a lame way to spend 1/7 of your life.
~Author Unknown

I love Fridays, and I'm not alone. Most people associate the last day of the workweek with feelings of relief, relaxation, and anticipation of good times to come in the weekend ahead. You know there has to be something special about a day when the feeling of celebration that accompanies its arrival is even commemorated in the name of a restaurant chain!

And so I, too, celebrate Fridays. After dropping my son off at school I head to Starbucks, to pick up a coffee treat of one type or another. Then instead of driving straight home I generally take a long route through the most scenic roads I can find, which usually includes my favorite corner of the local state park. On and on throughout the day I find myself smiling and happy for no other reason than that the day's name starts with an "F" rather than an "M," "T," or "W."

When I pick my son up again hours into the afternoon we high-five physically and vocally, our chorus of "FRIDAY!" resonating at least as loudly as our hand slap. Then we point out to each other the signs of beginning celebration in the college town we drive through. We see footballs being passed on fraternity lawns, hamburgers being thrown on grills, people parked on front porch swings, and parties everywhere swinging into action. Sometimes it seems as if the whole world is celebrating Friday!

The other day I emerged from a doctor's office happy over a positive

Treat Yourself | 159

prognosis in a health situation I was concerned about. My good mood was amplified by the signs of spring that were bursting all around me — flowers blossoming, birds singing, bright sunshine warm upon my back. I was suddenly ready to celebrate, and java-scented thoughts wafted through my brain. I whispered the word "Cappuccino!" and headed for the specialty coffee bar that was conveniently located just around the corner.

My mind rebelled. "What are you doing? It's Tuesday! Coffee treats are reserved for Fridays!" And suddenly I realized how ridiculous that line of thinking was! Why should Fridays be any more special than any other day of the week? Why waste six days while waiting to rejoice on the seventh? Minutes later I was walking back to my car with a big grin on my face and a raspberry mocha in my hand.

A small victory, to be sure, but it's also an accurate example of how many of us live our lives. We're waiting for conditions to be right before we allow ourselves to enjoy our time here on earth. Maybe when we finally graduate from college and get a job it will be time to celebrate, or perhaps when our toddlers are old enough to be in school all day. We'll rejoice when the car is paid off, or enjoy life when we're finally able to retire. And in that waiting we waste so much of the life that God has given us and the happiness that can be found in our todays. What if we moved a little of that "Friday feeling" into our rainy-day Mondays, our gloomy Tuesdays and our mid-week Wednesdays? Surely our lives would be much happier as a result.

It's interesting to note that T.G.I. Friday's isn't open for business on just the last day of the workweek! No, they celebrate all week long and into the weekend.

So should we.

— Elaine L. Bridge —

Guest Treatment

You're worthy of it all. You just have to believe you are!
~Tony Gaskins

My mom had guest soaps in the bathroom. In a home with very few luxuries, those tiny roses of avocado green and lemon yellow represented something special to her; they were something she wanted to keep nice for our guests. So she kept them in a covered glass container, where they would be safe from the many sets of little fingers in our household that needed washing. Only the guests never used them. We never used them. Those soap rosettes decorated the shelf in the bathroom for as long as I can remember. There they stayed, displayed until dust caked in the crevices of the soap petals, and the roses lost their luster. But they were never used. They were saved for guests.

Fast forward to my adult married life. We were visiting my in-laws when the marriage was still shiny and new. New traditions, new family members, and new relationships were just beginning to be forged when I received the gift. It was casually given. No big deal; everyone got one. It was just a bar of soap, a chunk of green marbled glycerin, lightly scented and wrapped in cellophane with a lovely label proclaiming that this soap had been handcrafted by an artisan who just happened to be my new brother-in-law. That soap was only a few ounces, but I carried the weight of it for years. It was guest soap.

It was too pretty to use. It was proudly set out to be looked at — but not used — for about a week. My practical husband did not see the point of it cluttering up the countertop. So it found a new home, wrapped and cushioned, set aside in my scarf drawer. There, its gentle scent would drift between the layers of nylon and silk, and waft up to greet me when I opened the drawer. With its cellophane wrapper and label intact, that bar of soap was a hidden gem that gently reminded me of nice people and nice things whenever I saw it. My life went on. My children grew. An empty childhood bedroom became a craft room, and in this newly created space there was a glassed-in display shelf — a place for the soap. It found a new home.

I loved my craft room. Bright and sunny, soft and cozy, it was filled with quaint furnishings and things I cherished. When I got sick, the craft room became my recovery room. I could rest there surrounded by happy memories. As I got better, I took inventory of my life, and of my surroundings. And, I saw the soap.

I saw something that was meant to be used, not admired. Long ago it was given to me, a simple gift of special soap. Except that I had decided I wasn't special enough to use it. Cancer changed that. I took that carefully wrapped soap off the shelf and opened it with a sense of childish delight. The scent was as lovely as I remembered it to be. However, without its wrappings, the glycerin was rather dull, and as I stood there with that hazy chunk of soap in my hands, I wondered what all the fuss had been about. Then I ran it under water.

It was transformed, and so was I. The running water turned the soap into a shining jewel in my hands. The surface became slick and the colors gleamed. The irregular angles gave texture to the glycerin rotating between my palms as the suds slipped through my fingers. A regular bar of soap does not feel like this. No, this was something different, something special. So I took my time, savoring each sensation, totally immersing myself in the moment. As I concentrated on the bubbles building between my hands, reveling in the feel of the flowing water over my skin, the ritual of washing my hands transformed into a meditative experience. I let it all go. I felt my troubles washing away with those tiny bits of foam. It became a small moment of pure joy. My heart was at peace; I felt pampered and loved. After all those years, why had I been waiting to use it? I was waiting for me.

Cancer was an unwelcome visitor in my life, but it taught me to live. So, from now on, I will use the guest soap. And while I'm at it, I might as well use the good towels, too.

—Paula Klendworth Skory—

The Life You Save May Be Your Own

*People who love cats have some
of the biggest hearts around.*
~Susan Easterly

My cat Belinda loved to lie on an old rug right by the patio door. In that spot she could bask in the sun without actually going outside. She and I had no interest in danger. But when her life was threatened by illness, I faced her danger, and learned something about myself in the process. The life you save may be your own.

Belinda was eleven years old when she stopped eating, started losing weight, and developed a series of lumps on her stomach. A biopsy that cost $400 revealed mast cell tumor disease, a form of cancer. "She's going to die in two months without surgery," the vet told my husband and me. The operation would give her more time, but at more than $1,100, it sounded extremely expensive.

My husband teaches college classes and I'm a paralegal. We've never had children, but our budget felt pretty tight. After paying our mortgage, car payments, school loans and regular bills each month, there wasn't much left. At least that's what I believed.

I thought about the fact that Belinda was an animal. Where would we draw the line in taking care of her? She and her sister Magda had always been expensive, high maintenance girls. Each of their files at the vet ran to two volumes. We had just paid for Belinda's biopsy. The price of this surgery probably made it reasonable to say "no more." She'd had a good life, starting with her rescue from the tree where her wild mother had hidden her when she was a kitten. We wouldn't let her suffer; we would put her to sleep. It would be merciful and prudent. We would stay within our budget, keep our life manageable.

But something felt wrong. At first I couldn't put my finger on the problem. Then I knew. Grief was flooding through me. Knocked off balance, I sat down hard in an armchair and closed my eyes. Memories came. I saw Belinda and Magda as kittens exploring my apartment like eager little scientists.

Then I saw Belinda after her first flea bath, a small, bedraggled creature, her wet fur stuck together in clumps. I had expected her to run from me as soon as I lifted her out of the sudsy water. After all, she and her sister had only been with me a few days. When she didn't bolt, but instead mewed around my feet, I scooped her up into a towel, and rubbed her dry. In those moments, an unexpected tenderness broke open within me. When I bathed Magda, I felt the same.

Thinking of Belinda, with her light orange stripes, and black-and-white Magda sitting clean and dry after their baths took me back into an older memory: my dark-haired sister Rachel and blond-haired me eating bologna sandwiches in the kitchen after school. But this was a painful memory. I remembered my mother coming home from work late, opening the refrigerator, and yelling at us for eating too much. She was a widow who worked hard to support us, and it must have seemed to her that food vanished like snow in the sun, that there was never quite enough of anything. My overwhelmed mother did the best she could, but life with her was all about scarcity. I spent my whole childhood feeling too expensive and high maintenance. Rachel and I have always wondered if we were worth it.

Sitting in the armchair, I opened my eyes. "Mom," I said aloud although she had died years before, "I know just how you felt because I feel the same way." As an adult, it was easy to point to my checkbook as the reason for pinching pennies, when the real reason was an emotional habit — a feeling of poverty that I carried with me always.

And I still felt a strong doubt about whether needy little creatures were worth the expense.

For so long I hadn't questioned my view that the glass of precious water was always half empty. Now, thinking about Belinda, I realized that my view was life-threatening — to her, and to me. I hadn't been in a bad car accident or been thrown from a boat, but my life — my faith that I was worthwhile, and that I had enough to risk giving — was in danger just the same.

"Mom, I know you loved me the best way you could, but I'm going to make a different choice here," I said.

I realized how much I loved Belinda, and what it meant to me to love her, to feel generous towards her. Somehow it was a way of believing that even expensive, high maintenance creatures — those who need surgery and cat food and those who needed bologna sandwiches — were worth it. Giving Belinda the surgery would be an act of faith, and a first step in trying to change my emotional habit.

My husband and I paid for the surgery. Our vet told us about a credit card for pet healthcare that charges no interest if the balance is paid off within a number of months. For me, trying to kick my scarcity habit in little steps, knowing we wouldn't have to pay interest helped me feel calmer about the expense. The new piece of plastic dubbed the "Cat Credit Card" took its place in my purse, and the line item "Vacation" disappeared from our budget for the year. I realized that even having money for "Vacation" in our budget meant I was luckier than I thought.

Belinda's surgery was long and difficult. The vet found another tumor. When I came to take her home she was shaven and weak like a concentration camp survivor, with so many stitches I didn't know how I was going to hold her.

Her recovery took every ounce of strength and patience Belinda and I had. There were many times I doubted my husband's and my decision. But even through the hours and days when all I could do was watch and wait for Belinda to heal, my leap of faith felt more and more right. Not only did she recover and share her sweet presence with us for eleven more months, but I felt I had found a pathway out of a dark and lonely place.

After those months, the cancer returned and it was clearly time to let her go. Now I often think of her, especially on mornings when I realize she's visited in my dreams. My memories of her help me find that pathway out of scarcity and doubt over and over again. Breaking habits is an act of faith. Belinda is my reminder that generosity benefits the giver most. And she lets me know that she was worth the gift and so am I.

— Rebecca Josefa —

Big Red Divorce Boots

*Give a girl the right shoes,
and she can conquer the world.*
~Marilyn Monroe

My divorce day had finally arrived. After a painful two-year separation that included several reconciliation attempts, our divorce was a reality.

I thought my ex-husband and I had done everything the "right way." We met when we were in high school, but didn't date until he was a third-year medical student. We waited to get married until he was well established in his residency and had our first child only after he was in a successful practice and we were financially stable. I loved my husband, our children, and our life.

In my mind, we had the perfect life, and nothing would ever change our storybook existence. I was insufferably self-righteous, smugly believing my place in Utopia was secured because of my own decisions and actions.

Pride goeth before a fall, and the plummet from my self-created pedestal was far and hard. My husband's unexpected request for a divorce left me shaken to the core. An unwanted and painful epiphany emerged through the darkness — life wasn't as simple as I thought. The good guy doesn't always win, and sometimes the "happily ever after" we assume is our rightful destiny takes a very unexpected turn.

Treat Yourself

People are fallible, and even when we think we've done everything according to the book, things may go terribly awry.

Shame and embarrassment at being the first amongst my friends to get a divorce led me to create a wall of silence and loneliness. I shared my situation with very few people. Even when I did, I presented a façade, a lie that said I was handling things well. My inability to admit weakness and what I perceived as failure left me alone on my divorce day. If this had been the movies, I would have had a posse of friends cheering me up at a margarita-laden lunch. But since this wasn't *Sex and the City*, I headed to the mall alone.

I wasn't normally a shopper, but the need to be among people who didn't know me and wouldn't ask questions drew me to the windowless, impersonal structure. I wandered around the mall obsessing about marriage regrets and consumed with worry about the future. The stores and the people I passed were merely a backdrop for my personal movie of sadness. I was heartbroken and couldn't imagine how I was going to pick up the pieces of my shattered life. But, for the sake of my young daughters, I knew I had to find a way out of the dark.

Through my self-pity, a vision of bright red and black cowboy boots appeared. As if they were on a pedestal, surrounded by an unearthly glow, the boots beckoned me. Never in my life had I even thought about wearing cowboy boots, yet I heard a voice seeming to come from my mouth directing the salesclerk: "Size ten, please." As I coaxed my long, city-girl feet into the unfamiliar feel of the boots, I sensed the possibility of novel adventures. These buttery soft, brightly-colored leather boots were the symbol of a new beginning, a different life. I walked around the shoe-store floor envisioning a future that included swing dancing in the arms of a tall, dark cowboy, dressing in clothes that didn't involve elastic waists, and experiencing the world in a way I'd been shielded from in my previously insulated life.

Absurd as it sounds, those boots were the catalyst for a transition from the life of a suburban, married mother of two to a single mother ready to take on whatever challenges were surely awaiting. I felt empowered. My mopey shuffling turned to confident strutting in those big, red boots. My 5'10" height became elevated to an Amazonian, six-foot level of strength. Floating out of the store with a big box of boots in my arms, I was poorer financially, but rich with feelings of renewal and possibility.

I wore the red cowboy boots almost constantly for the next year, designing outfits around them and even dancing the Country Two Step with a tall, dark cowboy. Fondly referring to it as my "Western Mommy" stage, my daughters remember hearing me walk down the hall of their preschool, knowing it was their mommy approaching by the "stomping" noise of the boots.

I like to think that my little girls felt safer when they heard my sure-footed, cowboy-boot stride. Their emotional security was dependent on me, and they needed to know their mom was strong enough to take care of them. We were still a family, and despite the changes, I was determined we wouldn't be broken.

Before long, I was able to put my magical boots farther back in the closet. Soon, I stopped wearing them all together. I was healing, as if the big, red cowboy boots' power had created courage in me, and I was moving forward bravely.

Over twenty years and many closet purges later, the magical boots still reside in my closet. They represent strength and independence, and the decision not to be a victim of sadness and bitterness but to take charge and move forward. The red boots were my touchstone, my talisman, as I became stronger than I imagined possible. Like Dorothy in *The Wizard of Oz*, I had the power all along; I just needed my own version of her shiny red shoes to discover it.

— Diane Morrow-Kondos —

Chapter 7

Find Your Fitness

Cleansing the Soul

*Everyone who has run knows that its most important
value is in removing tension and allowing a release
from whatever other cares the day may bring.*
~Jimmy Carter

The crisp air stings my face. While I lace my shoe, she circles me with anticipation. The sun winks a sleepy greeting and I stretch my arms to the clouds above me. I breathe in the fragrant morning and exhale with intent. It's time to begin. I move forward and she responds, taking the first steps in this well-practiced routine that never ends the way it begins. My footfalls are heavy next to hers. We struggle to find rhythm in this dance we've done a hundred times. Our warm breath escapes in front of us.

The smell of licorice tickles my nose while dawn creeps up on the still and silent Earth. The hillside glistens with dew; the skyline, freshly painted, meets the mountain's outline. The colors are more vibrant than at any other time of the day. I'm breathing deeply, and I slow our pace. She is always too anxious in the beginning. I hear my shoes on the pavement and the clinking of her collar.

It isn't long before we find our stride and move in unison. I feel my body lighten as the worry and stress of life falls from my shoulders and is carried away by the breeze. My faithful partner runs silently beside me, often glancing in my direction. Is she happy? Is this process as healing for her as it is for me?

Now moving as one, I loosen my hold on her leash. I relax and extend my limbs. Momentum carries us up and down the country hills effortlessly. I feel like I am floating and my mind is flooded with thoughts and ideas. I notice the sounds of birds now echoing in the trees. The sun has fully risen and beams down. Deer stand statuesque in the distance, watching us. I'm thankful for their quiet stance; she doesn't notice them.

We follow our well-worn path and sometimes find a place of euphoria, unexplainable and intoxicating. Our pace quickens and the air no longer feels cold against my skin. We are lost in time. Time is not always my own, but in this moment, it is. Only I will say how far I go and how long I run. There are no interruptions. No demands on my time. When I run, I am not Mrs. or Mom. I am a writer, a runner. Limits only exist if I've set them for myself. She is content just being with me.

This moment carries me deeper into a sense of self. I feel I could run forever. However, life awaits my presence. We slow our pace and begin our journey back. Now, free of all burdens, I am inspired by the day; I am ready to take on all that life might throw in my direction. Slowing to a walk, I take a deep breath and release her. She hesitates to leave my side.

I whisper "go home." She, so obedient, turns and runs up the drive.

As I take my final steps through this ritual, I reflect. I feel strong and energized. Renewed. Running, my addiction, has worked its cleansing magic on my soul once again. I am now ready to enjoy what I love most — being a wife and mother.

— Machille Legoullon —

Strength to Be Strong

Take care of your body. It's the only place you have to live.
~Jim Rohn

It's 7 A.M. and I am standing with 160 pounds on my back. I squat one. Two. Three. I slam the barbell back onto the rack and load on more weight. The sweat dripping down my face reminds me that I am a strong woman.

I move to the deadlift station. Can I handle eight sets of deficit deadlifts after ten sets of heavy squats? Of course I can. I am strong.

Rewind to before I discovered lifting. Growing up, I was constantly scrutinized. My family moved to America from Romania. Sometimes they would tell me that I had gotten fat or that I had a huge pimple on my face. They would pat my belly and ask, "When's the baby due?" or "Did the shirt come with the stomach?" They thought they were being funny, that they were showing affection for me.

I didn't care when I was growing up — at least, I thought I didn't care. I would get upset when the boy I had a crush on had a crush on other girls, but I never thought it was because I was ugly or fat.

But then, as adolescence went on, I started to believe that I *was* ugly and fat because I had acne and I couldn't fit in my neighbor's clothes. Other girls around me started "dating" boys, while I couldn't even get someone to come over and jump on my trampoline with me,

Find Your Fitness

let alone take me to a movie or give me a scandalous hug and kiss on the cheek.

Fast forward to college. At this point, I had alternated between being skinny and fit or being fat and lazy. I had gone through periods when I wouldn't eat anything and periods when I would eat everything. I felt like I couldn't control how I felt about myself because I couldn't control how I looked.

I started working out and logging my food. Counting calories isn't bad as long as you are eating enough to sustain you. I wasn't starving myself; I was just making sure I wasn't eating so much that I was gaining weight again.

I would go to the gym and lift or I would go on runs. But I never felt like a real runner or a bodybuilder or anything that actually made me feel good about myself. I was too focused on trying to fit into smaller pants and making sure I would never have to buy a shirt bigger than a size small.

Though I was technically eating right and exercising, and I had lost some weight, I still hated my body. If I weighed in one week and I had only lost half a pound instead of a full one, or if I didn't lose anything at all, I would binge on frosted sugar cookies, rationalizing that dieting wasn't working anyway. I fluctuated between eating right and eating poorly, and I was really hard on myself when my mile time was slower than the day before or when I failed a set of squats on a weight that I should have been able to do.

After a while, I stopped doing my weight loss program. I would go to the gym with my boyfriend, who is a powerlifter and personal trainer, and I would do his workout instead.

Being able to say I weigh a certain amount would probably feel pretty good. But saying I can squat 185 pounds is a completely different feeling. I weigh about the same as I did when I started, but now I have more muscle and my weight is distributed differently.

My focus is on being strong. Strength in the weight room can lead to strength in all areas of life. If I can lift hundreds of pounds, I can handle rejection. If I can lift hundreds of pounds, I can handle the uncertainty of the future, and I can definitely handle not having

Find Your Fitness

society's idea of the "perfect" beach body because that is not what matters. Now I know I can handle anything.

Focusing on my strength rather than my weight has actually helped me manage my weight. When I lift more, I can eat more and without gaining weight. By lifting, I build muscle and redistribute my weight. My legs are still big and my thighs still touch, but now my quad muscles show when I'm standing and I'm proud that they're so big.

It's 7 A.M. and I stand with 160 pounds on my back. Every squat is a reminder that I am beautiful, that I deserve to feel beautiful, and that above all else, I am a strong woman.

— Nicole Christine Caratas —

Finish the Race

*When anyone tells me I can't do anything,
I'm just not listening anymore.*
~Florence Griffith Joyner

In 2010, I experienced multiple life-changing setbacks within a short period of time. My marriage ended after seventeen years, I got laid off, a dear friend and mentor died, and I had an adolescent child who was facing circumstances that were beyond my ability to fix. My physical and emotional health suffered as I attempted to keep my mind straight in the midst of overwhelming pain and uncertainty.

From the outside, my smile, energy and personal accomplishments made others believe that life for me was great, but at night, I took the mask off. That's when I prayed, journaled, and cried myself to sleep.

I made a decision in 2013 that every year I'd do something I'd never done before. Life is a race and "Just Keep Going" became my mantra. I made a decision to LIVE! I started walking in 2013, completed my first 5K in 2014, finished my first half marathon in 2015, and blew my own mind when I conquered a full 26.2-mile marathon in 2016. This was in addition to writing a second children's book that was featured on FOX 5 news. Life was great for a while.

Then I took my dad for a visit to the ER after a cough that had lasted nearly two weeks. Right there in the exam room after only a chest X-ray and CT scan, the attending informed us that the cough was likely related to my dad having what appeared to be stage 4 lung cancer. "Wait... what?"

We had absolutely no idea. The ER physician had delivered the news assuming we already knew my father had lung cancer.

I remember the tears streaming down my face as we drove home from the hospital. My dad asked me to play "Baby Face" on Pandora and we both sang. I cried the entire ride home while singing to him. That was our thing, singing together in the car.

Daddy lost his battle with cancer in 2017. This loss shook me in a way that was far more painful than my combined experiences in 2010. It would've been so easy to fall right back into a state of depression, but my spirit was stronger than it had been back then. I went through my grief but I wasn't paralyzed by it. *Just Keep Going.*

In August 2017, keeping with my decision to be adventurous and ambitious, I decided to sign up for a triathlon. I was curious about what it would require, so some friends joined me on a road trip to see a triathlon that was taking place in the boonies of Maryland. I saw women going into the water and thought, *Are you sure you want to do this thing... there are ducks in the water! And, you don't know how to swim, fool!*

I started pre-training in February 2018, which was the anniversary of my father's transition. I learned from the past that I have the power to make anniversary memories what I want them to be! Feel what you need to feel but don't fall back into a depressed mindset!

I had a minor setback in April after breaking my leg during a run. This meant an interruption of my training. I took the recommended time off to heal and then got right back into my routine. From June through August, I had no pain and no complications. Two weeks before race day, my leg started aching. I was already tapering my training, so I just decided to slow it all the way down and take a break. I'd come too far to drop out.

My nerves weren't as bad as I thought they'd be on race day morning. I had focused on preparing for the swim portion of the event more than biking and running. The goal was to touch land. *You can do this, Temeka... you know how to swim!*

My anxiety eased up when I saw my coach Lloyd Henry and

teammates Kandis Gibson and Maxwell P. Blakeney. *All you have is a half mile… just swim one buoy at a time.* I stepped into the water with my wave and two minutes later, we were off. I was talking in my head the entire time, reminding myself to sight the buoy so I'd know what direction to swim. When I raised my head to sight, I couldn't see because of the fog. *Just Keep Going.*

I finally make it to the first turn but not without having to flip onto my back for a brief recovery position. I did this several times during the swim. The lifeguard in the canoe asked if I was okay. "Yes, I just need a minute."

When I finally made it out of the water, I discovered I was the last person to exit the lake. "How in the world did that happen? There were at least four other waves that came after me. Oh well, I finished without quitting, freaking out and getting pulled.

It was time to move onto the bike portion no matter how tired I was from swimming. *Just Keep Going.*

Kandis helped settle my nerves once my feet touched land. She walked me up the stairs near transition so I could switch into my cycling gear. Thank God for friends. Christy Fenner had introduced me to the world of triathlons; her words of inspiration and encouragement the evening before resonated in my heart now. When I arrived at the transition area, I saw that my bike was the only one there… out of 500. I silenced my thoughts and repeated, *Just Keep Going.*

I took off and heard the volunteer say on the radio, "The last bike is now out of transition." I was too determined to be embarrassed! I started singing Mary Mary's "Can't Give Up Now" in my head.

For a long distance, I was by myself on the road but then I saw other participants. I started passing folks. That last hill was a monster. I had to clip out and walk with my bike, but I didn't stop. *Just Keep Going.*

At the top of the hill, I saw my village which consisted of my fiancé, coach and teammates. Coach was ringing that cowbell. Their presence gave me life and a burst of energy. I hopped back on the bike and made the turn toward the second transition. I saw my children standing on the sideline yelling "That's my mommy… Go, Mommy!"

I survived the swim and the hilly bike ride. Running would be a

Find Your Fitness

breeze for me. I could do a 5K in my sleep, that is unless I got a cramp in my quad. I never had this happen before during a race. I was rubbing my leg and running at the same time. I turned the corner and saw the finish line. The cramp was gone and so was I! I flew as fast as I could.

I thought I could do it and I did! I swam, I biked, I ran.

"Look at me, Daddy. I'm a triathlete!"

— Temeka S. Bailey —

Time for Health

*For me, running is both exercise and a metaphor.
Running day after day, piling up the races,
bit by bit I raise the bar, and by clearing
each level I elevate myself.*
~Haruki Murakami

Anyone with five kids will agree with me: It's easy to find excuses to skip workouts. Back when Laurie and I were dating, I told myself, "I have a serious girlfriend. I want to spend all my time with her." While we were engaged, all my spare time went into wedding prep — or emotionally supporting Laurie while she did all the wedding prep. Once we were married, I wanted to be home with my new wife. Then we started having kids, and spare time disappeared quickly.

In the blink of an eye, I was in my mid-thirties with five kids and I hadn't worked out in over a decade. I didn't consider myself overweight except at my annual physical when the doctor told me an average male of my age and height should weigh about 40 pounds less. "How would I lose this weight?" I wondered as I left these visits. I was almost relieved when, a few minutes later, I got a call from Laurie and got distracted by one or more of our kids needing to be picked up somewhere or needing a few things from the grocery store.

I justified my health and being out of shape with a sense of pride. I was a devoted husband and father who wanted to spend his time and money on the family and not on himself. Then I got a job at an

Find Your Fitness

office with a personal trainer, Rose, who gave group sessions during the lunch hour in a conference room that had been converted into a gym. There were treadmills, elliptical machines, and a set of dumbbells. So, with money and time no longer issues, I started working out two days a week.

It started slowly. I spent the session walking on the treadmill because I found it less grueling than lifting weights. After a few weeks, Rose adjusted the speed and incline so I was forced into some light jogging. I might have pushed back and lowered the settings, except she was so encouraging. If I had a good session, she said, "You're doing great." If I had a lousy session, she said, "Don't get discouraged. Just keep showing up."

I wanted to impress her, so I told her I wanted to beat a 10-minute mile.

"That's a great idea!" she said.

On a dry-erase board, she tracked the time it took me to complete a mile each day. I memorized the speed settings and increased every day by a few seconds. A 15-minute mile became 14. Two minutes of jogging became four. At each session, Rose greeted me with a big smile and said, "How much are you gonna beat yesterday's time by today?" I got inside 11 minutes and planned exactly which day I'd finally beat 10 minutes. When that day came, I felt so anxious I could barely eat breakfast or concentrate on work all morning. At the session, Rose gave me a big high-five. "Today's the day!" she said.

I felt terrible throughout the run. It must have been my nerves. But I powered through. When I got to the final fraction of the mile, I accidentally pulled the emergency stop pin. Rose, my workout partners, and I all shared a collective groan. "Well," Rose said, "you can try it again at our next session."

Two days later, I couldn't wait to hit the treadmill. I was ready. I was hungry. And when I hit the mile marker at 9:59, the gym erupted. I was so amped up I could have run another mile. Rose let me enjoy my victory for the rest of the session. Then at our next session, she said, "So how long will it take you to beat a nine-minute mile?"

"Are you insane?" I asked.

Find Your Fitness

"Nope!" she said. "You can do it. Just keep training like you did for the 10-minute."

I soon beat the nine-minute mile, and then the eight-minute. Perhaps my proudest accomplishment was that I continued to improve after I got a new job and stopped training with Rose. Laurie encouraged me to find a gym close to my new office and continue to work out during my lunch break. I frequently texted Rose my progress, especially when I beat a seven-minute mile, and ultimately a six-minute mile.

During this entire time, Laurie encouraged me constantly. She bought me Dri-FIT clothes and little workout tools to use at home. She noticed if I went more than a couple of days without a run. "Your mood is dropping," she said. "Why don't you go for a jog? You'll feel better when you get home."

Running and working out also became a way to bond with the kids. I took them with me to boot camps regularly. When I played football with my sons and the neighborhood kids, my boys told their friends to line up against me. Their friends clearly saw my gray hair and thought I wouldn't be a problem, so I surprised them when I kept up. They told my sons, "Dang, your dad's fast."

"Yeah, he beats us all the time," my sons said.

At my most recent physical, the nurse took my pulse and blood pressure. "I'm just curious," she said. "Are you a runner?"

I was stunned. "Yes. How did you know?"

"Both your pulse and blood pressure are very low."

I was so excited that I felt lightheaded. As soon as the nurse left the room, I frantically texted Laurie the news. "That's great!" she responded. "You should treat yourself to something. Oh, you should get yourself something at the grocery store because we need a few things for dinner tonight."

— Billy Cuchens —

Cereal for Dinner

When you take care of yourself, you're a better person for others. When you feel good about yourself, you treat others better.
~Solange Knowles

I was too tired to make myself dinner. I'd just eat the kids' leftover cereal off the highchair tray. I bet I'd lose some weight doing this anyway. That's how I used to think. I actually thought this was a brilliant plan and called it the "Cereal for Dinner Diet." Back then, I knew nothing about nutrition, and this was one of my misguided attempts at dieting after I had put on some postpartum weight.

Of course, the Cereal for Dinner Diet failed, as did all my other attempts. I knew nothing about how to lose weight in a healthy way. I'd spent years caring for my three children, completely ignoring any self-care. Educating myself about nutrition seemed too lofty a goal when more pressing matters were at hand, such as three toddlers sticking beans in each other's ears and noses.

With two-year-old twin daughters and a three-year-old son, I never took a break. Often, my husband would return from work and find me still in my pajamas, wrestling little bottoms into diapers, with kitchen dishes stacked to the ceiling. One day, he came home and found me lying like a corpse on the kitchen floor with streaks of make-up all over my body. "The kids got into my make-up drawer," I said as I lay there defeated. "I didn't have the strength to stop them."

"It looks like a deranged clown attacked you," he said. "Go out for a while. I'll watch them."

I washed the make-up off and left the house for a walk. I passed a gym in the neighborhood. I averted my eyes. Healthy people went there — people who spent time investing in themselves. This was not me. As I turned to get as far away from that place as I could, I saw a sign advertising a six-month fitness challenge. I continued my fast walk in the opposite direction, but that sign stayed on my mind for the rest of the walk and during the following days.

I can't say what finally motivated me to go sign up for the challenge. Oh, wait. Yes, I can say. It was a ten-minute period in which my son threw his spaghetti plate straight up, lodging noodles and sauce in the overhead light fixture as the twins exploded into their diapers in unison from the startle. I could feel my soul deflate. As soon as my husband got home from work, I said, "You're in charge."

I made a beeline to the gym, marched straight in and said, "Fix me." It was the first time in three years I had chosen to do something for myself.

I was assigned a trainer, Emily. She was young and fit and had the energy of a person who did not have three young children. I wanted an IV with her energy. She asked what my goals were for the six-month challenge. I said, "I want to lose fifteen pounds." I should have said, "I want to take my life back. I want to be healthy so I can be a better mom for my kids. I want to feel powerful." But I could not verbalize such high ambitions at that point in time. I still had spaghetti in my hair.

Emily handed me the heaviest weights I had ever lifted in my life and said, "Okay, so in six months you will compete in a bodybuilding show."

I struggled to push the weights over my head and grunted, "You mean one of those shows where the women pose on stage in little bikinis?" She nodded but was not really paying attention to me. She was looking for a car or a building for me to pick up next. I tried explaining, "No, I don't want to do a show. That sounds scary. I just want to lose fifteen pounds." She pretty much ignored my protests, and we jumped into weeks of strict workouts and nutrition planning. I

Find Your Fitness

figured that, at the end of six months, I would just have to disappoint her and tell her I was not going to do that show.

Over the next six months, I learned so much about my body. I thrived in the gym. The pride I felt after my workouts was beyond what I had ever experienced. I watched my body composition change as I learned about food. I ate in a smart way that gave me energy, built muscle, and reduced fat. As it turns out, eating whatever is left on your kid's plate is not a great nutrition plan.

Emily forced me to focus on myself — my wants and my needs. By doing that, I became a much better mother and wife. I had more energy for my family. My lingering postpartum depression lifted. I felt mentally and physically more in control and powerful than I ever had.

At the end of the six months, I looked and felt amazing. Emily handed me a pamphlet for the upcoming show. It was time to break the news to her. "I appreciate all you've done for me, Emily. I really do. I look and feel better than I ever have, but I'm just too scared to do it." For once, Emily stopped trying to locate heavy items, looked me in the eye and said, "The old you is talking."

I thought about the old me, unhealthy and depressed, lying on the kitchen floor and striped with make-up. I compared that old me to the confident, proud woman today who had decided to spend time investing in herself. I thought about which one I wanted my kids to know and which one I would want them to be. My ears could not believe what my mouth was saying when the words "I'll do it" came out.

Emily and I jumped into weeks of preparation. There were posing, hair and make-up, and swimsuit-fitting sessions. By the time the show arrived, I could not believe the woman who confidently walked across the stage. It was a complete transformation of my former self. The mental and emotional benefits that came from this experience enriched me far more than the weight loss I had achieved. I lost pant sizes, but I also gained unwavering confidence and emotional control. Most importantly, there was a shift in how I thought of myself.

In the past, I had put my needs behind all others, but I learned I am a person worthy of investment. This makes me a better person, and those around me are better for it, too.

As the years passed, I became a fitness trainer. I now work with many people who were just like me. I teach them what I learned from taking time to care for myself. I watch these people become powerful, and it is just as rewarding to share this message with them as it was for me to receive it. Cereal for dinner no more!

— Shannon McCarty —

Off the Ropes

The unending paradox is that
we do learn through pain.
~Madeleine L'Engle

I imagined a teaching campaign in China or an afternoon at a soup kitchen in my hometown. I never dreamed God would call me to a boxing club.

About nine months had passed since I'd filed for divorce. My college sweetheart, the father of our then one-year-old daughter, disclosed the news of his affair shortly after our five-year anniversary.

From stay-at-home mom to single mom, my life began changing faster than I wanted it to. My husband moved out ten days after his reveal, and I was on my own, trying to raise a soon-to-be toddler and turn my erratic career as a freelancer into something stable.

I had everything to fear, it seemed. How would I pay the bills? Could I keep my daughter home? How would I help her cope with our suddenly un-normal life? But when I began looking at my world through eyes of faith, I realized how much I stood to gain.

I had lived up to that point crippled by self-esteem that completely depended on what others thought. If someone said I was pretty, I could believe it — for the moment. And I would try to recreate that moment over and over with the same hairstyle or make-up or outfit, or all three. If a man showed me affection, I could believe I was worth it — until he decided to write me off because he was too busy or tired, and I was left to agonize over what I did, or didn't do, to make him suddenly turn away.

I had no sense of who I was or what I was worth outside of other people's opinions.

My self-esteem hit rock bottom when I found out about my husband's affair. As we sat in his truck in the front drive of our house — the house we had purchased together four years earlier, the house we had made plans to fill with different flooring and new furniture and more children one day — my stomach ached, and my body shook with fear when he said the words no spouse should ever hear. And as much as I hate to admit it, the first and only thought that ran through my head that night was, "I don't deserve any better than this."

How did I get there? I asked myself this over and over in the months that followed. But the more important question I began to ask was, *How do I get out?*

The old saying is true — God answers prayer in mysterious ways — and for me, He answered my prayer for self-esteem by sending me to a boxing club. I'm the kind of girl who does yoga and Pilates, not boxing. I watch *Chopped* on Food Network, not *Fight Night*. I hate conflict and cringe at violence. But on a Tuesday night in November, I found myself learning about wrist wraps and strapping on red gloves.

I hit the bag as hard as I could. I kicked until my shins bruised. I landed jabs and uppercuts and hooks until my knuckles began to bleed. When I left that night, my whole body hurt — in the best kind of way. I had pushed myself to do something hard, something completely new, something I never thought myself capable of.

There's a saying in boxing that a fighter's "on the ropes." That means he's (or she's) trapped, pushed against the ropes by his opponent and dangerously close to defeat. I think that's where I was in the final months of my marriage. *I'm not a fighter. I'm not strong.* Those are things I had said to myself over and over. Those are things I would have kept saying had I stayed home that Tuesday night, like I wanted to, and done yoga and watched *Chopped*.

God called me to a strange place so I could hit and hurt and learn something about myself that He knew all along: I am worth it. I am beautiful, inside and out. I can fight when I need to. I am strong. I now

Find Your Fitness

believe these are the best gifts I can ever hope to give my daughter. She'll never have a perfect life or the ideal family, but I hope, when she looks back on her childhood one day, she'll be able to say she had a mom who showed her what she's worth and how to fight to protect it.

— Rachel R. Thompson —

The Joy of a Mortal Body

Yoga is the perfect opportunity to be curious about who you are.
~Jason Crandell

I started doing yoga in college. I was naturally flexible, so it felt like an easy form of exercise. I could already touch my toes, balance on one leg, and twist myself into eagle pose. Usually, I wouldn't even break a sweat. I wasn't particularly committed or regular in my practice, though. I didn't even own a mat. Since I went so rarely, it just made sense to rent one at the studio each time.

Fast-forward a few decades. I graduated, started working, got married, and moved to Montreal. My husband Derek and I had three kids: two girls and one boy. My third pregnancy especially took its toll. My hips hurt, my legs cramped, my back ached, and my neck felt stiff. My obstetrician tracked my weight on the same chart she'd used for my previous pregnancy, so I could see month by month how I was gaining weight more quickly this time around.

Fast-forward a couple more years. Our kids — Sonya, Leena, and Arjun — were now seven, five, and two. The hurting, cramping, aching, stiffness, and discomfort from my third pregnancy had never completely gone away. My birthday is at the end of March. I had always used it as a time of self-reflection, and this year I realized I was feeling worn down. If I didn't do something, I'd probably break.

Right around that time, the yoga studio around the corner advertised a thirty-day hot yoga challenge for the month of April, which sounded appealing in the chilly springtime. But thirty days straight? I wasn't so sure.

But I wanted my kids to know the version of me that used to be full of energy and stamina. I kept thinking about how I could make it work — sixty minutes for each class, plus ten minutes to the studio, five minutes to shower, ten minutes home — ninety minutes minimum per class every single day for an entire month. Was that realistic? When would I do this? The mornings were already jam-packed trying to get us ready and out the door. Fitting in exercise during the workday had never panned out. That only left the evenings, but I didn't want to miss out on dinners and bedtime snuggles. And I couldn't imagine doing yoga after the kids were asleep, when I was bone-tired and didn't want to leave the house.

Hot yoga is intense. The theory behind the heat is that it makes the heart work harder, the body sweat more, and the joints and muscles loosen, allowing a deeper expression of each posture. The first time I tried it in my twenties, I had to lie down on my mat for the second half of class so I wouldn't throw up or pass out.

I told Derek, "I haven't worked out twice in a row since..." I really couldn't remember.

On April Fool's Day, which was a Saturday, the kids and I went out for breakfast. The yoga studio was on our walk home.

"Mom, why are we stopping?" Leena asked.

"I need to do something," I said.

Sonya wrote my name on the wall chart where I'd eventually put a sticker each day I showed up for class. I paid the non-refundable fee for the 30-Day Hot Yoga Challenge. That night, after Sonya, Leena, and Arjun were all asleep, I went back to the studio for Day One.

Turns out I could no longer reach my toes — or even my ankles. I lost my balance on Warrior One when I tried to reach my arms overhead. My spine did not want to twist or backbend or forward fold. I was no longer made of rubber, but rigid plastic that might crack in half if I wasn't careful. But I felt proud of myself anyway and excited that I was in the studio, finally doing something for my body and myself.

I texted Derek: "Signed up for 30-Day Yoga Challenge. Want to do it with me? Laura can babysit every night after kids asleep."

Laura was a college student, our go-to babysitter. She'd agreed to a discount rate for the month.

"Sure. Let's do it," he texted back. Derek had recently recovered from a bout of sciatic nerve pain. His physiotherapist told him he had very tight hips and needed to work on his flexibility. Both of us were gradually falling apart, and we needed to take drastic action.

The second class felt more brutal. I was still sore from the first class. I did not want to go back, but I did. On Yoga Challenge Day 4, Derek came with me. At first, I was a little worried about how much I'd be sweating and how ridiculous I'd look in my tight workout clothes. Then we started the practice, and I got too busy with my steady yoga breathing and trying not to fall over. I only had time to focus on what my body was doing, not how it was looking. I swapped one kind of self-consciousness for another.

"I had trouble with the balance poses," I said on our walk home — in case he'd missed me toppling out of standing bow pulling pose.

"Pigeon felt great," he said. "My hip was really open."

Taking on 30 Days of Yoga had a big ripple effect throughout my life. It became a key habit that created other habits. I drank more water. I became more mindful about what I ate. Heavy, greasy food did not feel good during class. I did laundry more regularly to deal with my sweaty workout clothes. I made sure the living room was tidy for Laura every night. I focused better at work. I started feeling more in control, less helpless about change, more open to challenges even outside of yoga. I found I was more patient, kind, and thoughtful.

Day in, day out, even when I didn't feel like it, I kept showing up for myself on the mat. I did miss a few days in April, but overall I was consistent. Yoga is now a crucial part of my life. And even as I get better, I find new ways to express each pose, even ones I think I know already. This same practice echoes throughout my life — from trying new recipes to seeking new experiences or accepting bigger challenges at work.

Find Your Fitness

There are people in my class who can do headstands and crow pose and double pigeon. Their bodies are supple, lithe, and graceful. But instead of feeling defeated, I feel inspired.

For a long time, without really acknowledging it, I'd lost the joy of being in my body. By ignoring and masking the pain I'd allowed myself to live with on a daily basis, I'd numbed myself to other feelings as well. Now, through yoga, I've found my way back to that joy again, to appreciate the here and now, to connect with myself, to access the fullness of human experience. It isn't always comfortable or easy, but it is full of revelation and opportunity for second, third, and fourth chances — as many as we are willing to give ourselves.

— Mitali Banerjee Ruths —

Running for My Life

*If you want to live, you must walk.
If you want to live long, you must run.*
~Jinabhai Navik

I am sweeping my maple kitchen floor, my triathlon finisher's medal swinging back and forth in rhythm with the broom. Abbey, my five-year-old daughter, runs past me on her way to the back yard, her shoulder-length blond curly hair bouncing behind her. She stops and turns to me. "You still have your medal on. Did you know that?"

I laugh. "I am planning to wear it all day long." She giggles at her silly mom. "Tell me again, did you win?" I try to explain to her that I did not even come close to winning. She glances at my medal again, shakes her head and exits the patio door.

Did I win? I ponder the question. In my mind, I won the moment my face lowered into the lake water, cold enough to warrant a wet suit. Now I stand here having showered off the dried salty layer of sweat from my 750-meter lake swim, my 20K bike ride and my 5K run. What I have not showered off is the three-digit number marked vertically along my left arm or the sense of achievement. I keep glancing at the black numbers marked on my skin. I did it. I completed my first sprint triathlon. I feel strong and fit. I have demolished another mental barrier about my limits.

The phone rings and it is my sister-in-law calling to congratulate me and ask about the details. I put the broom in the closet and take the portable phone onto the deck and into the warm, sunny June afternoon. I hold the phone against my left ear, my left elbow and my right forearm rest along the railing of the wooden deck. I watch my dark-haired three-year-old son, Alexander, playing in the sandbox, sitting on the corner seat so he doesn't get too dirty. Abbey sits smack in the middle of the handmade, blue, wooden sandbox, running fingers and toys through the sand. My husband putters in the yard, staying close to Alexander, who can sprint to the road faster than any of the athletes that crossed the finish line ahead of me.

My sister-in-law is congratulatory and supportive. After I have broken down the three events and expressed my wonder at being able to do this, she asks, "Why do you do this? Why do you push your body this way?" She is curious and concerned, but not judgmental. We are the same age and she is a fit mom who likes to run but not race, so this level of commitment has her bemused. My tone is joking, but my words are dead serious. "I am running for my life."

How else can I explain it? Most simply, the endorphins bring me joy. But more than that, I need to complete something. I need something I can check off my list. I need something with a tangible reminder, like my medal. Motherhood does not offer many of these things. For all moms, motherhood is complicated, all consuming and never ending. For me, it has also meant one overwhelming medical challenge after another. My motherhood triathlon includes: Abbey's cancer diagnosis at eleven months, a life-threatening allergy for Alexander, and now, likely an autism diagnosis for him. I know my sister-in-law is worried that this athleticism is pushing my tired, middle-aged body too hard. Some days I wonder the same thing.

I struggle to explain how pushing my body is positive. Painful and tiring at times, yes, but positive. It is unlike the year I pushed my body while caring for Abbey when she was diagnosed with a rare form of leukemia that required a year of intense, tortuous treatment. It is unlike living in that hospital room with no windows for almost six months. It is unlike how my body managed to carry a pregnancy to term while living in that hospital. It is unlike when my infant son, my twenty-month-old daughter and I all slept in a single hospital bed

Find Your Fitness

for days on end while my husband returned to work to support us. It is unlike breastfeeding a new baby whose small, dark head lay cradled in my left elbow while my right hand caught vomit with a cardboard fish and chips container as my daughter on chemotherapy retched in bed beside us.

Running, biking, swimming — this pushing is good and necessary.

The exertion is rebuilding my body and my spirit, drained from that year of chemotherapy and the times my daughter almost died. My training flushes away the fear of a relapse, at least for the minutes that I am running, swimming or biking. What I do not say to anyone, even my husband, and what is only a whisper in my soul is that this exercise will make me strong in case I need to guide her through treatment again. If she relapses, I know I will need every ounce of strength I can mine from these muscle fibers.

The first time through cancer treatment I was naïve. I did not know the script. I did not know that my New Balance runners would sit ignored in the closet of her hospital room. I did not know that living in a windowless hospital room and dealing with daily, sometimes hourly, medical crises while growing a baby inside me would drain all my energy. I did not know there would be no time or stamina left for a rejuvenating run.

Now I know what childhood cancer looks like. That knowledge is terrifying. I know chemotherapy can erase my baby's lips, replacing them with yellow blisters. I know what it is like to change my baby's diaper with gloves because her waste is toxic. I know that some kids who leave the oncology ward do so with physical or mental handicaps. I know that about half the children admitted to that ward will die, no matter what the statistics say. I know that my only hope of surviving in that world again is to build my physical body into an endurance vessel.

So I swim twice a week — on Tuesday night when my husband can watch the kids and on Saturday morning at seven when I can be home before the family is out of their pajamas. My runs are squeezed in between my son's appointments with a speech therapist, Early Intervention and my daughter's kindergarten. My bike sits on a training device in my basement so I can ride when kids are in bed. In the pool, I don

Find Your Fitness

the mask of just another mom in the blue Speedo swimsuit, a woman in training, training for fun and fitness.

During treatment, another chemo mom assured me that I would carry the cancer experience with me as a medal of strength. "If you can do this you can do anything," she said. So I keep training to make sure that remains true.

— Sue LeBreton —

Chapter
8

Channel Your Inner Warrior

My Cape's Under My Cardigan

Life shrinks or expands in proportion to one's courage.
~Anaïs Nin

You can't see my cape underneath my cardigan.
You can't see the "S" inscribed on my chest.
You don't notice the look in my eye,
As I win at life and pass you by.
What you see is a woman, composed and cheerful,
Not an individual you view as being fearful.
Not that I would do any harm,
But I'm strong and solo, no one on my arm.
You can't see my fire and passion to win
Behind the delicate face and friendly grin.
You can't see my drive and my will to inspire,
To empower myself and achieve what I desire.
I stand up proud and tall, and with all of my might,
Get what I want while doing what's right.
We all have it in us; men are not better.
Just remember that cape tucked under your sweater.

— Ashley Dailey —

Remember to Breathe

Nobody can go back and start a new beginning, but anyone can start today and make a new ending.
~Maria Robinson

I stared into the barrel of that pistol, and my muscles froze. Lot's wife must have felt like this when she first looked back at Sodom. My eyes, not yet turned to salt, locked onto the would-be shooter's face. His tight-lipped grin sent my mind whirling into a "what's-wrong-with-this-picture" search. The strain of his grin reduced his eyes from spheres to almond slivers, full of nothing but black pupils. Seconds felt like hours as I remained focused on those pinpoints. How long would it be before I stopped breathing? Then I noticed I had already stopped.

I had come into the bedroom from the bathroom and found the lights on in the middle of the night. He was lying on the bed. He looked so comfortable, leaning on pillows propped up against the headboard, with his arms resting gently against his chest and his legs under the blanket. His hands were together as if in prayer, but pointing straight toward me, beneath cold steel, a pistol aimed slightly upward in a trajectory that would have pierced my sternum. He wasn't breathing either.

Would he shoot me? Would he really do it? I thought back to a day, four years earlier, when we had said to each other, "Till death dc us part." Then I thought about the bruises that had come and gone over those four years, bruises that had gotten increasingly larger and more difficult to conceal with each succeeding incident, harbingers of today. And I remembered the marriage counselor who said, "If you go back to him, he will kill you some day."

I recalled one time when he had told me about hunting, how he loved the power and how he liked it when the deer looked at him just before he fired his rifle. How after he'd lock on, he'd make a noise to get the deer to look his way. What a rush he got seeing its fear. It was so much better than the actual kill that the execution was anticlimactic.

Then it struck me. He was savoring my fear, prolonging his enjoyment before the anticlimactic event. The more I let him see my fear, the more likely he would shoot me. I couldn't get his weapon away from him, but I could take away his power.

"What are you doing?" Air had moved up from my diaphragm into my larynx, tickled my vocal chords, spilled across my curling and undulating tongue, and exited between my lips. I used that exhaust to unfreeze my muscles. My feet moved from their set-apart, broken-stride position and came together. My bare heels and toes sank into the plush white carpet. My shoulders reset. I was firmly grounded and breathing again, and I wanted to keep it that way.

I saw his chest fall. He set the gun on the night table.

Whatever inkling of love that had lingered in me for my husband died in that moment. Three days later, after he left for work, I stuffed my clothes into large, black trash bags and squeezed them into my car. I tied a mattress from the daybed onto the roof and moved into an unfurnished apartment thirty miles away. I went back to work the next day as if nothing had happened. Then I went back to school, finished my undergraduate and graduate degrees, and advanced in my career. Eventually, I remarried, and I retired.

This happened to me almost a half-century ago. But if you read the news, you might think it happened only yesterday.

— Marilyn Haight —

Bad Mama Jama

*I think that whatever size or shape body you have,
it's important to embrace it and get down!*
~Christina Aguilera, Marie Claire

While I was working as a tutor at Piedmont Technical College in Greenwood, South Carolina, I worked with a student named Darla. When I first met her, she couldn't look me in the eye while talking to me. She also had problems with anxiety and got so nervous around people that she literally shook. Basically, she was a mess.

As I tutored Darla in math, she began to open up and share her background. She had previously been a swimsuit model and had won swimsuit competitions run by some mainstream companies. In fact, she met her ex-husband at one of these competitions. At the beginning of their marriage, she said, she had been like a trophy for him and he loved showing her off to other men. As their marriage progressed, he became more and more controlling. A few years into their marriage, Darla got pregnant. After giving birth, she had trouble losing weight. This angered her husband and he became even more abusive. After years of his abuse, Darla left.

By the time I met her, Darla's self-esteem was shot. Prior to her marriage, she equated her value to her looks. Now weighing more than she ever had before, and having been abused and belittled for years by her husband, she thought she only had value as a mother.

She shared that she was attracted to a gentleman we both knew.

Channel Your Inner Warrior | 203

Unfortunately, she was sure that because he was so attractive and she had gained weight, there was no way he would be interested in her.

The curious thing was that Darla saw beauty in me. She said she wished she looked like me. Now, I am way bigger than Darla. We aren't even close in size. I'm not an average plus-size woman; I'm super-plus and I've got hips and thighs for days. And even though she didn't know it, the guy she liked was hitting on me daily. So I knew it wasn't about looks. It was all about Darla's confidence.

One day, as we walked into the Teaching and Learning Center for a tutoring session, Darla commented that when we entered the room, every man turned and watched me. I knew this was my chance to show her something that would begin to shift her thinking.

I asked Darla, "How did I walk into this room? Did I walk in like I owned the building? Did I walk in with my head up and shoulders back like I was the baddest thing moving, like I heard "She's A Bad Mama Jama" playing just for me? Or did I walk in with my head down like I was afraid or ashamed of who I was?"

"You walked in with confidence," Darla said.

I asked her if I was the size of a model, or if I was one of the larger women in the room.

"You are a larger woman," she said, "but it didn't seem to matter. You are beautiful and everybody knew it."

Then I told her something that I would repeat to her many times in the coming months and something that I have shared with many women since then. "The thing that will always command attention is confidence," I said. "I walked in here like I was the baddest thing moving, and in their minds they wanna know what I know that makes me walk with such confidence. A real man is looking for a real woman, a whole woman. He's not looking for some broken down woman that he has to piece together. A real man, a King, is looking for a Queen who can rule and reign with him. A real man is looking for a real woman who knows who she is and loves herself."

I know Darla didn't believe me, but she smiled and nodded. Every time we met to go over her math, I would take the opportunity to build her up and tell her how awesome she was. That semester ended and I continued to tutor her in another math class, making sure to speak life into her every chance I got. I often wondered if my words were sinking in.

Time went on and Darla graduated and I thought I would never see her again. Then one day, about six months after graduation, Darla came to campus for career counseling and came looking for me.

I couldn't believe my eyes. The woman who couldn't look me in the eye when we first met, who trembled from nervousness and never smiled, was now smiling from ear to ear. She looked amazing!

The Darla I knew rarely took time with her appearance because she felt like her weight made her unattractive, so why try? Now she had her hair and make-up done and was wearing the cutest outfit.

But that smile told the real tale.

Darla ran and hugged me. She thanked me for everything I said and did for her. She told me that it took some time, but one day it clicked; she realized she was worthy of living an awesome life and she decided to do just that. She told me that she would never forget what I had done for her and that she was making a deliberate effort to make the same type of impact in her daughters' lives.

Also, she'd gotten up the courage to approach our mutual friend and was waiting to see if he would make the move to call her. And then she said the best thing of all.

"I hope he calls, but if he doesn't, I'll be fine. That just means there's someone else out there who will appreciate me for who I am. If he doesn't call, it will be his loss."

"Girl, you are so right," I said. "And you know why?"

Without missing a beat, she said: "Yes! 'Cause I'm a Bad Mama Jama!"

— Regina Sunshine Robinson —

Never Underestimate Yourself

Do not underestimate the "power of underestimation."
They can't stop you if they don't see you coming.
~Izey Victoria Odiase

"YOUR BED NEEDS ME." The words screamed at me in white capital letters from the red two-inch button my boss handed to me.

Standing with him in the conference-room doorway, I looked at this married father and struggled to frame my refusal in words that wouldn't offend the man who had the power to fire me. "Uh... I'm a bit... uh..."

He moved closer. "I just thought you'd be interested," he said.

"Well, I'm not," I replied. Then I pocketed the button and escaped into the room now filling up with people. Safety in numbers!

Later at home, I tossed the button into a drawer. I had handled Jim's unwanted sexual attention before, but this was a new low. I had ignored his lustful looks, brushed his hand off my cheek, sidestepped him in the hallway, left the door ajar when meeting with him alone, and exited the elevator early when he was the only other occupant. But things weren't all bad. Recently, he had offered me a promotion that would increase my income and advance my career. I was highly motivated to manage the new project — and him.

A few weeks later, Jim called the staff together for an announcement.

206 | Channel Your Inner Warrior

The new project was ready for kickoff, and he was promoting Kevin to lead it.

What? Jim was not promoting me, but my male colleague? He was punishing me! Payback for rejecting his sexual advance.

I returned to my office furious but controlled. Performing my work on autopilot, I persevered. A couple of days later, I spotted the slogan button again. "YOUR BED NEEDS ME." It was as if it stood up on its hind legs and shouted, "See me!" And suddenly, I did see. I had evidence — physical evidence — of Jim's sexual harassment.

When I went to work the next day, the button went with me. This wasn't the dark ages; it was 1988 — just two years after the U.S. Supreme Court ruled that sexual harassment met the definition of employment discrimination under Title VII of the Civil Rights Act of 1964. Now, for the first time, legal means were available to help workers fight sexual harassment. My employer had provided training to help employees identify it and established procedures to help us report it.

After a quick phone call, I was in the Human Resources office, where a counselor heard my story, examined the button, and explained the procedure for filing a discrimination claim. The first step was to consult my departmental Equal Employment Opportunity officer in an effort to resolve my complaint at the lowest possible organizational level.

That process required that I, in the presence of a witness, inform Jim of his specific sexually harassing behavior and state how it had harmed me. If he failed to apologize and propose a remedy, I would report this when I filed my discrimination claim. This would trigger a fact-finding internal investigation that could drag on for months. Jim would be presumed not guilty during the inquiry, so I would continue to work in the same department with him.

The next day, my departmental Equal Employment Opportunity officer listened intently to my story. "Wow! The arrogance of power!" said Bob, handing the slogan button back to me. "Let me know when you get your meeting scheduled with Jim. I'm in!"

That night at home, I assessed my risks. What if Jim apologized and proposed a remedy? In that unlikely event, I would consider his proposal. What if he denied giving me the button and reduced my

Channel Your Inner Warrior

charge to a he-said-she-said dispute? I would willingly match my story against his. What if I filed a claim and lost? I would be transferred to another department to separate two employees who had a litigious relationship, but with my record of outstanding performance appraisals, I wouldn't be fired. What if I won? I would be awarded whatever I could negotiate—at a minimum, transfer to another department. Either way, I would be rid of Jim, who wouldn't be fired because he was part of the power establishment.

But the process could take a huge emotional toll. Did I have the nerve for a face-to-face confrontation with Jim? Yes; I had nothing to lose. Could I navigate the stress of working in the same confines with him during a months-long investigation? Yes; once I turned the corporate spotlight on him, never again would he risk being alone with me. Additionally, my personal support system was strong. My teenage daughter would be my cheerleader. My pastor had already voiced her support, as had my private lawyer and my rock-solid love interest, the man who would later become my husband.

The next day, I made an appointment for Bob and me to meet with Jim. When I went to Bob's office to collect him for the meeting, he opened his suit jacket and showed me the voice recorder hidden in his inner pocket. "Recordings are admissible in court when one of the parties knows he or she is being recorded," said Bob.

"Okay with me," I said into the recorder. Then we walked down the hall to Jim's office.

"I'm here to report something I'm troubled about," I said as Bob and I sat facing Jim at his desk. "I am unhappy about your sexual harassment and your failure to promote me, which has caused me loss of future income."

"What?" exclaimed Jim. "What are you talking about?"

"This button," I said, holding it up for him to see. "Do you remember giving me this?"

"Oh, that," he said with a dismissive wave of the hand. "Of course, I remember. But I didn't mean anything; it was a joke. You just misunderstood."

Bob and I glanced knowingly at one another. It was not an apology or a denial — just a classic blame-the-victim excuse. And an unwitting admission of guilt!

"No, I didn't misunderstand," I replied. "But you did. You misunderstood when you underestimated me. So I intend to file charges against you with Human Resources. And if necessary, I'll see you in court."

I filed my claim, and the investigation began, which included lawyers, interviews, questions, documentation, and three months of behind-the-scenes office warfare. Finally, I agreed to settle my claim and received everything I requested: transfer to another department, a promotion, and thousands of dollars.

What happened to the audiotape? Bob kept it. What happened to the button? I kept it. What happened to Jim and his job? He kept it. What happened to my job and me? I kept it, finishing out my career with the company.

Today's Me Too movement is a reminder that sexual harassment still exists. No matter what action the harassed person takes to confront it, that external action is driven by the internal conviction that drove me while on the leading edge of the legal battle against sexual harassment in the workplace. Never underestimate yourself.

— Carole Harris Barton —

Riding High Side

I can't control the wind but I can adjust the sail.
~Ricky Skaggs

"Ready to tack," the captain orders, and my first mate releases the sheets on the starboard side. I furiously pull them tight on the port. We are headed for the shallows where the current is not as strong. 5 knots… not bad for a boat her size. I grab the handle of the winch and give the sheets one last heave. The sails billow in the wind. I tie off loosely and sit back and relax for a moment before we tack again.

It is 7 p.m. on this glorious but chilly spring night. In the distance I see a flock of white swans taking flight parallel with our craft. The sun is casting a hazy yellow glow as swallows dance in search of their evening meal. I ponder grabbing my phone, but decide some things are better captured in the mind's eye than on film.

The past year has been a difficult one and the winter especially hard. I was in a tumultuous marriage and my self-esteem had taken a beating.

Then, a friend invited me to The LaSalle Mariners Club. They were empowering women by teaching them how to sail. What I saw as an evening of escape soon came to be my lifeline. With every rigging of the hanks and raising of the jib my resolve became stronger. If I could hoist a main and pull a boat out of chains, then surely I could pull myself up and get myself out of this mess as well. I soon discovered that when the body is busy, you're able to think more clearly. I began to trust myself and plan.

Now, as I sit here three years later, no longer merely a piece of deck fluff, I can truly say sailing gave me the confidence to leave my marriage. Riding high side with the wind whipping my hair I realize I am at peace. Every once in a while a wave splashes up to lick my face. I lean into it. I am refreshed. I am empowered.

— Robin Martin —

He Wouldn't Do a Thing Like That!

*If we don't stand up for children,
then we don't stand for much.*
~Marian Wright Edelman

"A girl reported that a certain boy had been hiding in the tubes at the school playground, and that he had been pushing the girls to do something inappropriate. She mentioned your daughter," the guidance counselor explained over the phone.

"Explain 'inappropriate,'" I demanded, trying my best to keep calm.

"I have spoken to your daughter, but she didn't open up about it," the counselor explained. "Perhaps you could talk to her tonight."

I began to tremble.

About an hour later, my seven-year-old daughter hung her head as she got off the bus. She refused to meet my gaze, pulling her pink hood over her head.

Choking down emotions, I hugged her tightly and kissed her forehead. "Rough day?" I asked.

"It was fine." She was pale. Her eyes were dark underneath and the whites reddened. Her lips pressed together so tightly that they were drained of color.

Normally, she'd talk excitedly about her day. Now she slowly walked beside me around the block and into the house.

212 | Channel Your Inner Warrior

Once inside, she went directly into the bathroom, closing and locking the door. That wasn't normal.

Then I heard her begin to cry and then turn on the running water to hide the sounds of her distress. I pressed my head against the bathroom door and breathed in deeply, sending all my love and energy to her. I wanted so badly to hold her but knew she needed this minute.

My intuition told me there was something more to this story, something deeper that had cut her. My daughter was not fine at all.

I stepped away from the door, overwhelmed by a feeling of helplessness. I prepared her a cup of tea and a snack, placing it on the living-room coffee table.

When she stepped out of the bathroom, her cheeks were red and raw from where she'd wiped away the tears. She looked so small and frail.

I patted the seat next to me on the sofa. As she sat beside me, I placed my arm around her shoulder. She leaned into my chest.

"Mama," she whimpered, shaking.

"I know, honey." We both began to cry.

When the tears subsided, we leaned back into the plush couch and pulled a blanket over us. This was something special we had always done, sitting this way. I wanted her to feel safe and protected.

"I need you to tell me what happened," I said, brushing her hair from her forehead.

"He was asking us to do things. I didn't know what he meant. He wanted me to touch him where I shouldn't. I said no, Mama, I swear I did. My friend got away, but he wouldn't let me go. And when I could get away from him, I did, but…" Her eyes locked on mine as she stammered.

The green pools reflected all the pain, hurt and shame I'd felt at her age when I'd been hurt by a great-uncle in a way that damaged me for a lifetime.

"I'm sorry," she replied, her voice full of disappointment in herself.

"It's not your fault," I gasped, covering my mouth as if it would hide from her how weak I felt in that moment. "Did you go tell an adult?"

"I did, Mommy. I told the playground aide."

Channel Your Inner Warrior | 213

"You did?" I was puzzled. The guidance counselor had said another girl had reported it. "What did she say?"

My daughter sniffled and looked down again. "Mommy, the playground aide said he's not that kind of boy and he wouldn't do that."

When I was seven and had been abused, no one had advocated for me. It was swept under the carpet, kept hush-hush. The incident was an embarrassment to my family. It was never to be spoken about, and I was left on my own to cope with my injury while the man who hurt me went on to abuse his own children.

That little girl buried inside me now rose up, ready to fight.

The next morning, I arrived at the school before the day started with my daughter next to me. "I am here to speak to the principal and my daughter's guidance counselor immediately," I demanded.

"I'm sorry, ma'am. They have yet to arrive," the woman in the office explained.

"Then we will wait." I planted myself on the bench outside the principal's office.

He arrived shortly afterward. "Do you have an appointment?" he asked.

"I don't think I need an appointment for this," I replied angrily. I looked at my daughter who thought so much of this trusted adult. "We can do this now, or I can go to the police. It is your choice."

"I see. I'll need a few minutes to do morning announcements and then I can fit you in." The principal was soft-spoken and evasive; he didn't seem like he was up for a fight for justice.

I returned to my daughter's side and squeezed her hands. "You are strong, my girl, so strong," I said to her. I kissed her head.

After avoiding us as long as he could, we were invited into a conference room with the principal and the counselor.

The counselor recounted to the principal what had been reported to her.

"I see, I see." The principal looked at the notes in the file she handed him.

My daughter cringed, embarrassed.

"This child is to have nothing more to do with my daughter," I explained.

"Well, Mrs. Jones, it's not like we can keep them apart if they are on the playground together." The principal looked at me, trying to appear firm.

I stared at him in disbelief before I stood, placing my hands firmly on the table between us. My daughter watched me with great interest.

I took three deep breaths to pull my thoughts together.

"I will remind you, sir, that this is 2017. My simple request is not unreasonable. First, let me state that by allowing this child access to my daughter, you are allowing her to be further victimized, if not physically then mentally. You are setting an example for all girls that boys can do whatever they want simply because they are boys. Do you have daughters, sir? Would you accept that?"

"No, of course not," he stammered.

"Secondly, my daughter went to the aide for help immediately and was told that he's not that kind of boy, and he wouldn't do that. I don't know what kind of training your staff is given, but there is no situation where that is a correct answer. I must demand she apologize to my daughter for her poor judgment. My daughter deserved better and deserved help."

The principal went to answer, but I raised my finger.

"This aide took away her voice. Of course, she wasn't going to tell you what she'd experienced when a trusted adult had already told her it wasn't possible." My face reddened as I glared at the principal. My voice raised slightly as my heart pounded in my chest. "Obviously, retraining on how to handle these situations is needed."

The expressions on the counselor and principal's faces changed as they looked at each other. They reflected both surprise and panic.

I looked at my daughter, who smiled with pride now. "The final point I must make clearly is that seven-year-olds don't just come up with this kind of behavior. This child's background must be investigated. I am angry beyond measure for what he did to my daughter, and what I imagine he may have done to other girls, but I know he learned this behavior somewhere."

"You're right, Ms. Jones. We are addressing multiple complaints, and I promise you we will look into it further." The counselor reached across and touched my hand. I looked back at her, surprised.

The counselor stood and walked around the table and over to my daughter. "Lily, I want you to know I am your friend. I will always be here for you. It doesn't matter what you need to talk about. I'm always going to make sure my door is open for you."

The woman's eyes welled with tears. She hugged my daughter. She stood then and took my hand in hers again. I saw in her brown eyes a victim and a survivor — the same as me, the same as my daughter. "I promise you, Mrs. Jones, that we are taking this seriously, and Lily will receive the apology she deserves from the aide."

— Michelle Jones —

Moment of Truth

Tackle problems with purity of personal power.
~Lailah Gifty Akita

I was in my early twenties, and life was not going well. Barely one hundred pounds soaking wet, with a dancer's body and a Catholic girl's demeanor, I'd been date-raped earlier that year and could not find my way.

Despite assurances from friends, I believed that I was to blame somehow. Maybe I'd given mixed signals. Maybe I'd dressed too provocatively. Maybe I'd simply chosen the wrong man.

As a consequence, my life became smaller and smaller. I didn't trust my own decisions, so I began to shy away from invitations. I became more and more of a recluse.

Except for college. While I worked all day to earn a living, night classes were purely for pleasure. Oh, I needed the degree and was certainly working hard toward its attainment, but my creative-writing class was a breath of fresh air. I'd found my tribe there. I'd found a community of like-minded souls who loved words and thrived in the fantasy of the worlds they could build and stories they could tell.

Each week, I looked forward to the three hours we would spend together. I slogged through my workdays for the embrace of that community every Thursday night.

Even when the professor announced that a potential rapist had been attacking women on campus, I was undeterred. There had been several attacks, all at night, all in the farthest parking lots. But it had been quiet for several weeks. The school was offering a security crew to walk women to their cars if they simply called at the end of class. Extra patrols were circling the campus, and the authorities were certain they would have the situation under control soon.

But inside the four walls of my creative-writing class, all was wonderful. On a particularly inspiring night, the class had been so deeply involved in a passionate critique session that we'd lost track of time. When we finally looked up, it was 10:15.

"Let me walk you to your car," offered one of my classmates when we realized the campus was empty. But I wanted to process our discussion and relished the short distance it would take to reach my car. Besides, both classmates were parked on the opposite side of campus. "No, thanks. I'm fine," I replied.

I began walking to my car. But as I stepped into the parking lot, I realized I'd parked substantially farther from the entrance than I'd remembered. Furthermore, I was startled to see that there were only three cars left in the entire lot. I quickened my step.

Then I heard the steps — behind me, for sure, but clearly catching up.

I looked back and saw a young man heading down the parking lot.

Maybe another late student, I thought. But my red flags were popping up.

I turned from him and kept my pace. I could hear his footsteps behind me and his labored breath as he walked. My heart began to beat faster. My palms became wet instantly. I could feel the menace in the air.

I walked quicker. So did he. I turned to look again. He was watching me as he hurried forward. He had no books, and we'd passed the last car before mine.

Only one streetlight lay between my car and us. Otherwise, the lot was dark, and we were isolated. Virtually no one was on campus. We were alone, and I was clearly in danger. With my head down and my arms wrapped tightly around my books, I realized, too late, that I made the perfect victim.

"Not again!" a voice screamed in my head. "How could I be so

Channel Your Inner Warrior

stupid? How could I...?"

And then it hit. Hot, red fury began to sweep through my being like a backdraft in a raging house fire. "No!" it said. "Not. Again." And, as that fire engulfed me, enraged me and expanded me to a size substantially bigger than my petite stature, I turned on my would-be attacker and... attacked!

"How dare you come after me!" I raged at him, dropping all but one of my books and going at him like a crazy woman, swinging my book like a club. "If you take a step closer to me, I swear I will..." And then I proceeded to tell him in graphic, not-for-the-faint-of-heart terms exactly what I would do with his manhood and where I would put it if he even thought of doing me any harm.

And, I knew I would have.

But more importantly, he knew I would have because his jaw dropped. He stopped. And then he turned and ran as fast as he could. All along the way, my totally-out-of-character-swearing pelted him with damnation and blasting curses as I scooped up my books and hurried to the safety of my car.

As I drove home, I knew I'd changed. I'd gotten a do-over. I'd repeated a situation where I'd been a victim and found a way to mine my strength. I'd been able to reach down and find a fury and a fortitude that I did not know existed and pull it up to incorporate into my new being.

And it hasn't left me since.

Several weeks later, a flyer circulated around campus with the attacker's picture on it. I didn't have to look at it. I knew what his face looked like. But, more importantly, I knew what it looked like when he was defeated. I knew what it looked like when I'd empowered myself to stop him in his tracks. I knew what it looked like when I permanently and forever changed myself from victim to victor.

— Susan Traugh —

The Chief of the Clan

*Each time a woman stands up for herself, without
knowing it possibly, without claiming it,
she stands up for all women.*
~Maya Angelou

When I opened the door to the factory, I was struck by the strong smell of oil and the clamor of machinery. I hurried through the factory, trying to get to my office without slipping or getting my high heels stuck in the old wood flooring. The catcalls started ringing out, as they did every day.

This was the second part of my college internship at a large helicopter manufacturing plant, and unfortunately it involved walking through the factory to get to the engineering offices. This was the 1980s, and when this type of thing happened, it wasn't considered harassment; it was just considered "boys will be boys."

The head honcho of this boisterous crowd was the man with an air whistle on his machine. In addition to his shouting, he would blow the whistle so loudly that everyone in the factory would hear. As it blew, the men in the factory laughed. This whole situation was humiliating, and I began to hate going to the offices. I hoped I would be transferred again soon.

Each morning, I walked quickly without making any eye contact and kept my head down. Back then, there was nowhere we could turn. Managers were well aware this was happening but did nothing.

Channel Your Inner Warrior

What was a girl to do?

After a while, I realized what made this annoying cycle hum. The ringleader, the man with the air whistle, seemed to delight in harassing the ladies. The more embarrassed the girls were, and the more they shrank away, the more fun the guys seemed to have.

Out of necessity, my idea was born. It would take some courage, but I had to stop this. One morning, as I walked through the factory door, I mustered up my courage. "Okay, deep breath, head up, you can do this," I told myself as I made my way around the machines. As I approached the chief of the clan, he began to holler and blow his whistle. I stopped right in my tracks and whirled to face him, looking him directly in the eyes. Startled, he stopped the whistle.

"Okay, you can do this," I told myself again.

Breathing deeply, I said aloud, "I just wanted to tell you that I wish you wouldn't do that. It's very embarrassing. How would you like it if someone did that to you or one of your family members? Do you have a wife? Would you like it if someone did that to her?"

I challenged him. I think I shocked him, and he looked down, now embarrassed himself.

"I'm sorry. I won't do it again. We were just having fun. My name is Tom," he muttered.

I met his gaze but smiled this time. "Okay, Tom, but it wasn't funny to me." I warned him one last time. "Let's just be friends from now on, okay?"

It seemed too easy, but it worked. By confronting him, Tom saw me as a human being. Sure enough, the next morning, Tom smiled and waved, and gave his horn two short, happy good-morning toots. I smiled and waved back. We continued to have this happy exchange for the rest of my internship. Mission accomplished.

— Elizabeth Rose —

Independence Day

Freedom is the oxygen of the soul.
~Moshe Dayan

I can still hear those defiant words blaring from the radio in my mother's Volkswagen sedan. Sitting alongside my mother as we scurried about the streets of our little town, running our usual errands, she sang along without missing a beat. She raised her left arm — the other firmly on the wheel — as if to accentuate the melody, and sang with the passion of someone who could relate to the woman described in the song, with the passion of someone with newfound freedom and independence.

From the frequent screaming and fighting, the abusive language, and the love/hate drama that had unfolded between my parents before my eyes, I knew that "Independence Day," written by Gretchen Peters, was more than just a popular song that summer. For my mother, it was the music of courage and self-confidence. For me, at the formative age of fourteen, it was the music that turned my world upside down.

The song's lyrics told of a woman's response to domestic abuse, seen from the point of view of her eight-year-old daughter. On Independence Day, while her daughter attends the local parade, the woman starts a fire in the house, and she and her abusive, alcoholic husband both perish in it.

The song has double meaning in that the woman was finally gaining her freedom from her abusive husband — thus, it was her Independence Day — and the events occurred on the Fourth of July.

Its message suggests that what the woman did was neither right nor wrong. Instead, it was the only way she could ultimately gain her freedom and, at the same time, protect her daughter from the violent home where her little girl had seen bruises on her mother's face far too many times.

"Let freedom ring, let the white dove sing... Let the weak be strong, let the right be wrong."

Those were some of the lyrics that my mother sang with the deepest passion.

My mother left my father that summer and never went back. A teenager at the time, I was initially angry about it all. The last thing I wanted to do was spend time with the woman who didn't seem to understand me and with the woman whose decision forced me to live in another house, to ride another school bus, to memorize another phone number, and, worst of all, to endure the financial limitations of a single-parent home.

As we continued about our errands that afternoon, I glanced over to the driver's seat at the middle-aged woman my selfish teenage self had begun to resent. With her long red hair, petite figure, sculptured face, and deep brown eyes, my mother truly was a picture of beauty. Although she seemed a bit overbearing and protective at times, she was my strength and I admired her. But she was increasingly down on herself. Inside the radiant beauty that most people saw was an increasingly broken, weary, and sad woman.

She tried to be strong for my younger sister and me, but I'd often see her cry and witnessed how the pain of ending that relationship drove her to a state of depression. I tried to be sympathetic, but there was little that I could say or do to help mend her heart.

Just the night before she had cried herself to sleep and, as we lay beside her, whispered, "I love you girls, more than you will ever know."

As I watched her sing that afternoon, I began to understand why that song was so meaningful for her. And I came to realize how much her freedom, her independence, and her ability to do what made her happy, really meant. I began to gain an appreciation for the sacrifices that my mother made, not only for her own well-being, but for my

Channel Your Inner Warrior

sister's and mine as well. Though we struggled financially, her courage and strength allowed us to live in a home free of fighting and verbal abuse. Her decision allowed us to stop living in fear.

When the song ended and she parked the car, she smiled as big as she could, and said, "I'll be celebrating my Independence Day on July 31st, not July 4th. Bring the fireworks."

It's been ten years since the day I watched my mother harmoniously sing along to "Independence Day" while en route to the grocery store. I'm no longer the teenager in the front seat, dependent on a ride to my destination. I no longer use my Sony Walkman to block out her high-pitched singing. But there's one thing that hasn't changed since that hot summer day in the passenger seat: the significant impact the song's message has on me.

When I hear the words "Independence Day," I don't always think about the fourth day in July, the red, white, and blue, or America the free. Instead, I salute those brave women who, like my mother, had the strength and the courage to make difficult and painful changes in their lives, changes that now face me as well.

Perhaps it's true that history repeats itself. Not long ago, when I left my alcoholic husband, I knew the same kind of pain my mother experienced nearly a decade earlier. Perhaps I should have paid more attention to the lessons of my mother, the lessons of my upbringing, and the frequent anguish of my childhood. But perhaps I was destined to follow in her footsteps, to make her mistakes, to feel her pain, and to develop her courage, strength, and independence.

I know she never wanted me to, but now I know. Now I understand. And as soon as I was able to roll the stone away, I had my Independence Day.

Coincidentally, I left my husband on July 31, 2010 — exactly eight years to the day my mother left my father. "Hard to believe," she said when she reminded me of our shared date. "Only now do you understand why it was so important for me to leave… for me, for you, and for your little sister."

Not long after our phone conversation, I came across that song, which I hadn't heard in years, on one of my late-night drives. Like

Mom always had, I turned up the radio and sang along with passion. And for once that day — probably even that week — it didn't feel so bad to be alone.

Let freedom ring.

—Ellarry Prentice—

Chapter 9

You Come First

Rebuilding a Life

Some people say you are going the wrong way, when it's simply a way of your own.
~Angelina Jolie

My decision to turn our 2,400-square-foot home into a 4,000-square-foot home, fully renovated and with three new additions, met with an interesting variety of opinions. Evidently, empty nesters in their early sixties weren't supposed to need a larger house, especially when the husband was being overtaken by dementia that began in his fifties.

We'd enjoyed living on our lovely, tree-lined country acreage in a traditional two-story home for the past seventeen years. I'd often tried to get my husband interested in adding on a room — or two or three — but that was never his thing. So, I paused my dream of getting to build a house in my lifetime, but I never abandoned it.

People around me offered up all the usual commentary in response to this aggressive and unique plan I was drawing up: Why don't you just build a new house for yourself somewhere, rather than go through all that tearing-up mess? Do you really need all that space to yourself? Why aren't you selling out and moving into a retirement community like I did?

My response to that last one stopped that person short. "Because my life isn't over yet. I still have things I want to do."

I ride the bike trails, mow our acreage, and do my own housework. I need to move, to get my hands dirty in flower gardens and generally stir the pot, trying new and different things.

When my husband's psychologist laid out the picture of what life was going to look like as his illness advanced, I saw our future die. The future we'd worked and saved for was never going to be.

I'd have to create a new life for myself without him.

As I contemplated the realities of it all, I knew I would not wait until I was too old, too sick or too tired to do something I'd been dreaming of for years. Ever since I was a small child, I'd loved Victorian-style turrets. There was a mystical uniqueness to the architectural form, and I'd always wanted one — or more — to be part of a house I lived in. They seemed like a space that a writer and reader should have.

As we didn't live in a historical neighborhood, the true Victorian turret wasn't going to work for our house, but my designer and I put together plans that included three new additions — and all of them would have a contemporary, hexagonal flavor. These would get me as close to having turrets as I could, and I was eager for the work to begin.

This was not a frivolous house design, however. I knew it needed to be a smart build, and we incorporated features that would make it easier for me to remain living here on my own as I aged.

As we'd had no bedroom on the first floor, I added a large master suite as one of the additions, complete with a zero-entry, walk-in shower, wider-entrance hallways and pocket doors. It's far easier to slide a door out of one's way when a walker or a wheelchair is part of the equation. Adult-height toilets were installed in every bathroom in the house.

The kitchen was gutted with plenty of maneuvering room left around the island. Pull-out shelves in all the lower cabinets were installed for easy access. A security system was added.

We lived on-site throughout the whole process — something else people thought I was nuts to do, but I wanted to watch my dream being built. To protect my husband from the chaos, I hired professional caregivers to come and take him out of the house every afternoon while I stayed behind to be accessible to the contractors, and sweep up and dust the small areas we lived in during the process.

It was a happy time for me to be around the action. This was going to be the only chance I'd have to do something like this, and I wasn't about to miss out on any of it.

Sometimes, I think my decision to build my dream house was my way of sassing back at The Universe for taking everything I'd assumed would be as we aged together. Perhaps it was my way of saying, "Oh, yeah? Just watch me. You aren't going to keep me from building my house."

I believe now The Universe was on my side. I was blessed with a talented and capable general contractor who took on the difficult build and hired the right crews — many who, over the eight months of construction, became friends of mine. We'd talk about their kids' activities, and they'd watch out for my husband if he was around. They showed concern for me when we had bad days.

Amidst all the drilling, hammering and sheetrock dust was this joy of a dream going up before me, juxtaposed against my husband's degrading health and a future together erased. It is a complicated dichotomy that the casual bystander cannot comprehend unless they stand in my shoes.

I wasn't going to be able to continue living in our home space the way it had been when we were a couple. I couldn't live in what had been. I had to make it new for the changing life happening to me.

My new home has become a sanctuary, not only for me but for family and friends, and new memories are made on a weekly basis.

I've come to realize there are expectations for women of a certain age who are alone. I want to shout from the top of my new turreted office to anyone who will listen: Do not wait. Do it your way. Let no one tell you how you "should be" at your age.

Building the house saved me in the year that was the hardest of my life. My husband's disease advanced quickly, and I was afraid I wouldn't get the house finished before I had to move him into a care facility, but we made it. He lived in the new house for a few months with me before that day arrived, and I'll always be glad that he did, even though he no longer remembers any of it.

— R'becca Groff —

What Breaks You

My willingness to be intimate with my own deep feelings creates the space for intimacy with another.
~Shakti Gawain

When I was twenty-one, I met a guy who I thought was "the one." Our relationship took off. We spent weekends together, attended parties from sunup to sundown, and exchanged cheesy text messages and phone calls when we were apart.

I put his needs first. I believed that pleasing him was my way of keeping him around. When he showed up—handsome, charming, confident, and open hearted—I couldn't believe that he would like someone like me. Soon enough, his likes, dislikes, and opinions became my own. It was unhealthy, and no matter how distanced I became from friends and family, I truly believed that it was love and these were the sacrifices that girlfriends needed to make.

One day, after not hearing from him all weekend, he called me at work and broke up with me. Just like that. He said he was bored and that I needed to figure out who I was. To say that I was crushed was an understatement. I felt like someone had just unplugged me, and I was slowly dying. I wondered what I had done wrong. It took many years to learn that asking that question was the root of the problem.

Fast-forward six years, and I am writing this from the headspace of a woman I never dreamed I would become. After the breakup, I found solace in yoga and meditation. It became a practice—a *sadhana*—that would pull me out of my self-sabotaging darkness and into the very lesson my ex-boyfriend was trying to teach me all along: be selfish. What angered me most in our relationship was the fact that he was always putting himself first. It made me feel unwanted, unseen, and unwelcomed, like I wasn't a part of his life plan. What he and the Universe were trying to teach me was that I wasn't a part of his life because I had never made it a point to be a part of my own.

He never lost sight of himself, and he was right. At the time, I didn't realize that he was giving me back a gift I had so easily tossed to the wind: myself.

During my time being single, I turned inward. In yoga, we call this *pratyahara*. Once all the distractions of the world fall away, and once you're rejected by someone, there's nowhere else to go. It's time to face yourself. I faced all of my demons, triggers, traumas, and dark corners that had never seen the light of day.

In 2014, I started my yoga teacher training, and then I taught my very first yoga class. I still get goose bumps and teary eyes reflecting back on a class full of my peers, cheering me on as I taught.

Yoga gave me not only a desire to get back to my own self-care and love, but it gave me my voice! Today, I teach, write, travel, and live my life with purpose, authenticity, and passion. Finally, I know who I am. And I know I would have never arrived at such a gift without the pain of being rejected in that relationship. For this, I am grateful.

I shed massive layers of the shy, reserved, afraid, and dependent girl I was at twenty-one. I took back the power I had ceded to men. And it was like coming home! The voice I used to teach yoga was the same voice I used to say "no" more often than I said "yes" now that I wasn't worried about being liked.

Somewhere out there, a like-hearted man will believe in the same for himself, and our paths will cross when each of us is ready. Gabrielle Bernstein, renowned speaker and author, always says, "The Universe has your back." And it does, steering us toward something bigger and better. Every single person we meet is our guide and teacher, especially the ones who bring us pain and trauma.

I'm a firm believer that the loves lost are our mirrors, showing us who we really are. Allow yourself to stand tall in that reflection and find gratitude for what breaks you, because what breaks you is also what rebuilds you.

—Aleksandra Slijepcevic—

Getting My Bling Back

*Love yourself first and everything else falls into line.
You really have to love yourself to get
anything done in this world.*
~Lucille Ball

I didn't think the word "bling" applied to me. I'm far from wealthy and my only diamond ring sits in a box. I know it is a commonly used word in the entertainment and fashion world and it comes from the imaginary sound produced when light reflects off a diamond. But for me, bling was a thing of the past, the victim of a debilitating disease.

I was the kind of person who counted her blessings. I read *The Power of Positive Thinking*, by Norman Vincent Peale, a hundred times. I believed the words of the Bible when it said, "I can do all things through Christ who gives me strength." So, when my doctor diagnosed my low-grade fever, joint pain, and fatigue as rheumatoid arthritis (RA), all my defenses came to attention. No way was I going to let it get me down like it had my grandfather and uncle. They had suffered until their will to live had vanished. With that in mind, I got busy looking for answers.

First, I found a rheumatologist whom I could trust. He put me on a combination of medications proven to reduce inflammation and improve mobility. He also recommended keeping a record of my pain to see if we were making progress or needed to make changes. Some drugs helped, but many that had helped thousands of other people didn't help me. RA had dealt me a hefty blow.

Still, I wasn't one to give up. I did my best to stay active and keep a positive attitude. RA wouldn't kill me, but I had seen for myself how it could diminish one's quality of life. I fought back with all my being. I had too much living to do.

Despite that, as time went on, the disease progressed and I became unable to work. Without an income, I faced a dim future. That's when my self-esteem began to crumble.

The decline started with little things. When a cheap pair of earrings hurt my ears, instead of buying better quality earrings, I made the decision to do without them altogether and let the holes close. Also, I got tired of asking my husband to fasten my necklace. It just wasn't worth it. And, when all my rings had to be removed because my fingers were so swollen, I gave up on jewelry for good. The bling was gone from my life.

The downward spiral continued as I cut out activities such as shopping and yard sales. They were no fun with my ankles and knees hurting with every step. Besides, what good would it do to buy cute clothes and shoes when the disease persisted? I was too self-conscious to wear dresses any more. Pantyhose were impossible to pull on. Tennis shoes with jeans or slacks would have to do for any occasion — even for church.

I had always enjoyed my hair at shoulder length and my husband liked it too. The problem began when I couldn't raise my arms over my head. Once again, I had to lean on him. Always the optimist, he never lost his sense of humor. "I never thought I'd become a beautician," he said.

When my hair was showing more and more gray, I opted to let it go. Never mind that all the women, and some of the men, in my family had colored their hair for generations to look younger. To me, nothing could be more aging than RA.

Since my teens, I had worn hard contact lenses. Now, I decided they were too much trouble, especially with my dry eyes. My eye doctor said my medicine was to blame and wanted me to consider soft contacts, but I passed up that offer too. With my crippled hands, I wasn't sure I could put them in or get them out. Glasses would have to do. I was in a tailspin.

Then, just when I needed it most, a good friend stepped in. "Why don't we re-pierce your ears?" Julia Ann asked. If anyone could inspire me, she could. Despite chronic back pain, she always managed to look great.

I couldn't see what difference it would make. "No. That's okay. I'm getting by just fine," I said.

"I'll bring my kit next time I come over," she said, unwilling to take no for an answer.

In a few days, she came back determined to get the job done. I was reluctant, but since she was so sweet and I didn't want to seem unappreciative, I agreed.

After she was gone, I looked in the mirror at the gleam coming from the tiny cubic zirconium earrings. Was it possible that I could actually be attractive again, in spite of my condition? Had I been letting my illness stand in the way of my appearance? Maybe if I did things to be more beautiful on the outside, I might feel it on the inside too. It was worth a try.

One thing led to another. I started looking for necklaces that would go on over my head and I added extenders or easy clasps to a few of my other favorite pieces; my friends took me shopping to find easy-on, comfortable, yet stylish tops and elastic-waist pants in stretchable fabrics; my husband ignored my argument that New Balance shoes were too expensive, so I ended up with several pairs of them in different colors; I found out I could handle soft contact lenses; and, my hair would soon have highlights and a much needed trim. At last, I realized what had happened over the years. Every time I had given something up, I had given up more of myself to the disease.

Today, thanks to Julia's persistence and the encouragement of many other friends, I'm getting my "bling" back. The changes wouldn't

You Come First

be noticeable to most people, but for my friends and family they are significant. Only, in my case, they won't see the light reflecting off a diamond. It will be coming from the sparkle in my eyes.

— Linda C. Defew —

Here to Shine

*You have to be self-interested in order to be selfless.
You have to put yourself first if you want
to be of use to other people.*
~Rachel Bartholomew

As an accounting professional, I know there are a few time periods each year when my life will be crazy. I can't schedule a vacation then, and I won't see much of my family or friends. I accept it and deal with it, as this is my chosen profession.

But when COVID-19 hit the U.S., my world flipped upside down.

Instantly, my role as a bookkeeper morphed from helping clients reconcile their ledgers to becoming their counselors. I became a shoulder to cry on. In some cases, clients felt I was their only hope to make it through the pandemic. They felt alone and scared, and they leaned on me.

The weight of that realization was so heavy I could hardly move. I was chained to my desk and computer for six weeks straight — ten- to twelve-hour days, seven days a week.

The enormity of what was happening took its toll. I couldn't let people down. I couldn't let clients lose their businesses because I didn't help. I couldn't leave them to fight this battle alone.

Nightmares became a regular part of life. I'd wake up in a cold sweat looking around the room, trying to snap back to reality. I lost weight. I didn't eat. My body felt as if it had been in a car crash. I didn't talk with friends or family. I just worked.

But one night I had a dream that not only changed my entire way of looking at this virus, but also changed the way I look at myself.

In my dream, I was running from someone — a stranger. I was running from room to room in an unfamiliar house. I didn't know where I was going. I was just running.

Random people from my work life appeared in my dream and said, "What are you doing?" Then I'd run out of that room and into another.

Someone else would say, "But wait, what are you doing?" Then I'd run out of that room, over and over, trying to find my way out.

The odd thing that stood out the most was the song playing throughout the dream. It was "Firework," written by Katy Perry and Ester Dean.

I woke up singing it. Okay, who doesn't love Katy Perry? But I found it curious. Why that song? In my nightmare?

I Googled it: "What does it mean when you dream about music?"

According to Dream Bible, "To dream of hearing music represents a theme to the type of emotions you are feeling."

These are the first lines of the song: "Do you ever feel like a plastic bag, drifting through the wind, wanting to start again. Do you ever feel, feel so paper thin, like a house of cards, one blow from caving in. Do you ever feel already buried deep, six feet under scream, but no one seems to hear a thing."

I felt chills. I'd heard that song a thousand times, but for the first time I listened to what it was saying. I actually heard the message.

It's easy to get lost in all the "have-tos" and "must-dos" in our lives. It's easy to get overwhelmed by the needs of others and want to help them. Until that moment, I felt that if I didn't drop everything and help someone in need, it made me a bad person.

But does it really? I run around on empty all the time, trying to fill up other people because that's what a good person does, right?

Maybe not.

My whole life, I've heard the saying: Love yourself before you can love others. It took a pandemic for those words to sink in.

My clients, friends and family are everything to me, but nowhere on that list of most important people is *me*.

238 | You Come First

I have to make time for me. I have to make time for what's important to me. And I have to find a way to be okay with that.

I'm starting to see that it's not an act of selfishness to take care of myself. If I take care of myself, I am a better, healthier, happier person for my friends, family, and clients.

I'm here to shine, but I can only do so if I take time for myself first. I need to make time for what lights me up so I can then shine for others.

I have to remember that I'm a firework. Fireworks are fragile. We have to handle them with care, or we could get hurt.

Now, I handle myself with the same care. Only then can I truly shine.

— Diana Lynn —

Being Intentional about Self-Care

I always try to remember that I'll be the best me I can be if I prioritize myself.
~Michelle Obama

In late 2011, my father was hospitalized in Kaufman, Texas. I was living 250 miles away in Houston, driving on weekends to be with him. He had been living with Alzheimer's for more than twelve years. My mom, who was much younger than my father, had resigned from her job to care for him full-time.

The doctor was making his morning rounds when I came around the corner. After listening to my dad's heart and his breathing, the doctor lingered in the room. The pause was long enough to become awkward. After glancing at the worried look on my mother's face, the doctor asked if I minded stepping outside with him to discuss a few things. I guess he thought I would be better able to handle what he was going to say.

He reviewed my dad's vitals and shared the results from a few tests they had run. I remember hearing the doctor say, "Unfortunately, Mr. Louis's health is beginning to decline rapidly. He could pass away at any time. It could be a week or a few months." Tears began to run down my face. My head immediately started throbbing, and I felt like someone had just placed fifty pounds of concrete on my shoulders.

I thanked the doctor for his great care and bedside manner, and then I burst into uncontrollable tears. The poor man couldn't leave. I remember thinking, *Why are you being so dramatic right now, LaQuita?* Then I thought, *When will I have time to plan a funeral? My plate is already beyond full right now.*

I managed to regain my composure and stuck my head back into the room to reassure my mother that everything was okay, and I would be back shortly after taking a work call. I felt as though I was about to have a panic attack. My heart was pounding, I could barely breathe, and my hands were trembling. I found the sign in the hallway pointing toward the chapel. I needed a quiet place to meditate, reflect, and gather my thoughts. It was obvious that I was hopelessly overwhelmed.

When I walked into the small, intimate room, I felt immediate peace. It became evident that I had allowed work-related stress, church ministries, marriage expectations, volunteer commitments, and family obligations to overwhelm me. I had become too busy to be still. I began praying and crying profusely at this self-discovery. I had simply failed to care for my own personal needs.

I asked God to give my family and me more time with my father to get things in order, both for myself and the needs of the family. Truth be told, my father had lived this long, in part, because of how he had taken care of himself. Even being over eighty years of age, the muscles in his arms and legs were still defined. He rarely ever raised his voice or showed any visible stress, and he always found time to read his Bible and say his prayers on his knees every night.

My father passed away four months later. Shortly after my father's burial, I began practicing daily downtime. My activities vary: fifteen to thirty minutes of journaling, prayer, quiet meditation, reviewing Sunday school lessons, or yoga flow movements. When I first started this process, I had to set the alarm on my cellphone to ensure I maintained a minimum of ten minutes because my natural response was to get back to being busy.

Five years ago, during one of my self-care sessions, God put it on my heart to start a nonprofit, Angels with a Mission, to provide hope and support to homeless and foster children. I was not sure how it was all going to come together, but I knew that I had to listen to

You Come First

the guidance I had received. I had always been an avid volunteer in the community, but starting my own nonprofit was a bit adventurous and sounded like a lot of work. I recalled that, as a little girl, I had watched my father grow vegetables year after year to pass out to the elderly citizens in the community. Aha! My dad had engaged in what he enjoyed doing—gardening—and was able to take the benefits from his hobby to bless those around him.

As a result of learning to be intentional about taking care of me, during my closet prayer time, the Lord reveals things for me to do. For instance, He places individuals upon my heart whom I might pray for or reach out to via a card or phone call. In the past, I would have been running around like a chicken with my head cut off trying to save the world. Now I know that if I will just take the time to be still, my heavenly Father will reveal specifics to me. He literally takes the footwork out of "finding my purpose" and delivers a clear roadmap for me to follow.

Maya Angelou once said, "If I am not good to myself, how can I expect anyone else to be good to me?" This is so true. I have learned to never get too busy to take care of myself.

—LaQuita Jean Starr—

Finding My Footing

*Self-care is giving the world the best
of you instead of what's left of you.*
~Author Unknown

I hung up the phone, put my face in my hands, and burst into tears. My husband, Richard, got up from the sofa to bring me some tissues and rub my back.

Since my father's death the previous month, this scene had become commonplace. I hadn't cried much when I knew he was in the hospital except for when I said my last goodbye, the nurse holding the phone to his ear, his breathing raspy and uneasy. I'd accepted that I couldn't go home to the U.S. for his funeral — a travel ban because of the pandemic left me stuck at our home in Japan — and I attended a visitation via video call with my mother, and my brother Bob and his family.

This time, though, the tears were for something completely different. My sister-in-law, Jenny, was rushed to the hospital the morning of my father's funeral. Always in fragile health due to her long-running battle with alcoholism, her heart finally gave out. My middle brother, Edward, barely arrived at the hospital in time to say goodbye. A recovering alcoholic himself, the double-whammy of our father's and his wife's death pushed him over the edge. He started drinking again.

My mother, stoic about my father's death, now sounded tired and exhausted when I spoke to her on the phone. My oldest brother and Edward hadn't spoken in more than ten years.

You Come First

That left me calling everyone. I worked with Edward's neighbor and sister-in-law to try and sort out help for him, make arrangements for the funeral, and try to persuade Edward to enter a recovery program. It seemed clear that I had to return home. This time, the mess was too big, and I feared my mother would be drawn in despite the danger of the pandemic and the unpredictability of Edward's mental state. However, if I went back, I wouldn't be able to re-enter Japan.

"I want to go home," I sobbed, "but I'm risking everything: my career, our marriage, our income."

"We can handle it," my husband soothed. "We'll be fine."

I appreciated his words, but I didn't buy them. Yes, we were fine financially, and our marriage was solid, but the future was far too unclear. If I left Japan and then was banned from re-entering from the U.S., I could end up unemployed, uninsured, and indefinitely separated from my husband.

"I'll think about it," I said, taking a deep breath. "I need to make another call."

This one was to my best friend, Kris. We had talked almost daily starting just before my father died, when the assorted meanings and implications of his death had been the sole items running through my head. Now, it was fear as well as anger at Edward and this disease, along with worry about the impact on my mother.

"Can I tell you what my mother heart says?" Kris asked after I spewed all of this, my voice cracking with emotion by the end.

"Sure," I said, reaching for a tissue.

Then, her voice low and steady, she made her case. By staying in Japan, I put myself in a better place, financially as well as emotionally, to support Edward and, in turn, my mother, as this long, slow crisis took its course.

We sat silently for a moment. Outside, I could hear the wind in the camellia bushes. I heard Richard making breakfast in the kitchen. Her advice felt wrong, but I promised to think over what she had said. Kris and I talked a bit longer and then signed off so she could go to bed and I could start my day.

I realized, as I sipped my coffee and mulled over her words, that

I hadn't exercised for over two weeks and had stopped meditating. My daily journaling focused only on this crisis. I was distracted and grumpy, falling behind on work. I was giving everything to this crisis, forgetting about what I needed to get through it.

After breakfast, I disconnected all my devices from the Internet and sat down to meditate. My mind jumped hither and yon as my breath came in rapid bursts, but I stayed put. Then, I set out for a long hike into the nearby foothills, eventually settling on a bench near a small temple, gazing out over the plain below to the sea. Overhead, birds chattered lazily in the trees. At my feet, an iridescent salamander sunbathed. Giant black butterflies, Alpine black swallowtails, floated past, and the old gray-and-white tomcat who lives on the mountain dozed on a picnic table. When the light waned, I headed down the trail to home. There was work to be done.

I established a schedule for calls and e-mails — nothing before 7:00 a.m. and nothing after 9:00 p.m. — unless it was an emergency or scheduled meeting. I resumed my daily meditation practice, and Richard and I took long walks together, pointedly not discussing my family unless absolutely necessary. I took on new writing assignments with an eye on income and keeping busy but also not overextending myself. I contacted a counselor. I did a lot of weeding in the garden, and when the gym opened again, I started swimming three times a week.

I still spent plenty of time on the phone and e-mailing with family, social workers, nurses, and doctors, as well as with Edward's neighbor and sister-in-law as we all tried to keep him safe until he might agree to enter a recovery program. Slowly, though, I felt myself steadying and my vision clearing. As the days turned to weeks and then months, smaller crises flared up, but I felt more able to meet them. Even now, there are still moments where I weep with my head in my hands, but when they pass, I find myself on increasingly solid ground. Firm-footed once more, I reach out to do what I can from where I am.

—Joan Bailey—

Giving Thanks by Letting Go

You've got to make a conscious choice every day to shed the old — whatever "the old" means for you.
~Sarah Ban Breathnach

I sneak away to my bedroom to make the phone call. I ease the door closed using both hands, being careful not to let the handle click. The house is full of the smell of roasting turkey. The table is set for nine with the inherited white china and my autumn-themed tablecloth and napkins.

Setting the table for special occasions is one of my favorite tasks. The silverware is polished and placed perfectly on either side of the plates. My grandma passed her silverware on to me, and my mother-in-law has added some of her pieces. I don't care that they don't match; I love that they come together in random order, just as families merge over time. Every time I pull them out, I think of holidays around Grandma's long table so many years ago.

My kids are home for the Thanksgiving weekend, and the usual quiet order of the house has given way to lively conversation and lots of extra work like loads of laundry. We are also hosting my son's girlfriend and her family in addition to my mother-in-law. It's our first time having our son's girlfriend for a holiday, and I'm excited. I can see our families merging in the future, which makes me happy. My mother-in-law is the only grandparent my kids really know; I'm happy she's here, too. My mom, however, is not invited to this Thanksgiving gathering. There have been too many holidays ruined by her drinking.

I've decided to call her today to ease my guilt, to tell myself, "See, I am a good daughter. At least I call my mom on Thanksgiving, even though I can't invite her to my home." I'm hoping she'll tell me that she is spending the day with my sister's family or maybe with her husband's kids. This will also help ease my guilt. I check the bedside clock: 11:45. I'm barely in time for my self-imposed noon deadline. After 12:00, Mom will usually have begun drinking.

My heart pounds fast. I take a deep breath. I know I should not make this phone call. The risk is high. My husband has cautioned me many times, after soothing away another set of tears. But I am drawn to do it anyway, just like a moth that is attracted to the light and his eventual demise.

I'm using the landline and have to look up her number. I think it's odd that I don't know my mother's phone number by heart. My hands shake as I punch in the digits.

"Hello?" Mom answers. My heart beats faster.

"Hi, Mom. I just wanted to say, 'Happy Thanksgiving.'" I can picture her sitting at her kitchen table, cigarette in one hand, pencil in the other. She's probably working on the last few clues of the morning crossword puzzle. Mom still has a thin but sturdy frame, but the years of drinking have given her a big belly. Her gray hair, which she refuses to color anymore, hangs down in long waves, framing her weathered face. She looks older than her seventy-one years, a life of sun, physical labor and smoking having taken their toll.

"Thank you. Happy Thanksgiving to you, too." Her voice is calm, maybe a little surprised to hear from me.

"So, what are your plans today?" I close my eyes, pushing my hope for good news into the universe.

"Not much. Just cooking a turkey for me and Richie."

"Oh. That sounds nice. Is anyone else coming over?" I ask cheerfully.

"No, just the two of us." First pangs of guilt.

"So, what else are you cooking?" I need to change the direction of this conversation.

You Come First | 247

"Oh, I'll make all the trimmings, too. You know how I like to cook."

"Yes. I'm sure it'll be delicious." She is a great cook.

"Are the kids home?" she asks.

"Yes, they're both home for the long weekend."

"Oh, that's nice to have your kids home with you." The guilt stabs me again.

"Yes, it's so great to have them home." Is she going to ask how they are, what they are up to these days?

"Well, I'll let you go now." She says "let you go now" as if she is the one who called, as if we've been talking for half an hour when it's only been three minutes.

I feel sad about her being home on Thanksgiving with only her husband to keep her company. I know that she will have a hard day taking orders and insults from him and wondering what all her kids are doing. Instead of easing my guilt, this call has only heightened it. I shouldn't be surprised.

I blurt out, "I love you, Mom." I have no idea where that came from. We don't say that or haven't in as long as I can remember.

"Okay," she responds. "Bye." Click.

"Okay? Okay? Who says 'okay' when their daughter says, 'I love you'?" I say to the empty room. "Who does that?"

I look out the window to the back yard. The lawn is damp with last night's rain, but the sun shines brightly. Yellow, orange, red, and brown leaves stick to the wet patio. A slight breeze picks up outside, and more leaves free themselves from the branches and drift down. How easily a tree rids itself of the things that it no longer needs. Without a thought, it discards the leaves that held a purpose all spring and summer but won't be needed for the winter while the tree rests and prepares for spring. It must do this in order to be strong enough to generate new growth.

I pace around my bedroom and ask myself, "Why have I done this to myself again? Why do I keep trying to get her to love me?"

But this time I do not cry. I think of the voices I hear in the kitchen: my husband and my two wonderful kids. They are laughing about something. I think about the phone calls I have with them, each one

You Come First

ending with "I love you" and a reciprocal "I love you, too." I think about the new lives they are both forging with their significant others and the "new" families we will add to our own; new branches to our family tree, new growth. I think about the day ahead and all the fun, warmth and laughter that we will enjoy.

I have more than I ever could have dreamed possible. The futility of my struggle with my mom hits me like a fierce autumn wind. I shake my head. It is finally as clear to me as the blue sky above: I will never get what I want from my mother, but I am finally okay with that. Just like those trees outside, I too must shed what I no longer need and prepare for the new season to come. I head back to the smell of roasting turkey, laughter, and hugs. I have so much to be thankful for on this day.

— Maggie John —

Surviving and Thriving

A thriving new beginning can be and should be a time for amazing engagement, growth, connections, contributions, and amazing possibilities.
~Lee M. Brower

I turned and buried my face in my husband's chest after the somber doctor told us, "Your breast biopsy showed a malignant lesion." My mind flashed to my mother, who put everyone's needs before her own, contributing to her death at age forty only thirty days before Harry and I were married. I wasn't going to make the same mistake.

I pulled myself together and wiped my tears with the neatly folded hankie Harry always carried, and we listened to the plan the doctor laid out.

For six months, my days were filled with countless medical tests and doctors' visits followed by two surgeries and thirty-three radiation treatments. Fighting for my life was a long, difficult journey, as the medications and radiation made me violently ill. When a dye the doctor injected into my tumor during surgery left my skin blue, I could only laugh. I looked like a Smurf.

In the waiting period between surgery and the beginning of radiation, I had the opportunity to travel to see our daughters. Both girls were upset they couldn't be by my side during my battle. When I returned home to start radiation, I had to grant myself permission to accept the meals and help with household chores that poured in from co-workers and even complete strangers.

My faith helped me find inner peace, a positive attitude, and the inspiration to carve out time for daily prayer. On my worst days, my beliefs kept me moving forward and focused, helping me to stay strong. My heart was touched as my name was added to dozens of prayer chains, something I had done so many times for others. Now it was my turn to receive.

It was only natural that as a woman, wife, mother and grandmother, I always made others my main concern. Reversing that role to one of care-recipient was a difficult transition. For the first time in my life, I had to make myself a priority. My survival depended on it. I went from being a strong, take-charge person to gratefully accepting the help offered by friends and family.

My self-care included splurging on weekly massages that soothed my ravaged body and helped me relax, something that would contribute to my recovery. As a bonus, my masseuse, a breast-cancer survivor herself, and I became great friends. She gave me advice on how to boost my immune system and also showed me how to massage the affected tissue to avoid the leathery skin that can result from radiation exposure.

When the radiation gave me cellulitis and I had a severe allergic reaction to the antibiotic, the members of a great cancer support group helped me sift through alternative options. These extraordinary women never missed an opportunity to share their experiences and encourage me. I had become a member of a sisterhood to which I never imagined I would belong.

Once on oral maintenance medication, my body reacted with thinning hair and unbearable aches in all my muscles and bones. My survival-sisters supported and comforted me to work through the pain and resist the urge to give up, adding a suggestion that I include water exercise in a warm therapy pool to my self-care routine. It gave me comfort when these caring women reminded me that it takes a village to combat this invader, and I was not alone.

Another wonderful thing my support group taught me was not to miss any opportunity to live life to the fullest. With that lesson firmly in mind, I planned something special to celebrate my survival. Despite being exhausted, on the day of my last radiation session, I boarded a plane for Disney World to join my daughters and grandsons. After all, it's the place where dreams come true, and I couldn't think of a better way to celebrate being declared cancer-free.

Later, while in the Magic Kingdom, I laughed and then cried as Mickey and Minnie swept my grandkids, daughters, and me into a group hug. It was as if they knew it was a new beginning for me.

I had done what I set out to do! I had taken care of myself so that I could have more years of memories with my family. Ten years later, I continue to pass on my energy and optimism while remembering to carve out me time. I count my blessings every day while I cherish the anticipation of thriving in every precious moment yet to come.

— Terry Hans —

Softness in the Vast Blue Sky

Underneath the hardness there is fear
Underneath the fear there is sadness
In the sadness there is softness
In the softness is the vast blue sky
~Author Unknown

When my son James was a baby, he was so beautiful. Everything seemed possible. Over time, it was clear to everyone but me that something was different about him, something to be concerned about. But I saw only magical uniqueness. Even when he was diagnosed with autism, I failed to acknowledge or to accept the loss of my dreams. I failed to see him for, yes, the truly magically unique child he was.

After his diagnosis, I was suddenly in a new world, a world I did not want to be in. A world I didn't know how to navigate. A world I only wanted to escape from. I denied the impact on my heart and on my life, and set out to force happy normalcy on us all. The alternative was simply more than I could bear.

There were lots of people to meet that I never would have crossed paths with. Experts. Parents. Doctors. Teachers. Specialists. Support groups. I was flooded with way too much information. I couldn't begin to sort it out. I was numb. No time for feelings. I had to function. I was alone with a son I loved who had a problem. I had to fix the problem. That is what I knew how to do and I did it very well. Fix problems. Find a solution. Make everything all right.

Someone said I should talk to Sherry, a mom/expert. Sort of the mother superior for all the novitiate moms. I took James to her house. She was so friendly. I thought she was happy because she knew how to make this all go away. She was going to share the secret cure with me. She had this great big smile on her face as she exclaimed, "I love autism!" Wow, I thought, will I ever love autism? I was pretty sure I wouldn't.

Many families look forward to the summer. Family vacations. Trips to the beach. Sports. Picnics. Cooking out in the back yard. Enjoying time with the kids. I don't remember it that way. Summers were a stressful time. Without the structure of school, James's autistic behavior deteriorated. He had frequent tantrums. He did not like to do what other kids enjoyed, so he did not have friends. He did not like to do what families like to do together, so family vacations were not something I looked forward to. I saw summers as opportunities to focus on the autism therapy du jour — auditory training, sensory integration, behavior modification, diet changes, homeopathic treatments, and on and on. With each summer, he grew older and my hope for a cure grew more desperate.

One spring I was talking to the child psychologist who worked with James. I was going over several options for the summer. One option I dismissed quickly by saying, "This one would just be fun." The doctor leaned forward until he was sure I was paying attention and said slowly and deliberately, "Fun... is... good."

I guess all those years of training paid off for him, because that was one of the smartest things I ever heard. I think that is when the healing began. When I realized that life in all its uncontrollable messiness held the promise of joy along with pain. That my child was like any other child — he wanted to be safe and happy, to learn and grow and have fun. That I was like any other mother — loving my child with my whole being, wanting to shield him from harm, wanting to prepare him for a life beyond me.

James himself helped me. One day, as he was looking at himself in the mirror, I heard him shout, "It's great to be James!" What more could a mother ask? I learned to delight in him the way he delighted in himself.

Is there any mother whose heart has not been broken by her children? By loving them so much, by worrying about them, by losing them, by finding them again?

One mom I know has a child with leukemia. Another has a child on drugs. Another's child died in a fire. A friend's daughter has morphed into bridezilla. Another has a teenager who is, well, a teenager. I have a son with autism.

What were we thinking when we had these kids? I have never regretted for a moment having children, but I have marveled sometimes that I don't. Surely I would regret anything else in my life that had caused me such heartache. Would any of us, if we really knew what we were getting ourselves into, have knowingly walked into this soul pain?

Amazingly, the answer, I think, is yes. There will always be a raw tenderness in my heart for James, a place sensitive to touch. A place of quiet grieving. And that's okay. I breathe into the softness of it, trusting in the basic goodness of the universe, the perfection of it all, the sunny brightness of the vast blue sky.

— Galen Pearl —

What I Deserve

One of the most beautiful qualities of true friendship is to understand and to be understood.
~Seneca

"Is Rob coming?" one of my friends asked over the loud music pumping throughout the club. The whole group of girlfriends at our table turned and looked at me. They waited for my answer. In my heart, I knew he wasn't coming. But I found myself saying, "Maybe, maybe later."

My friend smiled sweetly and said, "Let's go dance."

I knew what they were all thinking, but no one said a word.

I'd been dating Rob for a few months. He was funny, cute and kind. He had so many great qualities, but nailing down a time to see him was nearly impossible. He'd say things like "My work is unpredictable." "I might have the kids this weekend." "I'm not sure, but I might be going out of town." He never really knew when he'd be free.

I wanted to believe him.

As the night went on, I grew increasingly more doubtful that he'd show. Finally, the dreaded text came.

"Sorry, can't make it tonight. The kids are coming over."

My heart sank. Again.

I found myself torn. He was a hard-working, single dad. It was one of my favorite things about him. He was there for his kids. His whole life was about his girls. How could I be mad at that?

I'd try to tell myself, *See him when you see him. Enjoy time with him*

You Come First

when it comes. Go on with your own life. If he comes, he comes.

But the truth is, it made me feel unimportant. If he really liked me, he'd make time. If he really cared, he'd find a way. If he wanted to see me, he would.

Each time I'd get that last-minute excuse, my heart would break a little more. Each cancelation was a little dig at my self-esteem.

I left the club feeling dejected. *I can't keep waiting for this guy.* My head knew it. I just couldn't convince my heart.

The following weekend was my girlfriend Lyndal's birthday. A few girls got together to surprise her with a weekend away. We rented a condo in Friday Harbor. It's a sleepy little town, but it's beautiful — the perfect place to go with friends for quality time. And it was a welcome distraction from my boy problems.

We got into town, went out to dinner, and returned to our condo, where we drank wine, played games, and danced around the living room to our favorite songs. One by one, our friends went to bed.

Finally, it was just Lyndal and me. She looked at me as if she were reading my mind. "What's up with Rob?" she said.

"I don't know. Nothing," I said.

"Do you want to know why I married Jason?" she said.

"Sure. Why?"

"He shows up," she said.

I wanted to cry.

She continued, "He shows up. When he says he's coming, he comes. When I need him, he's there. He shows up." She looked at me lovingly and said, "You deserve that, too."

I'll never forget the look on her face — the way she made me feel that night. The love and kindness of her words melted my heart. I got it. I got it so clearly. "You deserve a guy who shows up."

She could have said Rob was a jerk. She could have said, "Don't put up with his wishy-washy crap." But instead she simply told me why she picked her husband: "He shows up."

It seems so obvious. But in the middle of it, I couldn't see clearly. I just felt confused. I felt my own self-esteem slipping away. But that's the thing about good friends — they won't let that happen.

You Come First | 257

When I got back to town, I ended things with Rob.

That night, a good friend taught me that I deserve someone who shows up. And now I know I will not settle for anything less.

—Diana Lynn—

Chapter 10

Reclaim Your Calendar

Speed Bump

You learn something every day if you pay attention.
~Ray LeBlond

For weeks, I checked the shelter website daily to see if her photo was still there. I had mixed emotions every time I began scrolling through the photos. I always hope that animals at shelters are adopted into loving homes. But this time, in my heart, I wanted our home to be the one this adorable cat moved into. If her photo was gone, I'd always wonder what happened to her. I'd also feel terrible knowing I didn't follow my heart and adopt her.

I didn't need to adopt another cat. It hadn't even crossed my mind until I saw the picture of this precious cat with short legs and an imploring expression that tugged at my heart. With all her cuteness, I was certain she would be adopted quickly. I was wrong. I'd been checking the website for at least two weeks, and she was still there. I knew her time was limited. When I couldn't resist the temptation to adopt her any longer, I called the shelter and told them I'd be there the following morning to adopt her.

My husband and I were at the shelter when it opened the next day. As we were walking to the area where the cats were kept, the shelter employee told us he stopped by every morning to visit with the cat we came to adopt. He described her as a real sweetheart.

As we approached her cage, it was easy to see why he started each morning with a visit to her cage. She wasn't bashful about wanting attention. As soon as the cage door was opened, she stepped right into my arms and secured a permanent place in my heart. Needless to say, she never returned to the cage.

After we brought her home, I decided to name her Smores. Her coat had all the colors of a s'more, and she was indeed a sweet treat. I soon realized that I should have named her Speed Bump, instead.

Smores came into my life at a time when every day seemed overly hectic. I felt rushed and overloaded with obligations. Smores brought a change to my daily routine. She made it impossible for my mornings to begin in their usual hurried manner. As soon as I got out of bed, she insisted I stop and pet her for a while. Just like the shelter employee, I couldn't disappoint her. She slowed down my morning routine just like a speed bump slows traffic. From the day of her arrival, Smores began creating beneficial "speed-bump moments" for me.

I have health problems and my husband had been trying to get me to take better care of myself and rest periodically throughout the day. Smores solved that problem. She has become my motivation for slowing down and taking breaks. She seems to sense when my energy level is getting low or my pain level is intensifying. During those times, she vocalizes her desire for attention or paces back and forth from me to the chair I typically sit in when reading or relaxing.

I used to put relaxation and quiet time at the bottom of my priority list. Days often ended without me ever getting to that last item on the list. Smores took care of that. The day we brought her home, she needed grooming desperately. Although I wasn't sure how she would react, I sat her on a footstool, talked to her softly and brushed her hair for a long time. She loved it. Every day since then, she has jumped onto that same footstool and waited for me to brush her hair. Brushing Smores is never at the bottom of my priority list. That time we spend together is calming and soothing for both of us. That's just one of the ways that Smores acts as the speed bump I need to reset my daily routine to a manageable pace.

I was mistaken in thinking I didn't need another cat. I needed help in getting my out-of-control days under control. I needed motivation to slow down and stop pushing my body beyond its limits. Smores

Reclaim Your Calendar | 261

helps me with those needs. I'm certain Smores and I experienced a dual rescue. Living with us, she receives the love and attention she desires and deserves, and I have a lovable, furry speed bump to keep my days from getting out of control.

—Veronica Bowman—

A Working Man's Chuck-It List

*The first step in crafting the life you want
is to get rid of everything you don't.*
~Joshua Becker

A bucket list is all about those ambitious tasks and exciting dreams you've been putting off until retirement. The list often includes goals you hope to accomplish and dreams you believe will complete your life. What would you like to do before you die? Attend Burning Man? Drive across the country? Ride a camel in the desert? Tackle a snowman? Play a zombie in a major movie? Hunt for buried treasure in Timbuktu? Crawl through hallways of lasers like a spy? Live in a van down by the river?

I'm a working man entering the later years of my seventh decade. My needs and requirements are small. I would like to rescue a kitten stuck in a tree and die a hero. That's about it. I'm not wealthy or ambitious enough for a bucket list, so I've developed a "chuck-it list" that contains objectives I'm willing and able to let go of. By this I mean anything that drags me down or holds me back from living a happy and comfortable life.

I've spent the last several months putting together my chuck-it list. I've thought about people I never want to meet (Madonna, Freddy Krueger, the inventor of My Pillow), activities I detest most (opera, golf, yoga), and places I wouldn't visit if you paid me (Iraq, Afghanistan, and Disneyland). There are many exotic places and unique experiences that I could care less about. When I wrote them down, a few really pegged my Ick-O-Meter. I'm certain that if I can cross some of this stuff off my list, I will be blissful and fulfilled. Here are a few things I'm giving the old heave-ho:

It's time to say chuck-it to wealth, materialism, and consumerism. I'm not interested in owning the latest iPhone or electronic gadget; I wouldn't use half their features anyway and I don't need to appear trendy. I drive a pickup made of rust and base my fashion taste on what doesn't itch or make me sweat. I don't care about "looking good for my age." Those who have seen me walking around the house in my underwear and sporting a three-day beard can attest to that. Most of the time, I resemble a guy who should be deep-frying butterballs at the county fair. I'm all for feeling energetic and vibrant. (Good health is important, right?) But as far as turning myself into sixty-nine-year-old eye candy, forget about it. A salad can only stay fresh for so long, if you catch my drift.

Higher education has to go. I'm chucking my degree in Philosophy from Humboldt State. What has it gotten me? My small life isn't really progressing toward anything. I haven't amassed a fortune or even risen above the day-to-day muck of a foot soldier. I've also become a little "squirrely" in my senior years. I hear voices and talk to myself a lot. Sometimes, I get into heated internal debates and don't always win. I wear a Bluetooth headset so I don't look completely crazy when I'm talking to no one.

How have I kept from being committed to a home for the mentally disturbed? It has to be a miracle. That's the only explanation.

Another item I'm chucking is "exotic" foods, starting with sushi. I once ate a ball of wasabi thinking it was avocado that had fallen out of my California roll. Gizzards are equally disgusting. I'll never eat them again. Kidneys are just as bad. They taste like pee. I'm chucking candy, too. Well, at least Reese's Pieces. I was recently eating a handful and thought I had dropped one on the carpet. I'm all about the five-second rule so I ate it, but immediately wondered what I had just eaten, as it made a rather sickening crunch between my teeth.

I think you get the point. I've only touched the surface of my chuck-it items. Chances are my list will continue to grow, and as it does, I will congratulate myself on all the adventures and experiences I get to avoid. That's me time at its finest.

— Timothy Martin —

Remember to Remember You

The Universe will never require you to set yourself on fire to provide heat for others.
~Clyde Lee Dennis

I hung up the phone and returned to scrubbing the kitchen floor. My brother Jason had just invited us over for dinner. Again, I had to tell him we couldn't make it; I had too much to do. Every morning, I made my to-do list. Every evening, each line was crossed off as done. The list was essential because there was always so much to do. But no matter what I did, a new list grew in the morning.

It was June 2016, and my wife Betsy had been diagnosed with liver cancer a month earlier. This was not our first journey with cancer. She was diagnosed with breast cancer in 1997, and it returned in 2008. Both times, I was her primary caregiver, and we'd beaten the disease. In the summer of 2016, I felt I was reprising a role I knew well. But this time, for some reason, I could not remember my lines or what to do once I stepped on stage each morning. I could've used some strong direction and a little stage managing.

But that's where the lists came in. I never needed the lists with the earlier cancer journeys. I just did whatever needed to be done next and then whatever came after that. This time, though, her diagnosis was more serious, and there was less she could do. The best advice I got as a caregiver was to remember the instructions regarding oxygen masks on airplanes: Put yours on first before trying to help someone else. But I forgot it that summer, and the next summer, and the next. I had helped save Betsy twice before, and I was determined to do it again. I was so determined, in fact, that I forgot about myself entirely.

In the evenings, we watched whatever shows on TV she wanted to watch and went to the films she wanted to see in theaters. I scheduled her chemo appointments and doctors' visits, CAT scans, blood draws, car inspections and repairs, and eye doctor and dentist visits. I had always taken care of the housework so that was nothing new, but now I was also taking care of the cat boxes for the four cats, scheduling vet visits, going over our daughter Emily's student loans, and struggling to do the bills—all tasks Betsy had routinely taken care of. Betsy always took care of so much and so well that I felt like an inferior replacement, an understudy to a much greater artist whose range I could never match.

By December 2016, the chemo had done its job, and she was improving. Throughout 2017, she was so healthy that I would have forgotten she had cancer if I hadn't been driving her to Friday chemo sessions and doctors' appointments. Even so, I had become used to my new role, and I continued to perform it, though not nearly so regularly.

Then, in May 2018, she woke up one morning with abdominal pain so severe that she couldn't move.

From then on, I was doing the high-maintenance caregiving daily on a far more intense level than in 2016 or ever before. I arranged trips from our home in New York for her cancer treatment in Philadelphia, took care of setting up all her procedures there, and got her back and forth between the hospital and the hotel. I made whatever food she liked, and I stocked the refrigerator with her favorite juices and snacks. I was haunted daily by the lines from a Lana Del Rey song about not feeling capable, of struggling to hold the one you love in your arms without letting them fall, of hoping to become what you need to be for someone you love.

This went on until August 4th when Betsy died peacefully at home, surrounded by her family. She was smiling. The great cancer journey was over, but my own journey was just beginning.

    I first became aware of the new phase two weeks after her death when I was out with my brother Jason, and he asked what I wanted to eat. I had no idea. The thought struck me as strange, but then I realized that for two years I had only eaten what Betsy wanted. When I ordered take-out, I would get what I knew she liked because she wouldn't eat it all, and I'd just finish what she left. I had no idea what kind of food I liked myself.

    I realized I knew absolutely nothing about myself anymore. What kind of shows did I enjoy watching? I didn't know. What movies did I want to see? I had no idea. What sorts of places did I want to visit? Not a clue. I had dived so completely into caring for her that I forgot who I was. I have absolutely no regrets over that impulse, but it should have been tempered with a little self-restraint and a lot more self-care.

    When we find ourselves in a situation like this, it's natural to move ourselves to second place. The person who needs our attention comes first. But we have to pause and realize that, if we're not taking care of ourselves, we're not going to be of much use to the one we love. I experienced eczema outbreaks, osteoarthritis flare-ups, gastro-intestinal problems, chronic insomnia, anxiety attacks, and hysterical toothaches throughout the time I was caring for Betsy, and even more so afterward when my grief found its outlet through physical symptoms until therapy helped me manage it better.

    I don't know if my story will have any effect on a caregiver out there going through what I did, but I hope for the best. I know, in my own case, I would not have given a second thought to this kind of advice in 2016 or 2018 because there was always so much to do, and those lists flowed relentlessly from the end of my pen every single morning. I realize now, though, I could have been better to me and, in doing so, would have been better for Betsy. I'm not saying I didn't do my best for her — I did — but I forgot to also do my best for me, which I know would have meant the world to the one I cared for.

—Joshua J. Mark—

Stop Juggling and Put Something Down

*If you prioritize yourself,
you are going to save yourself.*
~Gabrielle Union

When I left corporate life and started my own business, I thought I had it all figured out. When I made the decision to change my lifestyle and get fit, I thought I was on the right track. And when I purchased a second business, I knew I was doing the right thing. Slowing down never occurred to me. I was all about making things happen.

Over the course of three years, I programmed my brain to be in a state of perpetual motion. Even when I wasn't working, I was thinking about work. There was never enough time to get things done, and I feared I'd let someone down if I stopped long enough to relax. But the busier I got, the less I seemed to accomplish.

When the fatigue and brain fog set in, I told myself I just needed to work harder and get organized. But something was wrong. I was emotionally and physically exhausted. My Apple watch buzzed repeatedly in the night, warning me that my heart rate was over one hundred. My body ached, my head pounded, and no matter how much I exercised.

I was losing strength.

When I visited the doctor, the first thing she asked was "How's your stress level?" I shrugged. "Same as usual. Nothing new or out of the ordinary." But something was happening in my body. A multitude of tests and bloodwork revealed I had Graves' disease, an autoimmune disorder that causes hyperthyroidism, with symptoms that include accelerated heart rate, high blood pressure, physical anxiety, fatigue, and muscle weakness.

As Dr. Joy sat next to me to discuss the treatment, I said, "This doesn't seem fair. I've worked so hard on my health. I quit drinking, changed my diet and lifestyle, and lost weight. Things are supposed to get better, not worse."

She smiled sympathetically. "We'll get it figured out. Do some reading up on Graves' disease and take care of yourself." She wrote prescriptions for heart and thyroid medications and referred me to a specialist.

I scoured the Internet for information, articles and personal stories. I learned that autoimmune diseases cause the body to attack its own healthy cells. Disorders can be hereditary and are more common among women. In many cases, they are triggered and aggravated by stress. *How is your stress level?* I asked myself.

The following day, that question resurfaced when I bumped into an old friend. We hadn't seen each other for a while but were connected on Facebook. After exchanging hellos, Cindy said, "I just love following all the things you're doing. Wow, you've taken on a lot; you've got quite a juggling act. I don't know how you do it all, but you make it look good."

I smiled. "I have to admit, some of those projects I'm juggling are starting to get heavy."

"So, stop juggling and put something down. It's okay to tell people 'no.'" As we parted ways, she added, "It was good to see you. You look like you've lost weight; take care of yourself." She waved and disappeared around the corner.

For the next week, I thought about our short conversation. I reread online articles indicating that stress management played a part in controlling Graves' disease. And I made a list of everything I was juggling. I was running two businesses — each requiring a multitude of different tasks. My calendar was filled with online marketing, photo shoots, website design, copywriting and planning a huge regional event. On a good day, I'd squeeze in thirty minutes of writing the book I was working on. I barely had time to blink, let alone relax. But, somehow, I was managing to do it all. My commitment to do more, be more and serve more was too much. I examined the list. It was clear I didn't *want* to do it all. Something had to give.

Prioritizing was hard. I examined the juggling act and tried to decide what to let go of. I bid farewell to clients, explaining I was cutting back and lightening my workload. When asked to speak at events or take on new projects, I said "no." And I found someone to help me plan that big event. My calendar got a makeover, and I reminded myself it was perfectly acceptable to have white space on my schedule.

Until then, I didn't realize how much I'd missed the simple joys — little things that helped me relax and recharge, like long hikes, taking my dog to the park, visiting my favorite bookstore, and sitting on the back porch to watch the sunrise. Those things belonged on my calendar, so I started using an orange highlighter to block out time for myself. Those orange blocks are mine. They represent time to unplug, let my imagination wander, and focus on what's important.

Along with scheduled downtime, creative work found its way into my day. I blocked snippets of time for my writing and photography projects. Once I'd prioritized, it didn't take long for everything else to fall into place. I didn't know how, but I was more productive by doing less.

My calendar is still full, and my workload is still heavy, but I'm not buckling under the weight. I know my limits and when it's time to stop juggling. I've learned to be kind to myself. I start each day with meditation and end with gratitude. And somewhere in the middle, I savor a quiet block of time, reserved for just me. These little things play a big part in my wellbeing.

Perhaps this disease wasn't triggered by stress. Then again, maybe it was. Either way, the diagnosis has helped me reclaim my life. Dr.

Joy was right. We're getting it figured out. Gradually, I'm becoming a healthier, happier, more relaxed version of myself.

— Ann Morrow —

The Cleanup

*Having a simplified, uncluttered home
is a form of self-care.*
~Emma Scheib

I used to make the same New Year's resolution every year — to simplify my life and make time for me — but I was always too busy to stick with it for very long. Change is not easy for me. I liked helping people and hated to say "no" when I was asked for help. I was so overcommitted that it felt like I was dragging an anchor around all the time. I didn't have time to write, quilt, or just sit and read a book.

I often jumped in the car, backed out of the driveway and forgot where I was going. I once forgot my son! I had dropped him off for his swimming lesson and then gone on to do errands. When I got home, I thought, *Where's Darren?* Then I remembered where I had left him. I screeched into the parking lot, and he was sitting on the curb crying. I felt terrible, and I was cured… for a while.

I soon went back to overcommitting but became an avid list maker. That kept me a little better organized. If I did something that was not on the list, I would write it down just so I could cross it off! It made me feel more productive when I could see all the things I had accomplished at the end of the day.

I thought the lists would help me accomplish things more effectively so I would have time for myself each day. Instead, I felt tired all the time, and it was hard to fall asleep as I mentally went over my to-do list for the next day. I was stressed and miserable.

I was always doing five things at once but never felt like I was doing a good job at anything. Once, while hosting a meeting for my Girl Scouts' parents, I heard a little snicker or two every time I turned around to write something on the board. Later when I got home and changed my clothes, I found that when I rushed to get my pants out of the dryer, an extra pair of underwear had clung to the inside and hung over right in the back. I was mortified!

As I ran from task to task, I could never outrun the feeling that something was missing; that was real happiness, which seemed just out of reach. I felt like I was missing a key piece of the instructions on how to put my life together.

My real awakening came about in a strange way a few years ago. We were having the inside of our house painted and so we had to move all the knickknacks, curtains and accessories out of the painters' way as they moved from room to room. We put most of these items in the garage. We lived a simpler life — without stacks of magazines, photos and "treasures" — while our house was transformed with new, restful colors.

Somehow, we got along quite well without all the items we had collected over the years. We decided to think hard about what we would put back. Layers of lace curtains were replaced with simple, sheer curtains in the living room. Across the back of the house, we left the windows with just the lovely, wooden blinds that had been overshadowed by curtains before. My husband painted the old, crazed chandeliers black and they looked brand-new!

And so it went from room to room. We eliminated many decorations that friends and family had thoughtfully given us, because they made the rooms feel small and cluttered. Even though I hadn't wanted to hurt anyone's feelings, it was liberating to put back only the things we really wanted. The house felt so much more open, peaceful and beautiful.

When I started to hang our calendar back up, I noticed how full each day was. Every square was filled in. I decided to continue my decluttering with the calendar.

It was near the end of July, so I started "clearing" August and September. I kept doctors' appointments, family events and commitments to church. But I removed extra tasks I had taken on that left me very little time to relax, read or spend time with family.

At first, people were surprised when I told them in the most loving way I could that I wouldn't be able to help them. Over time, I got used to saying it and they got used to hearing it. Now, I think carefully before I take on anything new.

I am more relaxed, and I have found ways to help in advisory capacities instead. I also review projects via e-mail rather than committing to weekly or monthly meetings. The funny thing is that stepping back has allowed other people to step forward and realize their potential.

I still make lists to keep myself organized, but I am down to one page. I feel like I have blessed others by donating our unused items to charity. But, most of all, I schedule time for me each day—to do what I want. The uncluttered beauty of our home and schedule gives me great peace and joy.

—Judee Stapp—

Determined, Distraught, and Demented

Caring for myself is not self-indulgence, it is self-preservation, and that is an act of political warfare.
~Audre Lorde

As soon as I got home from the hospital I ran down to the basement and disconnected our home phone line. Then I blocked my father on my iPhone.

I'd already experienced his frenzied calls during the wee hours of the morning during the vacations my mother took, and I knew, because she was now in the hospital, the onslaught would only get worse. My mother had tried to be compassionate about my father's dementia, but after sixty-five years of marriage she didn't have much left to give. She'd been sneaking off on trips without telling her three children, leaving us to learn "Betty's in Mexico" from our anxious father. I'd finally persuaded her to disclose the trips ahead of time so I could hire someone to stay in their house to keep my father calmer.

Over the six days my mother was in the hospital my father became more and more frantic, calling anyone he could think of to somehow cure my mother and bring her home. When my mother passed, we rushed to tell my father in person before he found out some other way and had a heart attack.

Thus began one of the most stressful periods in my life. We could barely process the loss of our mother as we dove headlong into caring for a determined, distraught, and demented man. Dad was already quite feeble, and had to crawl up the stairs in the house, but he insisted on remaining in charge. He'd driven his tractor into a ditch while trying to plow the driveway; he'd recently driven an hour into New York City, undoubtedly going 40 miles per hour on the highway; and he was still trying to climb ladders and fix things. He was also visiting the bank almost every day, withdrawing large sums of money and then hiding the cash, forgetting where, and calling the police.

I quickly cobbled together a team of caregivers so that my father was never alone. That was a struggle, as he refused to have a new person come to the house. He knew two of the three women already, and the way I finally got him to agree to interview and hire the third one was to tell him that she was afraid of the steep driveway and he needed to help her by turning on the outdoor lights and greeting her reassuringly at the front door. Once I turned him into the person *giving* the care, he was okay with "interviewing" the caregiver I had already hired.

At the funeral, my mother's aide told me that in the ambulance my mother had said, "Allan killed me. Don't let him kill anyone else." I knew it was true. The stress of living with my father in his demented state had made my mother so unhappy that she'd deliberately disobeyed doctor's orders about her own health. In the hospital, she kept saying, "Just let me die." She didn't *want* to go home. When I went through her desk, I discovered that she'd known she was in renal failure and had done nothing about it.

Over the next couple of months, my brother and I pulled off a miracle. We got my father to "pick" the assisted living facility we had already chosen for him. But then the stress continued. It turned out that our father was not well suited to communal living. He refused to be alone in his apartment, so we had to continue the 24/7 care, now with four aides who I had to manage. He was often rude to the staff and other residents, unwilling to wait to be served in the large dining room.

After someone mistakenly programmed all the speed-dial buttons on his new landline phone, we continued to have a terrible problem with his calls. In addition to his three children, he had several elderly friends he'd call repeatedly to complain about his situation.

Eventually, I was able to change the speed-dial settings on his wired phone and his cell phone so that he only had everyone's cell phone numbers. That way, all of us lucky phone pals could block him. It took five months, but I was finally able to reconnect our home phone in the basement.

That day when I'd unplugged the phone was the beginning of my self-care. It wasn't selfish; it was mandatory. When you're trying to handle a cantankerous old man with dementia, you have to protect yourself. If you don't, you turn into my mother, fleeing to Mexico and neglecting her own health.

When I would review my "Blocked Voicemail" I would find dozens of messages from my father, spaced two minutes apart. He would leave the exact same message twenty times in a row, having no memory that he had just called.

I would call my father back for one phone conversation on the days I didn't visit in person. That was my rule. Two or three visits a week and one long phone call on my days off.

I tried to have fun with it. If my father had been perseverating too long on one topic, I would deliberately switch him to a new one. I'd even text my brother ahead of time: *I'm tired of talking about downloading Kindle samples because we've been on that topic for two weeks. So tonight I'm going to switch him to discussing where he bought his furniture.* That evening, I'd ask him about one of the pieces we'd moved with him to the assisted living, and we'd discuss his furniture for the next two weeks.

Texting my brother and sister helped, too. When the dementia got bad enough, I could text them without my father realizing I was doing it. I'd provide a running commentary on our conversations. We all deserve some comic relief when we are caring for someone with dementia.

My husband would comment on how patient I was when he heard my side of the phone conversations. They were endless loops, answering the same question or discussing the same topic a dozen times in a matter of minutes. That wasn't difficult for me. I was going to spend twenty minutes on the phone with him anyway, or an hour or two visiting him, so it didn't really matter what we talked about. He owned that time. If we covered the same ground twenty times in a row, fine.

If everything we talked about was utter nonsense, no problem. I entered my father's new reality. His ninety years pancaked into one flat continuum. He was still living with his parents… and he'd just come back from a business trip to Europe… and his mom who'd died in 1996 had just called… and my mother was away on one of her trips. I called his recliner "the magic chair." That chair took him all over the world. He told me he'd never traveled to Paris as much as he had during the past year.

Sometimes, it was even entertaining to hear how he would rewrite history. I learned that my grandfather, who ran a commercial real estate firm in Manhattan, had coined the term "the garment district" and invented the concept of designer showrooms. Probably not true at all, but I think I learned that my grandfather at least managed some commercial buildings in the garment district.

We started this caregiving journey more than four years ago and I have to say it is way easier now. Over time, the dementia worsened and it was like a hard shell cracked and fell off my difficult father, revealing a very sweet guy underneath. We moved him to an incredibly well-run memory care unit a year and a half ago. We'd been told that the move would be easy, and it was. The moment he got there he forgot about the two and half years he'd been at the assisted living. He thought he'd moved directly from his original house!

Now my father's in hospice and we don't talk about anything. When my husband and I saw him the other day for the first time in four months due to the COVID visiting restrictions, he was asleep in his chair and I couldn't wake him. I left him an old photo album from the 1930s and 1940s to look at with his aide. I retrieved the envelope of fake money I'd given him a year ago so he'd have some "cash" and feel secure. He doesn't feel the need for cash anymore, so I gave it to the front desk to pass on to another dementia patient coming up behind him.

The stress is over now. Dad's but a shadow of that determined

Reclaim Your Calendar

distraught man from four years ago. I feel like we did a great job for him, and a good part of our ability to do that came from strategically protecting our sanity and our own health. We took my mother's warning to heart.

— Amy Newmark —

The Pie Chart of Me

At times our own light goes out and is rekindled by a spark from another person. Each of us has cause to think with deep gratitude of those who have lighted the flame within us.
~Albert Schweitzer

The infamously rigorous International Baccalaureate program was always the most popular topic of discussion for everyone, from seasoned alumni to anxious Pre-IBers. Stories of sleepless nights sustained by cans of iced coffee and mental breakdowns at 1 a.m. were passed around like urban legends.

Those of us entering grade eleven didn't have time to be fazed. But the panic first started setting in when we received our physics lab on the third day of school.

"This is harder than anything you've done," our teacher chuckled—almost snidely—as he passed around the instruction sheets. "No one will get above ninety." My confidence was shaken as I looked at the page of tauntingly unfamiliar symbols.

With a heavy heart, I managed to make it through the rest of the school day. When I finally dragged myself home, my father only added insult to injury. Pointing out my lack of progress in the SATs, my dad reiterated for the millionth time that I would not be able to get into a prestigious American university without good SAT results.

The last straw was the e-mail from the Red Cross. As the vice

Reclaim Your Calendar | 281

president of my school's Red Cross chapter, getting rejected from the Regional Red Cross Youth Council was a possibility that never crossed my mind. It simply couldn't happen. Not only was the Red Cross my passion and inspiration, but it was also what I relied on to set me apart from all the other college applicants with ninety-five percent averages.

My future had seemed so bright and certain, yet in reality it was so fragile. Any small blockage could force me to veer off the narrow path to success. I felt like a rubber band — it can only take so much stretching before it snaps. After that e-mail from the Red Cross, I snapped.

I ran out of my room and the first person I saw was my mother, the woman who left behind her family, her friends, and her life in China to emigrate to a foreign country just so I could receive a better education and have a brighter future. The woman who gave up her highly esteemed job in Beijing and could only find a job as a part-time office assistant in Toronto. My mother had spent her life bringing me to the most advantageous starting point, and yet I did not have enough stamina to reach the finish line.

When my mom finally noticed me, I was already a sobbing mess. "What's wrong, baby?" she asked, her face a mixture of alarm and worry.

My answer was "everything," and so that's what I told her about. My mother let me blabber on and on.

After I was done, she stared at me with so much emotion in her eyes. Her brows were furrowed as she bit her lip. I recognized the expression on her face. It meant she had too much to say and didn't know how to get her message across, which rarely happened. The only other time I clearly remember seeing that look directed at me was when I was six and took a bouncy ball home from kindergarten. It was years later that I learned that, at that time, she thought she was a failure as a parent because I didn't understand the fundamental principles of integrity and honesty.

"This pie chart here," my mother began hesitantly after a long silence, tracing a circle into the felt table cover with her forefinger, "represents your time."

At this point, I was thoroughly confused. Rarely has my mother

Reclaim Your Calendar

chosen to use mathematics to prove a point; it just wasn't her forte. It was me, rather, who had such a dominant left-brain that I saw the world around me in numbers and statistics.

"Eighty percent is school work," my mom carefully darkened the majority of her impromptu pie chart.

"Ten percent is the SAT and ten percent is extracurricular activities."

It made sense. I mentally recorded everything my mom was saying.

"But most importantly, at one hundred percent," my mother's voice was starting to shake and she was tracing the circle so furiously that it was starting to look like a shapeless blob, "is your mental health."

I stared at her, a little dumbfounded, because that just didn't make sense. She looked back at me with the same look as when six-year-old me asked why it was wrong to take home the kindergarten's bouncy ball. It was a look that said "Trust me" in the most affectionate way possible.

"Nothing is more important than your health, Aileen. Why do we want you to go to a good university? Because you are more likely to have a good, well-paying career. Why do we want you to get a good job? Because you'll be less stressed if you're financially stable. This, right here, this is not healthy. This is not happy. If you feel so burdened by every little mistake and mishap along the way, then this isn't worth it. If you're happier working flipping burgers, so be it. There's absolutely nothing more important than your physical and mental wellbeing."

Maybe, to another girl in another family, such a lecture was the norm, but not to me. My parents did not immigrate halfway across the globe so I could be healthy. Yet I couldn't help the immense relief I felt in my chest. A rubber band doesn't have to keep stretching. A rubber band that wraps around your hair during the day and is allowed to rest on your nightstand at night won't ever snap.

That night, my mother and I stayed up all night chatting about my plans for the future, yet there was no impending sense of doom. The incessant fear of failure no longer seemed so terrifying.

To an outsider, perhaps nothing changed. I was still the girl who arrived at school at 7:30 a.m. to study before tests and stayed behind

Reclaim Your Calendar | 283

until 5 p.m. to get as much extra help as I could. Yet to me, everything changed. When I received a less-than-satisfactory result, there was no calm façade that crumpled as soon as I was safely hidden in a bathroom stall; there was only me carefully analyzing my mistakes so I could improve in the future.

I'm still reaching for the moon, but I'm no longer afraid. For I know that if I miss, I will land right in my mother's arms.

—Aileen Liang—

Itching for a Change

*Becoming acquainted with yourself is a price
well worth paying for the love that will
really address your needs.*
~Daphne Rose Kingma

I wanted to be a receptionist in a doctor's office when I grew up. As a kid, I played with a blue plastic phone and a calendar, answering the phone with a smile and filling in time slots for patient appointments. Fifty years later I am still filling in my calendar, but my plastic phone has been replaced by an iPhone and as a clinical psychologist I serve as my own receptionist. A vanilla candle on the corner of my desk perfumes the air with a subtle scent as I listen to life stories in forty-five minute intervals — sound bites of love, loss, dreams, and tragedy. Worn green leather chairs cushion our time together. I have a photographic memory for only two things: my patients' lives from one week to the next, and baking recipes.

One Christmas holiday a few years ago, my work stress was intensifying due to the difficulty of cases and the number of clients I chose to see in a day. It was a cold Thursday evening that I sat listening to a young woman recount a horrific car accident she had witnessed the previous night: "She flew through the air as the car careened around the curve and slid off the embankment. I knew it was my neighbor when I saw her red and green socks through my headlights as she hit the pavement. She always wore funny socks with her snow boots."

I drove home holding tight to the steering wheel, snow beginning to fall. As I opened our front door to the smell of baked potatoes, my neck suddenly became hot and itchy.

My daughter asked, "What are all those red spots, Mom?" A warm bath seemed to help but the next week it happened two more times after a long day of work. I realized I was itching for a change. I had to figure out how to simplify and live my next fifty years more peacefully.

Shortening my workweek and seeing fewer patients was only the beginning. More importantly my mid-day is now reserved for someone special whose self-care trumps all others. My blue yoga mat sits regally in the corner of my office, always a reminder of the importance of my own physical, emotional, and spiritual alignment. I steal away to a small yoga studio around the corner. It is my sanctuary where I connect to myself. I need to do that — it's at the core of my ability to help heal and connect with others.

Yoga is like putting on my reading glasses, allowing me to see what is closest to me, which can get blurred when caring for others. When I am centered and balanced, I can better read my patients' stories. A therapist's work is all about change and transition — both our personal growth and that of our clients. The inevitable pain and challenge of our journey is softened in yoga class as we experience a sweet calm in the transition between our in breath and our out breath and from one pose to the next. Standing poses challenge my balance, reminding me of the importance of finding that equanimity in our busy lives. I try to wear clothes that easily travel from one practice to the other, from mat to office, my seams holding the healing energy.

Like the soothing bath on a cold night just a few years ago, I now bathe in the light of daily yoga and meditation to sooth the inevitable rough spots in life. As I meet my true self on the mat I am better able to meet the truth in others. What an honor to hold on to the simplicity of that receptionist job I dreamed of as a child.

— Priscilla Dann-Courtney —

Making Time for Possibilities

Every new day begins with possibilities.
~Ronald Reagan

People needed me so I needed to tick off every item on my holiday checklist. No self-respecting Martha Stewart devotee would get caught dead without a checklist. Mine read like a NASA flight plan.

Do. Do. Do. I was so busy doing for others. With bread dough rising for our church bake-sale and cookie batter calling my name from the fridge, I had to keep moving no matter how exhausted I was. And that's how I landed in a heap at the bottom of the staircase when I was rushing to answer the phone.

The next thing I knew I was pulling myself along the floor inch by inch until I reached that phone. This time the mission was to dial 911.

My husband Joe arrived home from night school just in time to see the paramedics load me into the ambulance. By sunrise the next morning four stainless steel screws held my left leg together and a plaster cast stretched from my knee to my toes. Shattering bones is not for sissies.

No worries about the holidays though. I already had Christmas in the bag. Our tree glistened with soft twinkling lights and shiny glass ornaments while brightly wrapped gifts festooned its base. In the kitchen dozens of home baked cookies awaited distribution to friends and family. Procrastination is for lackluster elves and homemaker rookies. We wouldn't be missing Christmas, despite my broken leg.

What got me concerned though was when I heard the doctor say to Joe, "She'll be laid up for several months." Apparently he missed the memo announcing my status as linchpin of the Universe. When news of this catastrophe rippled through the realm, bedlam would follow. The world getting on without me? Impossible.

I sailed through the first day of my recuperation on a morphine-induced flying carpet ride. Resting comfortably in my hospital bed I could almost hear every bake sale, craft show, church committee, and volunteer project within a ten-mile radius come to a screeching halt. My inability to say "no" had made me a volunteer-recruiter's dream come true.

I always felt like a celebrity at work, church, the local neighborhood association, the nearby grade school, and the county resale shop to benefit the needy. That's the status you get when you're a volunteer junkie.

Now that I was laid up, that was all over. In the care of my parents the days turned into weeks and my mood swings ranged from grumpy to intolerable. How Mom and Dad put up with my insolence for so long I'll never know, but I clearly remember the day when they'd had enough. After one of my particularly surly remarks Mom came into my room, looked me right in the eye and said, with a healthy dose of candor, "Daddy and I are getting a little bored with 'sour-puss' being the recurring flavor of the day around here. You'd better figure out what's ailing you and fix it." Her eyes fixed on me. She meant business! I clenched my jaw and glared right back at her.

"What's wrong with me?" I shrieked, piercing a hole in the silence. I knew darn well what was wrong and so did she. I could no longer hide from the fact that the world marched on without me and never missed a step. No project, charity event or group volunteer effort collapsed without my tireless efforts. And that hurt me, a lot. Oh, how the tears flowed. I don't even know how I put it into words but somehow my mother got the idea and she sat down on the bed with a box of tissues in hand.

"Annie, you fell because you were so exhausted. You spread yourself too thin. You always have and you're not the only person who suffers

Reclaim Your Calendar

from it. It's very nice to feel indispensable. You know what is even nicer? A full night's sleep. Try it some time. If you don't, you'll be no good to anyone. It is possible to find balance, but not without taking a good hard look at what motivates your choices."

Mom delivered a dose of truth that was pretty difficult for me to accept, but deep down I knew she was right. I'd convinced myself over the years that no charitable project would survive to completion without me on the team. What a self-centered notion that was, and one that left me exhausted most of the time.

Through many more months of recuperation I spent considerable time contemplating the possibilities ahead me. I realized that I needed to choose my projects wisely. Along the way I not only stopped feeling sorry for myself, I rediscovered many simple pleasures that had fallen through the cracks. That little chat I had with Mom set me on the right path.

As I neared the end of my recuperation I signed up for a writing course, something I'd always wanted to do. Three days before my first class the phone rang. It was our church secretary. She was thrilled that I would soon be back on my feet. She asked if I would oversee a teen car wash event scheduled for the same day as my writing class.

"I'd love to, but I'm taking a class and I'm not available that day. Thank you so much for thinking of me. Goodbye." And I hung up the phone. I'm sure I sounded nervous, but still, I did it. I had said no. I made a wise choice. I had the power.

I still love volunteering, and work it into my schedule frequently, but I don't allow it to reign supreme in my life. Now I carve out time for me, just to explore the possibilities. Today I am a published author, an avid crocheter, and I play a mean game of *Scrabble*. I read for the sheer pleasure of it and spend many happy hours singing and recording Irish and American folk songs with Joe. I have a balanced life and look forward to every day knowing I will enjoy it rather than endure it. The possibilities are endless.

— Annmarie B. Tait —

No More Overtime

*Work expands so as to fill the time
available for its completion.*
~C. Northcote Parkinson

I sighed at the piles of dishes on the kitchen counter. A quick glance at the clock showed it was almost 8:30. I had just finished putting our daughters, ages two and six, to bed. I desperately wanted to play fairy godmother and wave my magic wand. Poof! Dirty dishes be clean. Poof! Floors be swept. Poof! Laundry be done.

But I'm no fairy godmother, and I certainly don't have a magic wand. No chance of enlisting help from my husband, either. I could hear Derek in the home office, still on the phone scheduling appointments with clients for the next day. There was nothing left to do but tackle the mountain of dishes. But as I fished bits of greasy chicken and mystery food gunk out of the garbage disposal, that familiar and weary discontent returned.

By the time I was wiping the counters, I was shooting furious glances at Derek. He was now relaxing on the couch, watching TV. Couldn't he see how much work remained?

I hinted through gritted teeth, "You know, I sure could use some help in here. Maybe dry these dishes. Or make lunches for school tomorrow."

"Not now, hon. I just sat down. I need a break. I'll help in the morning, okay?"

That was not okay. Couldn't he see I needed a break, too?

"Why don't you join me on the couch, sweetie? We'll finish in the morning."

"I can't. Can't you see how much still needs to get done?"

He gave me a suit-yourself look and went back to flipping through the channels.

I finished in the kitchen and stomped up the stairs. Derek was blissfully (or deliberately) oblivious to my resentment. By the time I was done with the laundry, it was past ten o'clock! So unfair. Yet another late night without a moment of downtime the entire day.

I was about to spit a sarcastic "must be nice" comment Derek's way when I considered maybe, just maybe, he wasn't doing anything wrong. He is a busy real estate agent and works many evenings. To be fair, he deserved a break. He deserved to end his workday.

That's when I had my epiphany: There is no official end to my workday at home. Even if I worked until midnight every night, I still wouldn't get absolutely everything done around the house. So why was I trying? A huge weight lifted as I recognized this futility. What a relief! Since I couldn't get everything done every day, I would just do my best and end my shift at a certain time. Right then I designated 8:30 as a realistic end time to my shift.

The next night looked a little different. After putting the kids to bed, it was already 8:15. Since I only had fifteen minutes until my workday ended, I tackled the kitchen with more enthusiasm than I've ever known. I didn't realize I could load the dishwasher, wash pots and wipe counters with such gusto. All the while I was glancing at the clock: 8:18... 8:24... 8:28 (woo-hoo, only two minutes to go!).

I never got to sweeping the floor or making our daughter's school lunch, but it didn't matter. My relief when I lit a few candles and sat on the couch with a cup of tea was worth it. When Derek came home late from work, he was rewarded with a peaceful, contented wife. No nagging. No stomping. No bitterness. It must have been a relief for him too.

Now I respect my schedule and usually end my shift on time. Nobody seems to care if the floors aren't swept or there's still a pile

Reclaim Your Calendar

of laundry in the morning. Somehow it all gets done eventually. I started delegating jobs to my older daughter, who's great at sorting clean laundry and putting away most of her own clothes. I've become more efficient with my chores, and more forgiving of myself (and my husband) when we don't get them all done.

Turns out I didn't need a magic wand. I just needed to set more realistic expectations and give myself permission to stop working overtime every day. Maybe next I'll start scheduling coffee and lunch breaks too!

— Anita Love —

Chapter
11

Do What You Love

Lisa Things

*Solitude is where I place my chaos to rest
and awaken my inner peace.*
~Nikki Rowe

By the time I was nearing my twentieth birthday, I had grown weary of the small tobacco-farming town where I grew up. I had to get out. Raised thirty minutes from Fort Bragg and having a father who was a career military man ensured that the Army was not a possibility. With not a penny in savings, the promise of life on the water, and its catchy slogan, "Join the Navy and See the World," I packed my bags and headed off for the open water.

Ironically, the only foreign soil I saw was Mexico, while stationed in San Diego, and the farthest I got away from my home was Hawaii. Four and a half years later, I returned to that no-stoplight town with two children and a divorce looming in my very near future.

Shortly after, I reconnected with my old college boyfriend and settled in for the long haul. A part-time job while obtaining my bachelor's degree in education, a husband, mortgage, and three more children that included a set of twins meant never having a free moment to spare or call my own. Five children under the age of seven ensured that my life did not belong to me anymore. A couple more fun-filled, completely chaotic years passed swiftly until a night came that shifted my world.

I sat in my living room... alone. My husband had gone out with his brother. I was supposed to have accompanied them. Arrangements for all five of the children were made for them to stay at different houses. My two oldest were staying at my best friend's house, and the three babies were staying at my parents' house for the night. So there I was, alone in a house that had been so completely filled for so many years, with no one to look after but myself. But what would I do?

My first thought was to hang out with my best friend, but she had a couple of my kids. If I were to go over there, it wouldn't be the escape night I had been hoping for. I thought about visiting my sister, but she had her own family. I could go visit my mom, but she had my other children. I sank back on my sofa and stared into the nothingness surrounding me. There was no one else to call, no one to hang out with who didn't have kids of their own and could get a sitter quickly. For the first time in seven years, I understood how dependent I had become on my family for defining my identity. Without them, I didn't know what to do with myself.

I dialed my parents' house almost in tears, and my mother answered the phone. I explained to her that I hadn't been able to make the trip with my husband so I would come and pick up the babies from her. She asked me to hold on a second, and the voice on the other end was suddenly my father's. He assured me that the kids were all right, and he and my mother were handling things just fine. He nudged me to go out and enjoy my evening, and I started to cry.

"Lisa, just go take a shower and get dressed. Go out and have fun. Go see some of your friends and take the night off."

His voice, so strong and sincere, made me break down even more. I explained my current dilemma, and that none of my friends could get away on such short notice.

"Okay, fine, then just go out and do something." The military tone was starting to creep into his voice.

I didn't want to go out somewhere alone. The club scene hadn't interested me in years, and you never quite understand the meaning of feeling alone until you are surrounded by a packed house of strangers.

Then he said it, "You know what? Just do Lisa things then."

"Lisa things?" I muttered through the sniffles.

"Yes! Lisa things: a hobby, a movie, an interest. Whatever it is that

Do What You Love

you want to do, but don't have time for."

"But I don't know what that is anymore."

"Well, I guess you have tonight to figure that out." Then he hung up. The Command Sergeant Major had given his order, and there was no refuting it.

I stood there a moment, dazed. "Just do Lisa things?"

A realization washed over me, practically drowning me in truth. I had spent ten years taking care of other people, and never having a moment of my own had caused me to lose myself.

That night, I stayed in. Ultimately, I spent hours with pen and paper making lists, pros and cons, journaling, and doodling in the side margins. Through those pages of notes, I began to see a new journey, a new path that I knew I needed to take. I would have to make some changes, and the first would be learning to ask for help.

When I awoke the next day, I made the rounds to retrieve my children. My father met me at the door with a knowing grin spread across his face. "So what did you do last night?"

"Not a whole lot really," I answered in a noncommittal fashion.

"Well, did you find your thing?"

"I'm working on it."

Four years later, the first of many novellas was published. A pressing of my father's thumbprint hangs around my neck with the words "Just do Lisa things" engraved on the back. I only wish that he could have shared that moment with me, as it was his much-needed advice that guided me to pursue my own interests. His words of wisdom helped me to understand that it was okay to be a person with dreams and interests, and still be a good mom, wife, and co-worker.

— Lisa A. Malkiewicz —

Following My Heart

*I don't focus on what I'm up against. I focus on
my goals and I try to ignore the rest.*
~Venus Williams

When I was seventeen years old, I dreamed of becoming a doctor, but my dream seemed unachievable. I am a first-generation American born to Jamaican immigrants, and the first college graduate in my immediate family. My parents instilled in my brother and me the belief that we could become anything we desired as long we worked hard, but I still didn't think that meant I could go all the way to becoming a physician. Perhaps it was because there were no black doctors around me to emulate, or perhaps it was because I didn't like science in school, especially physics, which was almost my undoing.

I decided to attend college in upstate New York and major in accounting. I enjoyed business, and accounting would give me a stable career. That decision led me to the world of investment banking and Wall Street. I had a very good friend with connections at Morgan Stanley and he managed to get me a temporary position on the trading floor when I graduated from college in 1991.

Talk about a different world! I had grown up in Amityvile, a small community on Long Island, and yes, the town featured in *The Amityville Horror*. It's the kind of community where everyone knows each other; I attended school with the same classmates from kindergarten through twelfth grade. We were very close-knit. My exposure to Manhattan,

Do What You Love | 297

forty miles away, was intermittent; my mother used to take my brother and me school shopping there once a year. But each trip increased my love of the city. I just knew that once I graduated from college, I wanted nothing more than to work in exhilarating and sophisticated New York City. And that summer, I got my wish!

Working on the trading floor of Morgan Stanley was exciting but temporary, and my goal was to find a permanent accounting position. I interviewed throughout New York City, and I eventually landed my dream position just six floors above the trading floor in the accounting department.

My eight years at Morgan Stanley and subsequent six years at Citigroup were great. I loved crunching numbers. However, deep down, I knew there was more for me to do. I could not pinpoint why I felt the way I did, but I knew that I possessed the potential to do more. I thought maybe the next step was to become a college professor. During my investment banking career, I obtained an MBA, and I thought the next logical step would be to teach business on a collegiate level. Then my father died, in June 2000.

His death was a seminal event. As previously noted, my parents told me I could do anything I wanted, but it was my father who gave me confidence. He had such high aspirations for his children. He used to say, "Randi, first you will get your bachelor's, then a master's, and then you will get your doctorate." I never paid any attention to him at that time, but somehow he instilled something in me.

Once he was gone, I knew, perhaps on a subconscious level, it was time to do more. Then, 9/11 occurred, just five blocks away from my office. After watching the destruction unfold that day, I realized that I needed purpose. Working as an investment banking accountant could be grueling at times; there were many times we would work on holidays or late on weeknights. I decided that if my work was going to take important time away from being with my family, it should at least be for a good reason.

Within a year, I was enrolled in pre-med classes at a local college. Somehow, I managed to work full-time and take courses such as Biology, Organic Chemistry and, yes, Physics! I aced my courses. Soon after, I took the Medical College Admission Test, the dreaded MCAT. My grades and MCAT scores were sufficient for admission to Stony Brook University School of Medicine.

I loved medical school, but it was challenging. When I enrolled in August 2005, I was thirty-five years old. There was only one student older than me. Medical school was a challenge, but I persevered and graduated on time. I went on to do my residency in pediatrics, which also was not a walk in the park.

When I decided to change careers, I knew I would be a pediatrician. I loved children and wanted my career to involve molding and guiding their health and wellbeing. I'm now a board-certified pediatrician serving the most vulnerable population of my community, back in Brooklyn where I was born. Yes, I made some major sacrifices, but I could not be happier.

If only my daddy could see me now.

— Randi Nelson —

Escaping Insomnia

If you do what you love, it is the best way to relax.
~Christian Louboutin

I honestly don't know why I set up the painting table. Even as I put out the paints and brushes, I felt foolish. I was a single parent, pedaling fast to take care of my four kids. I had no family nearby to help and little extra time after work and the kids' sports.

Even after I set up the table in our kitchen, we all knew I wasn't going to paint. It just wasn't going to happen. And it didn't.

All my days were the same. I got up, hustled the kids off to school, went to work, and then picked them up, fitting dinner in around their karate, softball and soccer. At the end of the day, I fell into bed exhausted.

Then the insomnia returned. I found myself wandering around the house at three in the morning. With nothing to watch on television, I cleaned the floors, made the kids' lunches, and tried to catch up on chores. By the end of the week, my checkbook was balanced, and the chores were done. That's when the painting table became more than a rectangular object taking up space in the kitchen. It seemed to call out to me.

I tried to ignore it. I told myself there were other things to do. But in those blurry hours when I should have been asleep, painting seemed like as good an idea as any. It was something to occupy my mind until maybe I could go back to sleep.

One night, I sat down, grabbed my brushes and painted. I did the same thing the following night, and then again, until a week had flown by. Most nights, I never went back to sleep, so it was easy to be dressed and ready for work before the kids got up. Every morning, I returned the brushes to their proper places and put my paints away. One morning — I must have been painting for two or three weeks by then — I sat down at the dining-room table and listened to the kids chatter as they finished their breakfast.

One of my girls turned to me. "Hey, Mom, you're nicer when you paint."

Before I could respond, another spoke up. "Yeah. Nicer."

At first, I was surprised that they'd even noticed. The painting table had become just another piece of furniture taking up space. Then my head swirled as I absorbed their words. Nicer? Did that mean I wasn't nice the rest of the time? My stomach flip-flopped as I pondered the implication. I wasn't a good mom — I was mean. My heart sank as I fought back the tears.

Finally, with a shaky voice, I asked, "So, I'm not nice normally?"

A chorus of voices followed, each child offering up his or her thoughts and explaining what they meant. Somehow, they'd noticed that I had been painting regularly, but they'd also noticed a change in me that I was unaware of.

Painting made me happy. They'd seen that and wanted me to know. Trying to ease my insomnia by filling the time with painting, I'd stumbled on a secret to taking care of me — just by letting my creative self come out of hiding.

And now, when days get long, work is too busy, and life wants to swallow me whole again, I can still hear their voices telling me how much nicer I am when I paint. They'd discovered something I might never have recognized: Doing what I like, even in small doses on a regular basis, is important. It makes me happy.

— Debby Johnson —

My Own Beat

> *Find what makes your heart sing
> and create your own music.*
> ~Mac Anderson

My pulse quickens as my feet take me closer and closer to the door. In my head, I can hear the words my kids keep telling me, "Do it, Mom. You never do anything for yourself. Just go set it up." I feel my lungs fill with air and release it.

What are you doing here? You're a single mom of five. You're fifty years old! My thoughts fight with my kids' words. Even so, it is as if I have no control over my feet. As if they are being urged along from somewhere deep inside me.

The minute I step into the house, my kids yell, "Did you do it?" Then they see the drumsticks in my hand. They start jumping up and down and then come hug me.

Wednesday comes, and along with it my first drum lesson. I walk through the door and head directly to the seating area in the back. My hands keep fidgeting with the sticks. I keep nervously looking at the time. I try to slow down my breath. I know the teacher will say I'm not the right type of person to play the drums. I turn around to see an older man looking at me.

"Stephanie? I'm Mike, the drum teacher," he says.

He leads me to a room about the size of a large walk-in closet. There are two drum sets, and he tells me to sit at the one closest to the door.

People make me nervous. That's the way I've always been. But Mike has a very calm manner about him, so I relax just slightly. Not only does he not tell me that I am the wrong type of person to play the drums, but he compliments me on how well I hold the sticks and follow along with him. I learn how to read a couple of simple sheets of music, but then my thirty-minute lesson is over.

Walking back to my car, I feel this energy beaming from within me. After taking care of kids and my family since I was twenty-two, it feels scary and amazing at the same time to do something that is purely for my enjoyment, something just for me.

With my practice pad set on top of a bucket in the living room, I practice as much as I can throughout the week. My fourteen-year-old daughter often complained that I never sat down with them, that I was always working around the house. But now with my lesson to practice, I finally sit down with them, talking as I practice my drumming. My second lesson comes, and I play the sheets of music for Mike.

I notice as I play that Mike's concentration becomes more and more apparent. When I finish the whole lesson without stopping, Mike says, "You played that perfectly!" He sounds amazed.

I explain, "Being a mom of five, I am used to moving and doing a lot. But now that my kids are getting older, and two have moved out on their own, drumming gives me something to focus that energy on. I find myself sitting for hours going through the rhythms."

After one week of lessons, I acquire a four-piece used Mapex Orion set. The guy who sold it to me used to tour with some big names and only sold it because he needed money to pay child support. It is big and very loud. I am, by nature, a quiet person — I work at the library — so it seems contradictory for me to pick drumming as something just for me. But I find as I sit in front of my set and beat out rhythms, something sensational happens. I become so focused on the drums that it is as if my expression of who I am comes out with every beat and rhythm. I am not nervous, shy, and quiet. I am a drummer.

As the weeks turn into months of playing, Mike convinces me to play at a blues jam where his band hosts the open mic.

"I'm so nervous. What will I do? What will I play?" I ask.

"You'll be fine. I've seen your self-confidence grow, and I see so much potential in you. It will be a simple beat that you know," he tells me.

How many times have I driven my kids to their competitions and watched proudly as they bravely went in front of judges and audiences? But driving myself to the jam, I realize I'm the one who has to be brave. For an hour, as my teacher's band plays the opening act for the night, thinking of my kids helps me to find strength within me. Clutching my sticks in my hands, I go over and over in my head what I need to play. Soon, it will be my turn.

My teacher goes up to the mic and makes the announcement. He says, "We have a special treat tonight. Stephanie will be on the drums for her first time playing with others and in front of people."

Walking up on the small stage, I inhale deeply and sit at the drum set. As I do, I look up and see that everyone has gotten up to watch me play. It is a little unusual for a woman to play the drums, but that is not all.

I am also a Muslim woman wearing the hijab (head scarf). It is a rare sight to see a Muslim woman playing the drums in hijab.

Facing me, Beau starts playing "Put on Your Red Dress" on his guitar, and soon I join in to keep the beat.

"A little faster," Beau says.

I speed up the beat; he smiles and nods at me.

I miss the first stop, but by the next one I get it. This is great! What a rush I feel when we finish, and everyone is clapping and cheering for me. I did it!

— Stephanie Doerr —

Self-Care Found in a Library Basement

The world was hers for the reading.
~Betty Smith

For the better part of the last decade, I've been a housewife. A mommy. An aspiring chef. A homeschooling teacher. A student. A founder of an organization for grieving parents. A querying novelist who usually wakes up to rejection notices.

I'm exhausted.

This year, I decided to make things easier. I got on a cleaning schedule so I wouldn't always feel behind. I gave myself time in the morning to brush my hair, shower, brush teeth, and get out of sweats or pajamas. Moisturize my face. Perhaps even paint my nails.

It worked great. For a week. Maybe two.

Then I realized that doing those things weren't my version of self-care. They were just personal chores to feel presentable. Picking out clothes, brushing hair, and moisturizing my face weren't calming. It was physical self-care, but I needed more. I needed mental and emotional self-care, too.

I started reading at night. It was my personal time to forget everything but the fictional world I was sinking into. But I was so exhausted from the day that I'd read two pages and fall asleep. If I managed longer, a dog would bark for attention. A cat would scratch at the door until

Do What You Love

I let it in. A kid would wake up and need to go potty. Relaxing? Not quite. Each time I brought a mug of chamomile tea to bed, it always went cold before I could enjoy it.

With kids home all day, being a one-car family, and working at home, I couldn't find anywhere that made me feel relaxed. My anxiety levels rose. Stress dreams caused me to grit my teeth, make my jaw sore, and tear up my mouth. I never felt rested when I woke. Even with a schedule, there were always more things I didn't do that weighed heavily on me. Should I have read the kids one more story when they begged for it? Did I have enough patience? Did I slow down and stop the endless chores to give them enough attention today? Did I remember to enjoy them enough, as time is so fleeting?

Then one of my personal favorite days of the year arrived — my library's giant book sale, where I usually come home with no less than a hundred books. I never missed the event — not for pouring rain, lack of vehicle, or a babysitter who calls last minute to say she can't make it. No matter what, I found a way to get there and be first in line. This year, miraculously, there was nothing standing in my way.

My husband and I were first in line with an hour to wait as the workers chatted in front of us. Then they said this was the last year. After more than twenty-five years, the people who ran it would be retiring. No one had stepped up to take their place. Certain that I had heard wrong, I glanced at the flyer, but there it was — where the announcement for next year's book sale date was, I saw a blank spot.

"This can't be the last year," I said to my husband. "I've been coming here for more than half my life!"

"You should do it," my husband said, pushing me forward with his elbow.

The idea instantly made me excited. Working at the library had been a lifelong dream. But instead of signing up, I laughed. "I can't do that," I said, rolling my eyes. "What about the kids? I'm already too busy. I can't stretch myself any further than I already am. This is a huge job, especially for one person."

"We could figure something out. You'd be perfect for this."

One of the leaders of the book sale walked over to check the long

Do What You Love

line. It was nearly time to let everyone in. I looked over my shoulder. So much of the community had turned out for this event.

"My wife is interested in volunteering to run the book sale," I heard my husband say.

I sent daggers at him with my eyes. As an introverted, shy person, I hated the attention I suddenly had when everyone surrounded me.

"You would?" one exclaimed. "Come with me. I'll introduce you to everyone before the sale starts."

I hadn't said a word yet, but my hand was being pulled, and I was being introduced to the team.

"Could you start on Thursday? We'll get you down to the basement where we keep all the books, and you can start sorting. We'll teach you how to do it. You could come down maybe two or three times a week to do it."

Two or three times a week? But the idea of seeing the library's basement, going into a place that was always locked, intrigued me too much to back out. One meeting couldn't hurt anyway, right? I'd give it a go.

The excitement of the book sale dimmed as this new prospect invaded my mind. I could finally work for the library. I could touch all the books. I'd be the one to choose which books went into the book sale. The event that I loved dearly would be mine to run.

Suddenly, I couldn't wait. The nervous part of my mind quieted as the eager part took over. For the next several days, it was all I could think about.

On Thursday, when I met the team, the nervous part vanished. I loved my role. I loved the team of library volunteers. I loved the basement that made my nose runny and needed a constant loud dehumidifier, with frequently damp floors from excess rain. I loved every single part of it.

I had been scared that it would be too much and take away time for the self-care that I desperately needed.

Instead, it became my mental self-care. Three times a week, first thing in the morning, I do my physical self-care chores. I get dressed, brush my hair and teeth, and put on my shoes. I say goodbye to my

Do What You Love

family and walk three and a half blocks to the library, where I say hello to the librarian and unlock the basement door. Once there, I get an hour or two all to myself. No one is there, just me and books. I spend the time in solitude around some of my favorite things in the world. I sort the books into boxes, looking through them and removing cute bookmarks to take home.

Getting alone time out of the house, in the place I've loved since I was eleven years old, and handling hundreds of books at a time, has become the perfect self-care I never knew I needed. By taking on the library job, I get a peaceful start to my day. Relaxed. Excited. On the days I don't go, I'm eager to wake up the next day and think about what amazing books are waiting for me.

I always heard that self-care looks different for everyone. Mine just happens to look like a hundred-year-old, dingy library basement covered in books.

—Jill Keller—

The Six Months Test

Your purpose should dictate how you spend your time.
~Brenda Johnson Padgitt

I stare out the window at the first roses of the season. Even their exquisite beauty doesn't register with me. Self-diagnosis reveals that I have a huge case of the "overwhelms."

Since I've retired, I've taken on too many activities to fill my so-called discretionary time. The result is that I have no time for myself — to finish reading the novel I started two months ago, go to lunch with a friend, or sometimes even return phone calls. My mild depression is certainly not life-threatening, but I can see no change for my schedule in the foreseeable future!

Where does my time go? At the end of the day, can I even account for my activities?

I somehow find the common sense to deal with this. I decide to evaluate what I would do if I only had six months to live. It's The Six Months Test. I make a list of all my activities other than those that involve my husband and home. It's a hodge-podge:

Tutoring
Babysit grandchildren
Church choir
Testing for a commercial college
Bible study
Sunday school helper

Writing
Writers' critique groups

Then I analyze it. What makes my heart sing? Where is my unique competence? What am I particularly suited for? Why am I doing some things and not doing others?

My determined focus is kids, and more specifically, writing for kids. With that in mind I put a "K" by all items that have to do with kids in my life, and an "A" by all activities that have to do primarily with adults. That helps me see if my activities are really in line with my stated focus.

There are other things to consider, too. Do I need income from any of my activities? Is the remuneration I receive from an activity enough to warrant my involvement? As a writer, I find that some projects take an enormous amount of my time and the pay isn't commensurate with the effort. So unless I write fast, ten cents a word will not make me rich.

Will an activity keep me in touch with the significant people in my life or will it hinder quality relationships? Will I still have time to do the things that keep love alive in my marriage?

Does an activity harmonize with my current interests or will it take me in an entirely unrelated direction? For example, I have been asked to collect donations in my neighborhood, and to help with costumes for the church play. Are these really things I would do if I had six months to live?

Probably the most important question I ask is, "Which of my commitments could others carry out if necessary? Which can only I meet?"

If I learned I had only six months to live, here's what I decided to keep on my list:

1. I would babysit. These are my grandchildren. We've mixed cookies together sitting on a beach towel on the kitchen floor. We make Play-Doh food to use in the playhouse, we rake leaf-houses together, and carve roads in the dirt. We have a mutual love affair going.

2. I would tutor. My remedial students have begun to like reading. Often, I am their number one fan. Of course, someone else could teach them, but no one can give them exactly what I do. Our interaction is unique, so I'd keep them as long as I could.
3. I would continue attending my Bible study class. I can study alone. I do, and I find it rewarding, but I would need the prayer support of the class members during my final six months.
4. I'd write because I must. God called me to take my life-long love of Bible stories and write them in simple and exciting ways for little children. It is my passion in life.

So, I have four things that passed The Six Months Test. Interestingly, these are identical to those I perceived as mine alone to do.

I put down my pen and slowly rock in my chair, processing my next steps. Because my mind has shifted off my pressure pile and onto my priorities and passions, this was time well spent. I can now grant myself permission, with certainty, to cut some activities at their logical termination points, and sever the cord immediately on others.

That simple test was just the attitude adjustment I needed. Now I can step outside into the sunshine and begin enjoying those first roses of the season.

— Pauline Youd —

Awakened by the Creator Within

*Don't die with your music still inside.
Listen to your intuitive inner voice
and find what passion stirs your soul.*
~Wayne Dyer

It was almost midnight on a cold winter night. I had just finished nursing my newborn son. I swaddled him in his blue and white blanket and placed him, protected from the world, in his bassinette near my bed.

I headed to the laundry room and put my son's tiny clothes in the dryer. How could one little baby create so much laundry? I finished the dinner dishes. On the way back to my bedroom, I checked on my two-and-a-half-year-old daughter, who was sleeping peacefully in her new big girl bed. Exhausted, I kissed her on the cheek and headed back to my room.

When I peeked at my son, his eyelids were fluttering. A smile flashed across his face. As I watched him dreaming, I thought about my life and my own dreams that seemed so long ago.

I kissed my sleeping husband good night and snuggled under the covers. Staying home with my children, nurturing them, and watching them grow was something I had always longed for. But during these pensive moments, I felt something deep stirring inside me. I could hear my creative soul whispering to me: "Remember your dreams. You

Do What You Love

promised yourself you would paint and write when you took time off from teaching to stay home with your children."

My saboteur within quickly chimed in: "You are too busy to do this. After all, you have two children and a husband who need you. You have laundry, cleaning, food shopping and an endless list of things to do. You don't have time to create and besides there is no money in art. Don't be selfish."

The seed for my dream of painting and writing was planted at a very young age. My mom was an avid reader who took my siblings and me to the library on a weekly basis. I fell in love with picture books from the very start. Sketching every character and making up stories in my imagination, I secretly dreamed of writing and illustrating a children's book. Now, my saboteur was trying to talk me out of it.

I listened to her and let her put an end to my foolish dream. I threw myself wholeheartedly into motherhood. I loved nurturing my children's minds and hearts, exploring nature with them and teaching them about their five senses. I also taught them to listen to the promptings of their most important sense of all — their intuition. Like my mom did, I took them to the library on a weekly basis. Once there, I got lost in the world of books again. I think I read every children's book in the library to my daughter. I also started a journal for each child and recorded our memories and their exciting milestones.

I was having fun, but still there were times when I felt my dream stirring deep inside me. I could hear my soul whispering to me in a powerful yet faint voice: "You must paint and write."

One day I was dusting my bookshelf. *The Artist's Way* by Julia Cameron, a book I had read several years earlier, caught my eye. I opened it and the first thing my eyes saw was a quote by Carl Jung: "Nothing has a stronger influence psychologically on their environment and especially on their children than the unlived life of a parent."

"Aha," I thought. Following my dream wasn't just for me. It was not selfish. I needed to listen to my dream so that my children would be able to listen to their own dreams. I realized I couldn't live my life through them. It wasn't good for anyone.

Still I tried to ignore my creative soul by keeping busy. The war

Do What You Love

inside me grew bigger, so big that I felt like I was going to explode. One morning, as I was in my walk-in closet getting dressed, it felt like my closet was closing in on me. I heard a faint yet powerful voice, which I later learned was my courageous inner warrior, state, "You must paint or drink heavily." I knew I had to make a choice. That day I called a local art center and signed up for an art class. I have been painting and writing ever since.

I am living my dream and modeling for my children that they must listen to their own. That is my gift to them.

— Christine Burke —

From Plumbing to Prose

If you put yourself in a position where you have to stretch outside your comfort zone, then you are forced to expand your consciousness.
~Les Brown

For most of my adult life, I worked as a plumber. But by my mid-forties, after surgery on both shoulders and years of chronic back and knee pain, I realized it was time for a career change.

This was easier said than done. I was a middle-aged master plumber with no college degree and a lack of marketable skills. That's how it seemed to me anyway. My wife saw things differently.

"How about becoming a writer?" she asked one evening.

"A few short stories published in small literary magazines doesn't make me a writer," I replied. "Besides, I make more in an hour of plumbing than I have for all of my short stories combined."

Undeterred, she said, "There are other types of writing. I think you're talented enough to do it."

Well, that made one of us. But because my wife is usually right, I started searching online for writing jobs where I could utilize my knowledge of plumbing. I honestly had no idea these types of jobs were even out there, but I soon began writing home-improvement and plumbing articles for a couple of content mills. These companies were

Do What You Love | 315

sort of the bottom of the barrel and the pay was low, but it was a start and gave me a few writing credits to put on my resumé.

From there I moved on to freelancing for a couple of online HVAC (heating, ventilation, and air conditioning) companies. The pay was better and the work steadier. I still wrote the occasional short story, and even self-published several novels and a series of Maine humor books.

About a year ago, I wrote an essay about my son's high school graduation and submitted it to a parenting blog. It was accepted for publication and led to my having more than twenty essays published on various parenting blogs in less than a year. This was yet another market that I had never paid attention to. I expect it to continue because my sons give me a lot of material to work with.

This is a direction I never saw my life taking. In three years, I've gone from working as a master plumber to writing parenting posts. When I tell people who haven't seen me in a while what I'm doing now, they look at me in disbelief. I don't blame them; sometimes I don't believe it myself. I'd like to say I took the leap of my own accord, but it was a combination of injury and my wife's belief that drew me into writing as a career. Looking back, it's a move I wish I'd made much earlier in life. If only we all had a crystal ball. It just proves that some of the best things in life are unexpected.

There have been many benefits to such a drastic career change. The pain in my back and shoulders is greatly reduced. I don't come home from work every day complaining about sore muscles and cuts and burns on my hands. I no longer wrap my arms around toilets more often than I wrap them around my wife. And, best of all, I now work from home and get to spend more time with my family.

Of course, it's not all peaches and cream. It's been a little difficult financially, and I still don't make nearly as much money from writing as I did plumbing. But overall the pros far outweigh the cons, and I can happily say I'm the only person I know who's gone from being a plumber to a writer.

— Gary Sprague —

Warm and Familiar

Pearls don't lie on the seashore.
If you want one, you must dive for it.
~Chinese Proverb

After my mom died, I realized I had broken my two promises to her: One, that she wouldn't die alone, and two, that I would live life to the fullest. I failed miserably with the first promise, and as for the second one — to live life fully — how many of us actually do that? How many of us take risks and dare to color outside the lines?

We all have responsibilities, so when I told my mother that I would live my life to the fullest, deep down a part of me knew it was a lie. In fact, I was numb after she died. I had two small children, and each day I went through the motions of being a normal human being, but I knew I was a shell.

I worked as an assistant in a prison, and every night I came home to my family and little apartment in the city. It wasn't much, but the rent was affordable. And although the sounds and smells of city life rose up from the streets, our home was decorated like a cabin on a faraway beach. Seaside paintings covered our walls, seashells became centerpieces, and we even had a little wooden sign that said, "Beach Life."

I spent my days craving a new life while I kept fulfilling my responsibilities.

Unfortunately, those responsibilities involved a lot of despair. My

Do What You Love

office was set in the health care wing of the prison. Inmates would come and go for everything from spider bites to withdrawal symptoms. I met one inmate who was handsome in a rough sort of way. He always had an air of sadness about him, even though he said optimistic things. He would tell me of the mistakes he had made and that, above all else, he wanted a fresh start in life. He wanted to live clean. He wanted to see the sun rise again, eat a mango on the beach, and kiss a girl in the back seat of his convertible. Most of the guys there talked about big hopes and dreams, but I usually didn't believe them. This guy, however, seemed like he had a solid plan beyond eating mangoes. And this guy, unlike all the others, seemed to know what he had done wrong and was willing to fix himself.

I was happy for him the day he was released. He had made himself a promise that he was going to make changes, and he swore he would never see me again.

When he left, I felt a pang of something. Sadness? Jealousy? Although I could leave anytime I wanted, I was still drawn back to this haunting place that stayed with me, even when I left. I envied the inmates who would leave and never come back.

I continued however, doing the same thing every day. I went to work, and then returned to my cramped little apartment and dreamed of a different life while sitting among my seashell centerpieces.

One day, I had friends over for dinner. It was no big deal. No birthday festivities. No big party. Just a few friends enjoying each other's company and a bottle of wine. We laughed and joked about plans for the summer.

One of my friends said, "Who cares what we plan? This apartment is as close as Erin will ever get to the beach."

She and the others laughed, and I smiled while I seethed inside — mostly because I knew she was right. I knew that I had given up really living.

I went back to work — to the lockdowns, red suits and cinder-block walls with only tiny windows to let in the light. Would it be so bad just living as I was? I had a steady job and a roof over my head. And even though some nights the traffic would keep us up, we were

| Do What You Love

fine with it. We had gotten used to it.

And then I saw him standing with a few fellow inmates, laughing as they awaited their time to go outside in the yard.

It was *him*, and watching him laugh tore at my heart. Seeing him back inside was devastating.

I stood there for what felt like hours and watched him be carefree despite the fact that he was once again caged. When he noticed me, he smiled and waved, and then he walked over to say "hi," grinning from ear to ear.

"When did you get back in?" I asked.

"A few days now," he said. "Ya miss me?"

"I just thought I'd never see you again."

He shrugged then and leaned in a bit closer to me.

"My life is crap," he said. "Total crap. I'm swimming in crap twenty-four hours a day. But here's the thing: It might be crap, but it's my crap. All of it. And the crazy thing about crap is that even though it stinks, it's warm, isn't it? Warm and familiar."

And that was that, wasn't it? The truth behind why he and everyone else on the planet stay in their ruts and routines. Why we avoid risks and never color outside the lines. Because, even if we're sitting in crap, it's our crap, and it's warm and familiar.

My little talk with him changed me that day. I decided that my mother's death, although gut wrenching, was a powerful reminder of how precious life is, and we shouldn't be wasting even a second of it. I decided it was time to step out of my pile of crap and move on. I quit my job without knowing where I would be going afterward, and I packed up our belongings and moved to the beach.

It was a good step toward living a life I truly wanted. I didn't know what I was doing or where I was going, but at least I was doing it with an ocean view.

— Erin Hazlehurst —

Loving My Inner Child

You yourself, as much as anybody in the entire universe, deserve your love and affection.
~Buddha

A friend brought clothes over to my house. "I was cleaning out my closet and thought you could use these clothes."

"Thanks," I said. After she left, I searched through the bag. The clothes were clean, but faded, and the wrong size for me. I kept a couple of shirts that kind of fit, and donated the rest.

It wasn't long before yet another friend came over. "I have too many clothes," she said. "I thought you might need them."

Again I gracefully accepted them. Again, most were too big, but I kept some more shirts.

A couple months later, another friend showed up. "I lost weight and had to buy a new wardrobe. I thought these might fit you."

"Thanks," I said. My reflection in the mirror showed I had gained some weight. Did my friend think I was fat?

My friends were good people. But why were they always giving me their used clothes? I looked in the mirror at my typical outfit of jeans and an old shirt. I rarely ever bought myself anything new.

My priority was always my four children. I would give up everything so they could have voice lessons, dance lessons and money for a school trip. But me — I was their mom. That was my identity. I was the one who sacrificed, who took care of everyone else but me.

On a typical day I would berate myself. "I am so ugly and fat. I can't do anything right. I am a big nothing." These words ran through my head in a constant, negative tape that would never stop playing.

"No one loves me. Life stinks. I never have enough money. No one cares." I was a victim in life. I was a martyr. I was the one who sacrificed for everyone else so that my children could succeed. That was my job, wasn't it? Isn't that what moms were supposed to do, put themselves last? Moms were the ones who took the smallest piece of meat at the table and ate the ruined egg for breakfast. Moms were the ones who cleaned up the messes in life. Moms were the ones who told their children they could do amazing things. It was wonderful to watch your family living their dreams. So why wasn't I happy?

Because of me, my children excelled. Because of my sacrifices, the household ran smoothly. Yet, why wasn't I content?

Why, when I vented to my friends about how much I sacrificed, did they suddenly go silent and have to hang up the phone to answer the door? One by one, people began to get too busy to listen to me complain. I was a victim in life, and I desperately craved attention and validation for my martyrdom. Didn't the Bible say to love others more than yourself?

Then one day it dawned on me. It didn't. The Bible said to love others *as* yourself. I realized this one day and it floored me when the sad truth was revealed. I loved my family a lot, but I didn't love me. I constantly berated myself and said horrible things to myself that I would never dream of saying to anyone else.

One day I looked at my reflection. I thought of the little girl inside me who once had dreams of her own. I never did anything for her, not even setting aside a few dollars to buy her a new outfit. The cruel things I said to her on a daily basis were appalling. I would never dream of giving her singing lessons or sending her to a good college. I had given up on this little girl a long time ago. She felt sad and unloved.

It was then I realized I could change things. I had the power to change my life completely. Nothing was stopping me except for my biggest obstacle — me. My children were grown and happy and didn't

Do What You Love

need my constant fussing over them anymore.

I started loving the little girl inside me as much as I loved my own children. I stopped saying mean things to her. I looked at my reflection and said all the inspiring and nice things to me that I had said to my own confident children.

I changed "You're ugly" into "You're beautiful." I changed "Nothing good ever happens to me" to "Great things happen to me." I changed "I never win anything" into "I am a winner." I changed "I never have enough money" to "I have more money than I could ever need." I changed "I can't" to "I can." In the beginning it felt forced and fake, but after a while, as I kept repeating these new affirmations to myself, it became easy.

Miracles began happening. I faced my fears and chased after my dreams. I allowed myself to further my education, to work at losing weight, to pursue my career goals, and to buy myself some new outfits, without guilt. Soon, I was managing money better and rebuilding my life. Whenever I reached out to do something for myself, I found the resources to do it. Obstacles disappeared. It was amazing.

I stopped complaining about life, and soon my friends didn't mind talking to me again. Some of them actually looked forward to my phone calls. One of my friends gave me the highest compliment. She said I inspired her. Some of my fondest dreams were realized. When I graduated college in my forties, my children were proud of me. My success inspired my daughters even more.

And then, one day, I noticed that people weren't offering me their hand-me-downs anymore. They asked me where I bought the pretty dress I was wearing. The little girl inside me smiled. I was finally taking care of her too.

— L.A. Strucke —

Meet Our Contributors

Monica A. Andermann lives and writes on Long Island where she shares a home with her husband Bill and their little tabby, Samson. Her work has been included in such publications as *Sasee*, *Guideposts*, *Woman's World* and in several other *Chicken Soup for the Soul* books as well.

Joan Bailey is a freelance writer currently living in Japan where her work focuses on food, farming, and farmers' markets. She lives near the mountains with her husband and two cats.

Temeka S. Bailey is a licensed clinical social worker with several years of experience serving children. families, and communities impacted by trauma. She received a bachelor's degree in social work from Bowie State University, a master's in social work from University of Maryland, and a PhD in social work from Morgan State University. Temeka enjoys spending time with her family in addition to reading, swimming, biking and running.

Carole Harris Barton, author of *Rainbows in Coal Country* and *When God Gets Physical*, is retired after a career in government service. Her stories have appeared in *Chicken Soup for the Soul: Dreams and Premonitions* and *Mysterious Ways* magazine. She is a widowed mother and grandmother who lives in Dunedin, FL.

Bonnie L. Beuth received her Bachelor of Science degree, with honors, in Computer Information Systems. She works in the legal industry in Learning and Development and owns an international company she co-founded called LTC4. Bonnie is actively involved with the Booth Photography Guild and the Southeastern Photography

Society in her spare time.

Tamra Anne Bolles received her Bachelor of Arts in Journalism from the University of Georgia in 1988 and Master of Education from Georgia State University in 2000. She retired from Cobb County Schools after thirty years. She enjoys kayaking, hiking and dreaming about her very own cabin in Blue Ridge, Georgia.

Veronica Bowman is a poet and writer. She and her husband share their country home with their much-loved rescue dogs, cats, and chickens. She enjoys reading, gardening, and cooking.

Elaine L. Bridge is a happily retired former forester, stay-at-home mom, and grocery store cashier, grateful for the freedom now to plan her own days and enjoy life with her pets, three grown sons and their families.

Christine Burke is an artist, author, and health coach passionate about creativity and wellness. A former teacher with a master's in reading, she now teaches art, health, and writing. She studied under Brandywine artist Karl Kuerner and is a certified health coach. She has published three books, most recently *Create Your World*.

Nicole Caratas is a junior at Saint Mary's College in Notre Dame, IN. She is studying English Writing and Humanistic Studies and serves as the Saint Mary's editor for *The Observer* and the contributing editor for the *Saint Mary's Odyssey*. She enjoys reading, writing, history, good music, puppies, and donuts.

Rachel Chustz lives in Louisiana with her husband and three children. She loves reading, writing, music, and playing Mahjong. This is Rachel's fourth contribution to the *Chicken Soup for the Soul* series. She is also the author and illustrator of the children's book, *The Bubble's Day at LSU*. E-mail her at rachelchustz@gmail.com.

According to **Courtney Conover**, self-care is indulging in a long, piping-hot bath every Sunday afternoon. She's the author of the Amazon book series, *Confessions*, and also co-authored the novel *AI Turf* with her husband, Scott, a former NFL lineman. She resides in the Midwest. Visit her online at courtneyconover.com.

Billy Cuchens is the father of five through transracial foster and domestic newborn adoption. He lives with his family in Texas.

Ceil Ryan D'Acquisto is a wife, mom and nana of six living in the Midwest. After retiring from her nursing career, she started writing and blogging full-time. In 2019, Ceil received a certificate in spiritual direction and is currently serving as a spiritual director. Ceil enjoys spending time in nature, swimming, music and with family.

Ashley Dailey has always had a passion for working with children and a desire for all children to be comfortable in their own skin. She has a Bachelor of Science in Early Childhood Education and is the director of a childcare center. She enjoys the outdoors and creating new adventures with her own three children.

Priscilla Dann-Courtney is a writer and clinical psychologist and lives in Colorado where she and her husband raised their three children. Her columns have appeared in numerous national publications and her book, *Room to Grow* (Norlights Press, 2009), was her way to navigate the light, dark, and wonder of the world. Learn more at priscilladanncourtney.com.

Michele Ivy Davis is a freelance writer and photographer. Her stories and articles have appeared in a variety of magazines, newspapers, and law enforcement publications, and her debut novel, *Evangeline Brown and the Cadillac Motel*, received national and international awards. Learn more at MicheleIvyDavis.com.

Linda C. Defew writes from her home in Salem, KY. She started her own writers' group in 2009 with five people, which has grown to ten. They critique as well as inspire other writers to keep on keeping on. E-mail her at oldest@tds.net.

Stephanie Doerr received her Bachelor of Science in 1993 from Metropolitan State University. As a mother of five, she has homeschooled through high school. She currently works as a material handler at the library system in Colorado and enjoys playing the drums in her free time.

Britteny Elrick attended Regents College in London, England, where she began her freelance writing career. She is a business owner and aspiring author of non-fiction books. Britteny cannot resist: a sense of humor, anything Italian, confidence, or sweatpants. Or cupcakes. Learn more at www.wordsbybrit.com.

Meet Our Contributors

Molly England is a writer and therapist passionate about mental health and personal growth. Her work appears in *The Washington Post*, *HuffPost*, *Salon*, and the *Chicken Soup for the Soul* series. Connect with her on Instagram @willowofwellnesscoaching and visit willowofwellness.com.

Holly English is the author of several novels. She is the mother of three grown children who are practically perfect and the grandmother of four grandchildren who are definitely perfect. She is currently writing a western novel titled *Regret*.

Tanya Estes spent most of her career as a librarian and bookseller. Now she is a writer who delights in experiencing her son's enchanted world each time he says "Fee Fi Fo Fum" while climbing a tree. You can find her little family hiking through the woods of central Texas.

Kim Forrester is an award-winning author, holistic well-being educator and consultant. Kim blends science with spiritual philosophy to inspire fullness of living. She is the host of the Eudaemonia podcast, interviewing world-class experts about the traits and practices that allow us to flourish in life. Learn more at www.kimforrester.net.

Betsy S. Franz is an award-winning writer and photographer specializing in nature, wildlife, the environment, and human relationships. Her articles and photos reflecting the wonders of life have been published in numerous books and magazines. She lives in Florida with her husband Tom. Learn more at www.naturesdetails.net.

Kristin Goff is a retired journalist, grandmother of five, plodding runner and outdoor enthusiast (when she can force herself off the sofa). She enjoys traveling, trying new things and is grateful for the support of friends and family, who may laugh with her but not at her.

R'becca Groff is a former administrative assistant turned independent content provider. She has written on the topics of healthcare, business and financial trends, as well as local interest stories for her community, in addition to writing personal nonfiction stories for national anthologies and magazines.

Marilyn Haight survived domestic abuse and lived long enough to be willing to talk about it, though it is always uncomfortable to remember. She is a retired businesswoman, and the author of four self-help books and one book of poetry, which you may read about on her website at www.marilynhaight.com.

Wendy Hairfield has a B.A. in journalism from Temple University. After years in public relations promoting environmental programs, she is now a freelance writer who enjoys photography, biking, hiking, and gardening. She has a daughter and stepson and lives in the Seattle area with her husband and two tortoises.

Terry Hans, a retired dental hygienist and frequent contributor to the *Chicken Soup for the Soul* series, has published *Laugh, Rinse, Repeat*, an Erma-Bombeck-style collection of stories from the other side of the dental chair. Mother of two, grandma to four, and great-grandma of one, Terry loves spending time with her family.

Erin Hazlehurst is an award-winning screenwriter and self-published author from British Columbia, Canada.

Marilyn Helmer is the award-winning author of many children's books as well as short stories, poetry and articles. She recently self-published a collection of her short adult fiction titled *Birdsong on a Summer Evening* and contributed to *Stories to Chew On*, a book of fifty-word stories published by her writers' group, the Wellies.

Teresa Hoy shares her country life with her husband and a fur family of rescued cats and dogs. Her stories have appeared in the *Chicken Soup for the Soul* series, *The Ultimate* books, *Rural Missouri* magazine, and *Guideposts*. In addition to writing, she enjoys reading, researching, volunteering, cooking, and traveling.

Linda Hoff Irvin is a psychotherapist in private practice who has been practicing for more years than she cares to admit. She is happily re-married and her son is doing well. E-mail her at lhofflcsw@gmail.com.

Anna Jensen is a British ex-pat who has lived in South Africa for almost thirty years. Her home, a few miles north of the city of Durban on the east coast, overlooks the Indian Ocean, from where she watches dolphins and whales at play while writing. Anna is the author of historical and contemporary fiction and has also published Christian devotions and inspirational poetry.

Maggie John lives in Northern California with her husband of forty years. Her most joyous days are the many weekends and holidays she gets to spend with her two grown children and their growing families. She edits and writes for local newspapers and magazines and has published two children's picture books, with hopefully more to follow.

Wife. Mother. Karate instructor. Just a few of the labels **Debby Johnson** proudly wears. As the mother of five she has plenty of tales to tell. Debby has been writing for as long as she can remember and has published several children's books. She loves to hear from her readers. E-mail her at debby@debbyjohnson.com.

Margaret Johnson-Hodge is the author of nineteen published works, many receiving national acclaim and making multiple bestseller lists. She has garnered rave reviews from the likes of *Publishers Weekly*, *USA Today*, and *Booklist,* to name a few. Learn more at www.mjhodge.net.

Michelle Jones left urban life to pursue her love of art, gardening and home canning. She is a devoted stay-at-home mom, wife and fur parent. Her free time is spent in libraries and wandering used bookstores for hidden treasures.

Rebecca Josefa lives in California and works as a paralegal. She and her husband go for walks and count cats they meet. On their best night so far they saw seventeen cats. Her current project is to read all the mysteries in her nearby public library in alphabetical order by author — after three years she is on B.

Shannon Kaiser is the best-selling author of eight books including *The Self-Love Experiment*, *Return to You*, and her latest, *365 Happy Bedtime Mantras*. She has been named in "100 Women to Watch in Wellness" by MindBodyGreen and is an eight-time contributor to the *Chicken Soup for the Soul* series. Connect with her on social media @ShannonKaiserWrites and on playwiththeworld.com.

Jill Keller lives in a small town in Southern Indiana with her husband and two children. She enjoys writing novels, French cooking, making desserts for her custom bakery, being a reborn artist for therapy dolls, and reading to her children. Learn more at kellerjf.wixsite.com/author.

Mimi Greenwood Knight says she blinked and her four kids were grown. She's empty-nesting it now with her husband, David, on a small hobby farm in South Louisiana where Mimi is teaching herself gardening, beekeeping, herbalism, and chicken wrangling.

Loren Lahav, author of six impactful books including Amazon Best-Seller, *Stay True: Own Your Badass and Beautiful Life*, a 36-year veteran of the stage, she has three impactful programs: OWN IT!, TRUE VOICE, and OWN It! in the Wild and a mastermind, TRUE Legacy Collective. Her companies include Stay True Creative Productions Agency and STAY TRUE Wellness Spa. Loren's passion projects include Super Hero Birthdays and Parawan Gap Dog Rescue. Her story in this collection originally appeared in *Chicken Soup for the Soul: Time to Thrive*, which she coauthored.

Sue LeBreton is a health and wellness writer whose articles appear regularly in regional parenting magazines in Canada and the U.S. The unexpected challenges of her parenting journey have included cancer, autism, life-threatening allergies and diabetes. She uses self-care and humor to help her on her parenting journey.

Machille Legoullon is a children's book author, wife, and proud mother of four boys. She is currently working on her first middle grade novel and has completed a picture book manuscript she is hoping to publish soon. Machille is extremely involved with her sons' school and the family business. E-mail her at writerinside@comcast.net.

Aileen Liang is a grade 11 student who is primarily interested in science and literature. She enjoys baking, writing, snowboarding, and playing with her little sister in her spare time. In the future, she would like to become an optometrist and travel the world with her family.

Sydney Logan is an elementary school librarian and the best-selling author of six novels. A native of East Tennessee, she enjoys playing piano and relaxing on her porch with her wonderful husband and their very spoiled cat. Learn more at www.sydneylogan.com.

Ilana Long loves sharing life stories in the *Chicken Soup for the Soul* series. She is the author of the romantic comedy, *PICKLEBALLERS* (2024) and *PICKLE PERFECT* (October 2025). Ilana enjoys singing, writing music for guitar and piano, adventure traveling, swimming, and hiking.

Diana Lynn is a freelance writer and small business owner in Washington State. This is her fourteenth story published in the *Chicken*

Soup for the Soul series. She is currently working on her third book.

Anita Love is passionate about leading people to sacred peace, comfort and joy in a chaotic world. She can be found hiking her local mountains, designing greeting cards to revive the art of snail-mail, and hosting silent retreats on nearby Bowen Island. Anita lives in Port Moody, BC with her husband and two teen daughters, and can be reached at anitaloveswords@gmail.com.

Diane Lowe MacLachlan is a graduate of Hope College and a student of life. The grateful mother of three amazing, adult children, a lovely daughter-in-law, and grandmother to her first grandchild, she loves to enter into the stories of family, friends, and strangers and to find joy in everyday things.

Lisa A. Malkiewicz writes from a little plot of country, tucked away in the North Carolina Sandhills. She acquired her B.A. in Education after serving in the Navy for some years and teaches full-time online. To relax, she hikes, paints, sews, and of course writes.

Joshua J. Mark is Content Director for the online site World History Encyclopedia. His wife, Betsy, passed on from cancer in 2018 and he now lives with his two Beagles, Sammie and Jamie, in rural New York State.

Robin Martin is an internationally acclaimed children's picture book author and poet. She recently received the King's Coronation Medal (2025) in recognition for her children's book *Someone You Love Has Cancer: A Child's Guide to Understanding*, available on Amazon. This Medal is given to people who have made a significant contribution to Canada or to a particular province, territory, region or community of Canada, or have made an outstanding achievement abroad that brings credit to Canada.

Timothy Martin is an author and screenwriter living in Fortuna, California. He has contributed to over two dozen titles in the *Chicken Soup for the Soul* series. He is the author of ten screenplays and numerous children's novels. Please feel free to email him at whiteshaft@yahoo.com.

Shannon McCarty writes humor articles to keep herself sane. She is a software trainer by day and wine mom by night. She has three lovely and spirited children: Tess, Tabitha and Riley. Shannon and her family live in Austin, TX.

Dennis McCloskey has a journalism degree from Ryerson University in Toronto. He has been a full-time freelance writer since 1980 and is the author of several books, including the 2008 award-winning biography, *My Favorite American*. He lives in Grimsby, Ontario, with his wife, Kris. E-mail him at dmcclos71@gmail.com.

Author of *Grace in Tension: Discover Peace with Martha and Mary*, **Claire McGarry** regularly contributes to *Living Faith* and *Mornings with Jesus*. Living in New Hampshire with her husband and three kids, she endeavors to fish for more people for God through her speaking engagements, writing, and blog ShiftingMyPerspective.com.

Aja Moore-Ramos is a writer, storyteller, and former educator based in Philadelphia, PA. She firmly believes in the power of the pen to expand our horizons. Aja holds a BFA in Writing from Emerson College and an MS in Education from Hunter College. When not writing, she enjoys spending time with her three children, meditating, and exploring new cities. One of her lifelong goals is to become a New York Times Bestselling Author.

Ann Morrow is a writer, photographer and seventeen-time contributor to the *Chicken Soup for the Soul* series. Additionally, her work has appeared in online publications and national magazines. Ann's passions include dogs, hiking and bookstores. She is currently working on a memoir.

Diane Morrow-Kondos writes a weekly blog about her adventures in grandparenting, which can be seen at www.tulsakids.com/Grand-Life/. Diane has a B.S. and an M.S. from Oklahoma State University. Diane's book, *The Long Road to Happy: A Sister's Journey Through Her Brother's Disabilities*, is available at all major bookselling sites.

Tina Muir, former elite runner and founder of Racing for Sustainability and Running for Real, is a leading advocate for sustainability in running. Through her podcast, book, and nonprofit, she empowers runners and race organizers to reduce their environmental impact while also championing athlete health and climate action.

Jonet Neethling lives in a small town in South Africa. She spends a lot of time outdoors and with her pets. Writing and reading are some of her hobbies. Running and cycling is the best time to think about stories and put them later on paper and then hide them for no one to read. Jonet is a loner and dreamer.

Randi B. Nelson, MD, MBA, is a general pediatrician, who hails from Brooklyn and Long Island, NY. She is a former investment banking accountant. In her spare time, she enjoys concerts, museums, theater, and traveling. She owns Wellcome Care Medical, which is a multispecialty practice in Far Rockaway, NY.

Sandy Newman received her BFA in Graphic Design from Auburn University in 1986. She works as a graphic designer in Lower Alabama. Sandy enjoys reading, learning, creating, travel, living life, and supporting the Auburn Tigers. War Eagle! This is her first published writing.

Tina O'Reilly loves the ocean and writing. She resides in Rhode Island with her loving husband, four children and two dogs. She loves to hear from readers. E-mail her at tinamoreilly@outlook.com.

Kristiana Pastir graduated from Syracuse University's S.I. Newhouse School of Public Communications in 2004 and has worked for Chicken Soup for the Soul in some capacity since 2008. She, her husband, and their four children live in Connecticut. Kristiana enjoys reading, baking, lifting weights, and having an uninterrupted conversation.

Galen Pearl is a spiritual guide, teacher, student, martial artist, writer, retired law professor, explorer of the world's wisdom teachings, and embracer of life's mystery. For more information about her books and access to her blog, please visit galenpearl.com.

Connie K. Pombo is a freelance writer and author of *Coffee Lover's Devotional: Take a Break from the Daily Grind*. She and her college sweetheart, Mark, embrace their salty, sandy, and happy life on Florida's Gulf Coast, where they enjoy sharing a large cappuccino at Back Alley Treasures on Anna Maria Island. Learn more at www.conniepombo.com.

Wendy Portfors is a previous contributor to three books in the *Chicken Soup for the Soul* series. She has a published memoir titled *Remembering Love*, and an anthology titled *Through My Eyes*. She enjoys golf, hiking and traveling the world with her husband Dave. They reside near the Rocky Mountains in Alberta, Canada.

A journalist in rural Minnesota, **Ellarry Prentice** studied travel and tourism. In addition to her work as a reporter for her hometown newspaper, she is a freelance writer and photographer, and an advocate for mental health and alcoholism awareness. She enjoys reading, volunteering, and traveling with her husband, Greg.

Connie Kaseweter Pullen lives in rural Sandy, OR, near her five children and several grandchildren. She earned a B.A., with honors, at the University of Portland in 2006, with a double major in psychology and sociology. Connie enjoys writing, photography and exploring nature. E-mail her at MyGrandmaPullen@aol.com.

Rebecca Radicchi is a freelance writer who lives in Atlanta, GA with her husband and four kids. She writes about adoption, faith, and parenting. She's written for *Today's Parents*, *No Hands But Ours*, and *iBelieve*.

Deborah Henderson Roberts enjoys writing humorous and inspirational pieces that draw on real-life experiences. She recently completed a historical fiction novel, and she has begun work on the sequel. Deborah makes her home in Florida.

Regina Sunshine Robinson is a motivational speaker, talk show host, publisher, and empowerment coach who wants to help you "Find Your Way Back to the Light"! Regina Sunshine shares her message of self-love, positivity, and empowerment in her writings including her latest book *Chasing Sunshine*. Her motto is "It's Not Over Til I Win" and she wins when she sees others winning.

Elizabeth Rose graduated *magna cum laude* from Sacred Heart University and is a member of a local writing group. Her interests include reading, cooking, and walking in the great outdoors with her family and dog. A native of New England, she enjoys the scenic beauty and changing seasons of the region.

Mitali Banerjee Ruths grew up in Houston, TX and now lives in Montreal, Canada with her husband, three kids, and their dog, Tux. Mitali has written several award-winning books, like *Archie Celebrates Diwali*, and two popular early reader series from Scholastic titled *The Inside Scouts* and *The Party Diaries*. Learn more at www.mitaliruths.com.

Jenna Schifferle is a Buffalo-based writer who drinks her weight in

Meet Our Contributors

coffee and asks too many questions. Her work has appeared in *Aurora Poetry, In Good Health, Syracuse Woman Magazine, Blink-Ink*, and others. Her debut poetry collection, *My Therapist Told Me to Write This: Poems for Our Daughters*, is now available.

Jonney Scoggin retired from the Los Angeles corporate world in 2011. He now lives on a forty-acre forest in southern Mississippi with his two Collies and spends his time working on his writing craft and capturing the world around him with photography.

Deborah Shouse is a writer, editor, speaker, and dementia advocate. She has an MBA but uses it only in emergencies. Deborah is the author of *An Old Woman Walks Into a Bar* and *Letters from the Ungrateful Dead: A Grieving Mom's Surprising Correspondence with her Deceased Adult Daughter.* Learn more at deborahshousewrites.com.

Paula Klendworth Skory lives in Washington, IL with her husband Chris where they raised their three (now adult) children. She loves art, reading, gardening and going on walks with her Corgi, Finnigan. She is a devoted grandmother who is grateful to find little moments of beauty to celebrate each day.

Aleks Slijepcevic is a meditation and journaling teacher, writer, and podcast host passionate about authenticity, healing, and self-expression. She teaches on Insight Timer, hosts the Soul Sessions podcast, and has authored *The Stories We Tell.* Since 2015, she's guided mindfulness practices and helped others find meaning through writing and reflection.

Gail Small is a Fulbright Memorial Scholar. She is the author of seven books and speaks internationally about joyful living and life choices. Travel is her passion, taking her to all seven continents. *Have Bikini Will Cruise* is her latest book. E-mail this motivational speaker and educational consultant at joyforgail@aol.com.

Gary Sprague lives with his family in Maine. His novels, including the humorous *Lettahs From Maine* series and the *Joe Walker* series, are available online at amazon.com/author/garysprague. He can be reached on Facebook @garyspraguewriter, and on Instagram @garyspragueauthor.

Judee Stapp is a speaker and author who loves to share her life experiences in an engaging and inspiring way. She has had eleven stories published in *Chicken Soup for the Soul* series and several in other publications. Judee is a wife, mother, grandmother, and great-grandmother! Email her at stappjudee@gmail.com.

LaQuita Jean Starr received her Bachelor of Science degree from Texas State University in San Marcos, TX. LaQuita and her husband, Youthel, have been married for twenty years. She is the founder of Angels with a Mission, Inc., a 501(c)3 organization to provides hope and support to the homeless, foster youth, and low-income families. Her living hero is her mother, Mrs. Emma Elie. LaQuita enjoys speaking, traveling, volunteering and tending to her garden.

Noelle Sterne (PhD) publishes stories, poems, essays, and academic and writing craft articles. Her *Challenges in Writing Your Dissertation* helps doctoral students fulfill their goals. In *Trust Your Life* Noelle guides readers to reach their lifelong yearnings. Gratefully pursuing her own, Noelle writes (almost) daily.

L.A. Strucke, a graduate of Rowan University, is a frequent contributor to the *Chicken Soup for the Soul* series. She's also published in *Guideposts, Highlights* and other magazines. Her interests include songwriting, working on her first novel, and spending time with her four children and their families.

Annmarie B. Tait resides in Harleysville, PA with her husband Joe Beck. Annmarie had been published in the *Chicken Soup for the Soul* series many times as well as in *Reminisce Magazine*, and the Grace Publishing *Moments* anthology series. Annmarie also enjoys cooking, crocheting, and singing Irish and American folk songs. E-mail her at irishbloom@aol.com.

Rachel R. Thompson lives just outside of Nashville, TN, with her husband and two daughters. Along with freelance editing and writing, Rachel serves as a high school English teacher and adjunct professor for a local university. She and her family attend St. Stephen Catholic Community. Connect with Rachel at www.RachelRThompson.com.

Tena Beth Thompson writes about life and shares her experiences with a touch of humor. Her first book, *Separation: More Than Just Surviving* for women was published in 2007. Tena Beth also contributed to *Chicken Soup for the Shopper's Soul* and *Chicken Soup for the Soul in Menopause*. Tena Beth resides in Las Vegas.

Susan Traugh used those writing classes to launch an award-winning career writing curriculum for special needs teens all over the world, nonfiction books, articles, and blogs in addition to her young-adult novel, *The Edge of Brilliance*. She's a homebody who loves reading, gardening, and visiting with her grown children.

Ann Vitale lives in rural northeast Pennsylvania, has a University of Michigan degree in microbiology, and worked in hospitals and research before joining her husband in their Ford dealership. She trained dogs and their owners for many years. She took the advice in her story and enrolled in beginning drawing and yoga classes. Ann also coaches novice writers who write family stories and occasionally lectures on history for the Montrose Area Adult School.

Dr. Tricia Wolanin continues to live a life of inspiration and creativity through her work as a clinical psychologist, sound healer, author, and yogini. After attaining her doctorate, the zest as a wanderluster emerged. Her passions include journaling, traveling, learning, and savoring moments with her tribe of loved ones.

Elizabeth Yeter is a teacher of students with visual impairments in Albuquerque, NM. She enjoys writing about her past and current adventures in life on her blog resuscitatingyou.com, which she started with her sister in 2019.

Pauline Youd is the author of twenty-three Bible story books for children and adults. Her background includes public school teacher, musical theater, and church choir and musicals director. She has served her community as a reading and writing tutor. Her family includes her husband, three adult children and four grandchildren.

Meet Amy Newmark

Amy Newmark is the bestselling author, editor-in-chief, and publisher of the *Chicken Soup for the Soul* book series. Since 2008, she has published more than 200 new books, most of them national bestsellers in the U.S. and Canada, more than doubling the number of *Chicken Soup for the Soul* titles in print today. She is also the author of *Simply Happy*, a crash course in Chicken Soup for the Soul advice and wisdom that is filled with easy-to-implement, practical tips for enjoying a better life.

Amy is credited with revitalizing the Chicken Soup for the Soul brand, which has been a publishing industry phenomenon since the first book came out in 1993. By compiling inspirational and aspirational true stories curated from ordinary people who have had extraordinary experiences, Amy has kept the thirty-two-year-old Chicken Soup for the Soul brand fresh and relevant.

Amy graduated *magna cum laude* from Harvard University where she majored in Portuguese and minored in French. She then embarked on a three-decade career as a Wall Street analyst, a hedge fund manager, and a corporate executive in the technology field.

Her return to literary pursuits was inevitable, as her honors thesis in college involved traveling throughout Brazil's impoverished northeast region, collecting stories from regular people. She is delighted to have come full circle in her writing career — from collecting stories "from the people" in Brazil as a twenty-year-old to, three decades later, collecting stories "from the people" for Chicken Soup for the Soul.

When Amy and her husband Bill, the CEO of Chicken Soup for the Soul, are not working, they are visiting their four grown children and their spouses, and their six grandchildren.

Follow Amy on X and Instagram @amynewmark. Listen to her free podcast — Chicken Soup for the Soul with Amy Newmark — on Apple, Google, or by using your favorite podcast app on your phone. You can also find a selection of her stories on Medium.

Sharing Happiness, Inspiration, and Hope

Real people sharing real stories, every day, all over the world. In 2007, *USA Today* named *Chicken Soup for the Soul* one of the five most memorable books in the last quarter-century. With over 110 million books sold to date in the U.S. and Canada alone, more than 300 titles in print, and translations into nearly fifty languages, "chicken soup for the soul®" is one of the world's best-known phrases.

Today, thirty-two years after we first began sharing happiness, inspiration and hope through our books, we continue to delight our readers with new titles almost every month, but have also evolved beyond the bookshelves with super premium pet food, a podcast, adult coloring books, and licensed products that include word-search puzzle books and books for babies and preschoolers. We are busy "changing your life one story at a time®" and doing it for the whole family. Thanks for reading!